LOGIC AND LINGUISTICS
RESEARCH DIRECTIONS IN
COGNITIVE SCIENCE
EUROPEAN PERSPECTIVES
Vol. 2

Logic and Linguistics
Research Directions in Cognitive Science
European perspectives
Vol. 2

Edited by
Helmut Schnelle

Ruhr-Universitat Bochum
Sprachwissenschaftliches Institut
Postfach 102148
D-4630
Federal Republic of Germany

and

Niels Ole Bernsen

Commission of the European Communities
Rue de la Loi 200
B-1049, Brussels, Belgium

LAWRENCE ERLBAUM ASSOCIATES, PUBLISHERS
Hove and London (UK)   Hillsdale (USA)

Published on behalf of the Commission of the European Communities by:
Lawrence Erlbaum Associates Ltd., Publishers
27 Palmeira Mansions
Church Road
Hove, East Sussex, BN2 2FA

Publication No. EUR 11116 Vol. 2 of the
Commission of the European Communities,
Directorate-General Telecommunications, Information
Industries and Innovation,
Scientific and Technical Communication Service,
Luxembourg.

© ECSC-EEC-EAEC, Brussels-Luxembourg, 1989

British Library Cataloging in Publication Data
Research directions in cognitive science: European
    perspectives.
    Vol 2, logic and linguistics.
    1. Cognitive psychology
    I. Schnelle, Helmut
    153

    ISBN 0-86377-112-2

Printed and bound by BPCC Wheatons, Exeter

Contents

General Introduction
A European Perspective
on Cognitive Science

Niels Ole Bernsen

ESPRIT Basic Research Actions
Commission of the European Communities
Rue de la Loi 200
B - 1049, Brussels, Belgium

The present volume on Logic and Linguistics is one in a series of five presenting the findings of a joint European study in cognitive science 1987-88. The study was organised and funded as a collaborative network by the research unit FAST (Forecast and Assessment in Science and Technology) of the Commission of the European Communities and comprised about 35 scientists from the core disciplines of cognitive science. The research disciplines represented in the network were: cognitive psychology, logic and linguistics, cognitive neuroscience, human–computer interaction, and artificial intelligence.

The aim of the network activity was to attempt a prospective mapping of research problems in cognitive science to be addressed over the next 5 – 10 years. Prospective judgment of course has to be based on firm knowledge of the state of the art but a presentation of the state-of-the-art of cognitive science as such was not our primary objective. This objective had already been addressed by a report presented to FAST in February 1986, *Cognitive Science in Europe* (ed. Michel Imbert et al.) and published by Springer-Verlag in October 1987.

As often happens in science nowadays, the dual aim of state-of-the-art presentation and prospective mapping realised through the FAST initiatives was linked to another, more practical aim, namely that of making sure that cognitive science finds its appropriate place in the European Community's long-term strategy for research and development in information technology. It is no doubt a pleasure to the contributors, and we hope to the European cognitive science community at large, that this has now happened to the extent that cognitive science has been included in the ESPRIT Basic Research Actions initiative, which forms the upstream, basic research complement to the European Communities ESPRIT programme in I.T.R. & D. In response to the first call for proposals for ESPRIT Basic Research Actions (1988), some $65-70 Mio. are currently being committed to basic research in cognitive science and artificial intelligence, computer science, and microelectronics. Moreover, now that European cognitive science is becoming increasingly visible, partly through the FAST and ESPRIT initiatives, it seems reasonable to expect an increase in cognitive science funding at the national level.

As part of the more practical aim of funding procurement, the network agenda also included surveying and commenting upon the current institutional state and the state of collaboration in European cognitive science. Results and, we hope, some timely recommendations form part of a separate report of the network activity (Bernsen & the FAST Network, 1988).

The overall view of cognitive science taken in the papers published in the present volumes is fairly comprehensive though not exhaustive. Choice of topics for presentation and discussion has been made with a view to potential long-term relevance to information technology. Authors have been encouraged to take a personal view of their respective fields rather than a more comprehensive, and perhaps less exciting, encyclopaedic view. Each contribution has been written in order to make it comprehensible to cognitive scientists from other disciplines.

Since the general characteristics of current cognitive science are not, as such, addressed in the individual introductions or papers, a brief sketch may be in place here.

Sometimes a new theory can provide a unifying perspective to a number of hitherto disparate scientific endeavours and thus motivate a potentially drastic regrouping among the sciences. This is the case in cognitive science, where a new theory of the most general type which I shall call a *research programme* currently has this effect. The new research programme offering a unifying perspective to large parts of the sciences of logic, linguistics, psychology and neuroscience came from computer science and artificial intelligence and had been gaining ground steadily since the 1950s. It consists of the general idea that intelligent agents should be looked upon as information processing systems, that is, as systems receiving, manipulating, storing, retrieving, transmitting and executing information. Some of the general questions to ask concerning intelligent agents according to this research programme are: what information do such systems have? how is it represented? how is the information processed? and how are the processes implemented? The theoretical language of cognitive science is that of computation and information processing.

The objectives of cognitive science are to define, build and test information processing models of the various sub-systems (and of *their* sub-systems) making up intelligent agency, whether human (biological, natural) or artificial, and eventually to make them fit together into general cognitive theories and systems. The knowledge obtained can then be applied in various ways. Examples of cognitive sub-systems are vision, speech, natural language, sensory–motor control, memory, learning and reasoning. Each of these sub-systems is highly complex and may be further broken down into a number of functional components. Today's limited-capacity autonomous robots and knowledge based systems having a (written or spoken) natural language interface are examples of technologically implemented steps towards more general systems.

In somewhat more detail, the research programme of cognitive science may be characterised as follows:

1. Intelligence or cognition is physically implemented. However, a central level of analysis is the description of cognitive systems as systems for the manipulation of representations. Representations may consist of discrete symbols or may be of other types such as distributed representations.

2. Widely different types of physical implementation are capable, in principle, of manipulating the same representations in the same ways: chips made of silicon or galliumarsenide, optical devices, mechanical, or hydraulic devices, organic–biological systems.

3. Artificial, i.e. non-biological intelligence and hyperintelligence is therefore possible, at least in principle. Cognitive science is an investigation of both biological and artificial intelligence.

4. The level of description at which cognitive systems are described as manipulating representations cannot be reduced to:

(a) the physical implementation of the system ;
(b) the behaviour of the system ;
(c) the conscious experiences of the system, if any.

5. Cognitive science is mechanistic. Intelligence or cognition, including semantics or meaning, and consciousness, is regarded as being produced by, in a wide sense, mechanical operations.

6. Acceptance of some version of functionalism. Functionalism states that cognition is constituted by the information processing functions which are physically implemented in the system.

7. Historically as well as in scientific substance and methodology, cognitive science is closely related to the computer and its information processing potential as studied by computer science and artificial intelligence. The paradigms of cognitive science still derive from contemporary computer systems, whether serial or parallel, classical or connectionist. Use of computer simulations is essential to cognitive science except for the few areas, like problems involving social or organisational aspects, where specific computer modelling is not yet feasible.

8. Cognitive science is multidisciplinary. Methodologically, cognitive science aims at increased collaboration and cross-fertilisation between disciplines, the central assumption being that this is the most promising way of accelerating the achievement of the research programme, and hence also of realising the application potential of cognitive science. If anything has become apparent over the last 20 years, it is that

cognition or intelligence are extremely complex phenomena whose investigation requires the full exploitation of a wide range of methodological tools. The basic idea behind the interdisciplinarity of cognitive science, then, is that each discipline employs its own *particular* methods in order to add *constraints* to the construction of *common* models and theories of the cognitive functions and their interrelationships. These models and theories are expressed in the common language of cognitive science, that is, in the language of the research programme and of one or other of the paradigms (discussed later). In addition, the basic idea behind interdisciplinarity assumes that each discipline could significantly contribute to the development of models and theories. So each discipline should, in order to belong to cognitive science, be concerned with both knowledge and processing (or competence and performance) in cognition, abstract programme and implementation, peripheral and central processes, sub-system integration, and the understanding of intelligent performance in complex, real-life tasks.

Present-day cognitive science is an interdisciplinary endeavour rather than a new science in its own right, and speaking about core disciplines suggests that insights from other sciences like mathematics, physics, biology, computer science, anthropology, and the philosophy of science, mind and language actually do contribute to the advance of cognitive science. Furthermore, numerous sub-disciplines exist linking the core disciplines together, such as computational linguistics, computational logic, psycholinguistics, neuropsychology, and so on.

9. Cognitive science is closely related to application, in particular, though not exclusively, to the application of information technology. Applications of cognitive science are of at least three types.

(a) Specifying information processing models of the various sub-systems making up intelligent agency is essential to the building of increasingly intelligent artifacts such as the coming generations of vision systems, speech systems, natural language interfaces, robots, and knowledge-based systems. Interactions between the various disciplines of cognitive science have in the past produced such important AI knowledge representation and reasoning techniques as semantic networks, production systems, and logic programming, as well as significant results in areas like vision, speech and natural language processing. Future interaction will have to face still other areas of research where humans continue to perform far better than current artificial systems, as in causal reasoning, reasoning about time, plans and intentions, learning, or fluent, skill-based behaviour.

(b) It has become clear that the actual design of information processing systems should go hand in hand with research on their interactions with human agents in real-life task situations. Through the computerisation of work in all sectors of society, information technology has become an important tool at the interface between humans and their work. Successful system design, whether of large control systems, computer networks, manufacturing systems, office systems, tutoring systems, speech and language systems, or expert systems, not only depends on the training of users but also on the systems' inherent adaptability to users. If a system's design is not successful, users are not likely to want to use it, and if they do use it, serious accidents may occur, as in nuclear power plants or large chemical installations. In this situation, cognitive science research is strongly needed in the interaction between I.T. tools, task domain and work context, the cognitive resources of users, and the new patterns of social interaction arising from the use of computers. Thus, the rapidly evolving field of human–computer interaction research could be included among the core disciplines making up cognitive science as being sufficiently distinct from, and somewhat orthogonal to, the others to merit a disciplinary label of its own.

(c) Although these two points describing the application potential of cognitive science for information technology have been central to the present network activity, it should be noted that they do not exhaust the application potential of cognitive science. The human information processing system can be damaged or inoperative in various ways and from various causes, with neurological and psychological disorders or loss of certain mental abilities as a result. Studying the system and its behaviour in information processing terms promises better ways for diagnosing, repairing, and retraining the system as well as better ways of supplying the system with efficient prostheses.

The aforementioned points 1–9 are by no means uncontroversial among cognitive scientists. And needless to say, interdisciplinary collaboration among traditionally separate disciplines is not uncontroversial either. What is interesting, however, is that points 1–9 currently do seem to represent international convergence towards a common conception of cognitive science.

A research programme is in itself nothing very important. What matters are the research paradigm(s) demonstrating the practical viability of the programme. A research paradigm consists of one or more successful, specific applications of the research programme to particular problems falling within its scope. These applications, *in casu* models of specific cognitive functions, are seen by the scientific community as evidence that the principles on which they are based might be generalised to account for a much larger class of cognitive phenomena, and possibly to all of cognition. The central scientific task, then, is to implement and test this assumption. Cognitive science currently appears to have to consider two different research paradigms. The relationship between them is not clear at this point and is subject to strong, ongoing debate (e.g. Fodor & Pylyshyn, 1988; Smolensky, 1988).

According to the *Classical AI* paradigm, an intelligent system's input and output consist of physical signals and movements, whereas a large central part of the information processing linking input and output consists of automatic computation over language-like, discrete, and combinatorial symbolic codes, as in conventional serial or more recent parallel computers (Fodor, 1976; Newell, 1980; Pylyshyn, 1984). According to the *Neural Network Computation* paradigm or the *Connectionist* paradigm, which has been strongly revived in the 1980s, computation over discrete combinatorial symbols exists to a lesser extent, or does not exist at all, in intelligent biological systems. Instead the complex cognitive abilities of higher organisms are based on the information–processing abilities arising from the collective behaviour of large populations of highly interconnected and very simple processing elements such as nerve cells or simple artificial processing elements. Consequently, it is maintained, cognitive scientists should develop and implement their theories of intelligent information processing in ways that resemble much more closely the way in which the brain actually operates (McClelland & Rumelhart, 1986).

Today, both paradigms can claim a number of successes in terms of concrete models jointly covering most areas of cognitive science.

This ongoing debate over research paradigms is a very real one because, at the present time at least, the two paradigms clearly do generate different systems providing different functional primitives (i.e. different elementary information processing capabilities) and possibly different behaviours.

Thus, the virtues of connectionist systems include their ability to rapidly acquire and apply large amounts of knowledge in noisy situations not governed by rigid laws but by context–sensitive regularities having many exceptions. And the paradigms generate importantly different directions for research and different technologies, and tend to attract different core disciplines of cognitive science. Thus, many researchers in classical AI tend to be sceptical about the opotential of artificial neural network systems, despite the success of similar systems in nature; others do not doubt the importance for AI of "massive parallelism", but argue that connectionist systems do not really represent an alternative research paradigm, only a specific way of physically implementing classical cognitive architectures. Logicians and most linguists tend to disregard connectionist systems, whereas many cognitive psychologists and virtually all cognitive neuroscientists, who never really adopted the classical AI paradigm anyway, tend to embrace the neural network computation paradigm as the first firm basis for realistic models and general theories of cognition. The formal language of the classical AI paradigm is that of symbolic logic and algebra, whereas the formal language of the connectionist paradigm is that of dynamic systems theory belonging to mathematical physics. Also, researchers studying the peripherals of cognitive systems like speech, low-level vision, or movement, all of which involve considerable signal processing, appear to be more strongly attracted by neural network computation than those studying central processes. Not least, this latter point has led many cognitive scientists to believe that the two paradigms really are basically different cognitive architectures, but that they are compatible in the sense of being apt to model different types of cognitive function or different parts of cognitive functions, such as voluntary, introspectively accessible, attentive, and controlled processes versus skilled, automatic, pre-attentive, probably massively parallel processes. Research in the next 5–10 years will no doubt result in important attempts to integrate these two approaches or paradigms of cognitive science.

Two interrelated themes dominate the network findings and cut across the distinction between scientific substance and methodology. These themes can be viewed as constituting some central tendencies of current research covering all the core disciplines of cognitive science. Since the themes or trends are based on prospective analyses of most areas of cognitive science, from research on vision and speech to research on natural language, logic, and reasoning, they appear to form a stable pattern. These trends should be encouraged by an appropriate research policy.

The themes are *integration* in theory, computer models, and actual working implementations, and *real-world validity* of theories, models and applications.

The theme of integration covers the following aspects:

Integration of different cognitive functions;
Integration of cognitive sub-functions into cognitive functions;
Integration of models into more general theories;
Integration of partial models into full models;
Integration and convergence of approaches, methods, and results from different disciplines;
A more theory-driven approach in traditionally experimental disciplines like cognitive psychology and neuroscience.

Integration clearly means a trend towards the construction and testing of general theories and towards increased interdisciplinarity. Moreover, as mentioned earlier, the possibility of integrating the two current research paradigms of cognitive science is currently the subject of lively debates.

The real-word theme covers the trend towards explaining, simulating and actually building larger-scale, more general-purpose, real-time, closer-to-real-life systems of speech and grammar, natural language and communication, vision, perception and movement or action, and problem-solving. This trend also receives strong support from human–computer interaction research, which from the outset has to face human information processing in complex, real-life situations. Real-world research in cognitive science contrasts with, e.g., research in cognitive psychology on the performance of abstract and ecologically meaningless tasks in the laboratory or AI research on system performance in "micro-worlds". The real-world trend marks an important step beyond these classical approaches in cognitive science and implies the disappearance from the field of the sharp, traditional distinction between basic and applied research.

The two themes of integration and real-world validity are closely related because, in a large number of cases, explanation and synthesis of performance in complex, real-life situations require an integration of different cognitive functions and systems, and of different approaches. The themes are also closely related to the technological applicability of models, systems, and theories because integration and real-world validity is what is needed, both in order to extend the range of applicability of systems and in order to adapt them to users. In many cases, computer simulations may function both as theoretical test-beds and as software prototypes of potential machines for technological applications.

Numerous examples of the above trends can be gathered from the network papers. I shall leave it to the reader to find these examples and to judge whether they are sufficient to justify the conclusions stated above. If they are, then it can confidently be stated that contemporary cognitive science in Europe demonstrates the viability of the research programme, the productivity of the research paradigms, the convergence of disciplines towards common models, theories and problems to the extent allowed by the existence of two different paradigms, and the potential applicability of results. Not everything is idyllic, however; nor could or should this be so within an emerging science. Most of the basic questions still remain unanswered, with the prospect that cognitive science may look very different in 10 years time.

I would like to warmly thank all network participants for their friendly collaboration during the past two years. We all learned, I think, that even today, large-scale, multidisciplinary European collaboration in science is not a matter of course, but something that requires a substantial effort. I am especially grateful to the leaders of the four "network institutions" and the Special Editors of the first four volumes in the series: Alan Baddeley (Cambridge APU), Michel Imbert (University Paris VI), Jens Rasmussen (Riso National Laboratory), and Helmut Schnelle (Bochum University). Without their judgment, vigilance, patience and collaborative spirit the network would never have been set up, let alone have produced anything. Derek Sleeman (Aberdeen), Special Editor of Volume V, entered the collaboration at a later stage and has demonstrated impressive efficiency in catching up with the work that had already been done.

We are all deeply indebted to Dr Riccardo Petrella, Head of FAST, whose sensitivity to emerging trends in science and technology first brought cognitive science to the attention of EC scientific programmes and whose dynamism, non-hesitant support, and constant good-will have made the network possible. I must personally thank Dr Petrella and the Danish Science and Engineering Research Council for making my one-year stay at FAST possible, and the EC's ESPRIT programme for allowing me time to complete the work while assisting in setting up the ESPRIT Basic Research Actions.

REFERENCES

Bernsen, N.O. & the FAST Cognitive Science Network (1988). *Cognitive science: A European perspective.* (Report to the FAST Programme.) FAST, EC Commission, Brussels.
Fodor, J.A. & Pylyshyn, Z.W.(1988). Connectionism and cognitive architecture. *Cognition, 28,* (1–2), 3–71.
Fodor, J.A.(1976). *The Language of Thought.* Sussex: The Harvester Press.
Imbert, M., Bertelson, P., Kempson, R., Osherson, D., Schnelle, H., Streitz, N.A., Thomassen, A., & Viviani, P. (Eds.)(1987). *Cognitive Science in Europe.* Springer-Verlag.
McClelland, J.L., Rumelhart, D.E. & the PDP Research Group (Eds.) (1986). *Parallel Distributed Processing* Vols. 1–2, Cambridge MA: Bradford Books, MIT Press.
Newell, A.(1980). Physical Symbol Systems, *Cognitive Science, 4,* 135–183.
Pylyshyn, Z.W.(1984). *Computation and Cognition. Toward a Foundation for Cognitive Science.* Bradford Books, Cambridge MA, MIT Press.
Smolensky, P.(1988). On the proper treatment of connectionism. *Behavioral and Brain Sciences, 11* (1), 1–74.

CHAPTER 1

Linguistic Research in the Context of Cognitive Science and Artificial Intelligence: An Introduction

Helmut Schnelle

Ruhr-Universitat Bochum,Sprachwissenschaftliches Institut, Postfach 102148, D-4630, Bochum, Federal Republic of Germany

1. INTRODUCTION

Linguistics is concerned with the structure and use of languages, and logic with the form and correctness of argumentation in ordinary and scientific language. We shall not discuss these two fields in general but only with respect to their connection with two related domains: cognitive science and artificial intelligence.

We thus will be less concerned with the technical details of logic and linguistics, but rather with the problems posed by relating the two, as they are traditionally conceived, to the sciences of cognitive processes. Particular questions to be posed are for instance how structure and use of languages are realised by psychological mechanisms or biological processes and whether particular abilities in language use and logical inference can be programmed or wired into information processing machines. The achievement of the required degree of detail, specificity, and applicability-in-principle would seem to provide a strong test for logical and linguistic research.

The last 30 years of research in logic and linguistics have brought a wealth of insight into the structure of more flexible, and hence more natural, systems of logic, and also into the more formally analysed parts of grammar and semantics. On the basis of this, much progress has been made in the computer implementation of these insights. The

1

contributions in this volume give introductions to the state-of-the-art in the formal analysis of flexible logic (van Benthem, Chapter 4) and linguistics (Klein, Chapter 3; Laver, Chapter 2), as well as logic and linguistics together (Guenthner, Chapter 5; Wahlster, Chapter 7).

But at the same time this volume attempts to present a broader perspective, in which an integration of formal structure with the structure of processing systems might be possible (see Laver, Chapter 2; Schnelle, Chapter 6).

Given that the relation of logical and linguistic structures to the problem of clarifying language and grammar as cognitive phenomena is a complicated one, it seems appropriate to introduce this problem first. I will start by presenting some of the technological expectations of the field and then move gradually to a discussion of the scientific problem areas which would have to be clarified in order to satisfy these expectations. I shall give an overview of the *scope of application* and of the *scientific knowledge* which is the basis for practical progress, explain the *subdivision of the field*, give an introduction to the *conceptual dimensions* of analysis, and, finally, of its *mathematical dimensions*.

2. EXTENDING THE LINGUISTIC AND LOGICAL CAPABILITIES OF COMPUTERS AND INFORMATION PROCESSING SYSTEMS

Computers, robots, control systems, etc., are tools and devices to help humans in solving certain tasks or even to replace them whenever this is desirable (such as in extremely tedious or time-consuming computational activities or in dangerous environments or situations). They may also be conceived as extensions of libraries, i.e. sources of knowledge, which—in contrast to ordinary books—are not passive stores, but a kind of active media, providing not merely relevant knowledge data but also tools for solving problems.

In contrast to traditional tools, these devices confront the designers with an additional challenge: they are potentially intelligent. This does not mean that they are as yet actually intelligent: If they were, we should be able to explain to them the tasks we want to be executed in an ordinary dialogue and order them to act as told.

We know that computers and robots that are currently available are a long way from having this intelligence. If we want them to execute certain tasks, we must program them. Why? Basically for two reasons: Computers do not understand natural languages and computers cannot find solutions for problems by themselves. We must perhaps qualify this: Some computers understand small fragments of natural languages applied to specific areas of knowledge and some computers can find solutions for problems in clearly defined limited domains. But the general statement still holds, as does the fact that only human beings have the command of languages; although monkeys have been taught the language of a 2-year-old human being. It is thus true that current computers can only obey orders if the requested task is expressed in a regularised, non-natural language, such as a programming language.

This contrasts with task specifications for humans. If I were to ask a mathematician to help me with a problem, he or she would have two tasks: first to translate my problem into a mathematical form and second to compute. It is the former of these two tasks which requires intelligence. It involves factual knowledge of the domain in which the task is to be executed and it involves the knowledge of ordinary language.

It was realised very early in the history of computing that computers can do more than just execute the trivial part in mathematical tasks, i.e. the computation of solutions specified by mathematical formulae. A century of research in formal logic has created the hope that the intelligent parts of task execution might also be reduced to computation: Reasoning in rigorously and formally defined areas has been shown to be amenable to computation and so has structural and combinatorial analysis of systems of expressions (formal languages). The fact that scientific knowledge is presented by expressions of theoretical or empirical content and rules of inference led to the *assumption that any knowledge and any behaviour guided by knowledge can be defined as formal representation and computation.* Should this not apply, *a fortiori*, to any form of intelligent behaviour?

The crucial proof that this assumption is correct must come from logic and linguistics. In which knowledge domains is it possible to define formal representations and inferential systems and in which is it possible to define computational systems which allow natural language access and provide natural language responses? The concrete part of this proof would consist in providing computers (or more general information processing systems, robots, etc.) with reasoning and language understanding. Optimism has been fuelled by the fact that, in contrast to earlier "taxonomic" analyses of logic and linguistics, it is now possible to show how the meanings of words, terms, and sentences depend on their formally specified context: words and terms have meanings within sentences, and sentences have meanings within theories specified by meaning postulates and factual laws. These insights were obtained on the basis of rigorously analysed mechanisms of symbol manipulation.

In spite of this optimism it soon became clear that the proof of having found the key to the understanding of intelligence is so formidable that it will not be able to be given in the foreseeable future, and has certainly not yet been given by formalist calculi. Many scientists believe that it cannot be given in principle, unless basic assumptions underlying present approaches are radically revised.

One of the reasons for this scepticism is as follows: In referring to the capabilities of a human problem solver we referred to the factual knowledge of the domain in which the task is to be executed and to the knowledge of ordinary language, and we implied that this knowledge would be fully specified by the formal structures of reasoning and of language. It is true that some factual and linguistic knowledge is necessary but it is by no means sufficient to explain real understanding. As has been strongly emphasised by some researchers (e.g. Winograd & Flores, 1986, with reference to the German philosophers Heidegger, Gadamer, and Habermas) human knowledge involves a huge framework of personal and social experience, and understanding problems as well as creativity in finding solutions presupposes this framework. Even formalised problems

LL—B

and solutions are in fact merely regularisations and regimentations of informal ideas. Unless we take steps to come to an understanding of these highly contextual ways of thinking, we will be unable to create systems which deserve the predicate intelligent in the ordinary sense of the term.

This pessimistic evaluation of some claims and expectations does not exclude the expectation that *very useful parts of this task might be solved in the near future and that knowledge-guided systems with natural language access could become available on computers or robots so as to allow successful communication in a limited context.*

Indeed, the *scientific basis for limited systems is already available*: Linguistic and phonetic research of the last 30 years has provided important insights into the structure of words and sentences and into the procedures necessary for their structural analysis and literal interpretation. Logical research has provided methods for the mechanisation of inferences, which allow the generation of the other sentences implied by a given sentence (in a given framework of understanding) and thus allow the programming of not only the explicit and literal sentence understanding but also of the implicit understanding and presuppositions. Many of these aspects have been presented elsewhere in this volume (van Benthem, Chapter 4; Guenthner, Chapter 5; Klein, Chapter 3, Laver; Chapter 2).

These methods can and should be extended from the limited linguistic domains on which they have been so far tested to larger sets of sentences. This implies the *development of larger dictionaries* containing the specifications required for formalised use in a programming context. In other words, the *basic insights of formal linguistics and formal logic* developed during the last 30 years *must be applied on a large scale*, using tens of thousands of words instead of a mere hundred.

However, these natural language systems will only become useful when *further aspects* have been incorporated, aspects usually reckoned as coming under the *pragmatic features of language use and dialogue*. That these features are extremely important in language use is elegantly demonstrated by the examples in Wahlster (Chapter 7). In other words, the natural language systems to be developed must try to *imitate the flexibility of language use*.

Some scientists feel that specifically designed natural language systems will only become an important component of computer systems when they allow the extended *use of spoken language* (automatic speech recognition and production) and thus add an additional channel to the visual screen and the tactile keyboard of a computer. The fact that the first systems which are presently being implemented will not yet understand language without particular constraints, i.e. are not as flexible in their understanding as people are, might create some disappointment in the use of speech systems, but users can still interact with computer systems by voice.

What has been said so far may be summarised in a few words: important methods have been developed for formally defining natural language systems and systems of logical inference and implementing them as systems of information processing. Their flexibility and scope has been extended theoretically and tested by implementations. Technological applications of these theoretical insights have been proven to contribute to the economic success of various products, e.g. in word processing and access to database systems. The conclusion seems to be obvious: *continuation and extension of presently fruitful research based on established principles of formal and computational logic and linguistics.*

In spite of this optimism about gradual progress in the field, many scientists feel that *the time is ripe for a radically new start* which deviates from the established principles of research in fundamental respects. They feel justified by the pessimistic evaluation outlined above and they challenge the very basis for the progress of the last 50 years. This attitude is not merely based on a general feeling of dissatisfaction but on very specific insights about the shortcomings of current approaches and how to avoid them.

In order to appreciate these shortcomings one must remember the conceptual origin of the progress of the last 50 years: the formalisation of rigidly constructed logical calculi for scientific discourse. The earliest inventors in the field (Leibniz and Frege) compared their logical instruments to the microscope and contrasted them with the ordinary language which had, in their view, a flexibility comparable to the eye. By this comparison they tried to apologise for the lack of flexibility of their calculi by simultaneously recommending their proposals for their virtues in securing scientific rigour.

It is certainly true that the ranges in which these calculi can be applied have been enormously extended, due to the ingenious proposals of people such as Chomsky and Montague. Even a certain degree of flexibility has been incorporated. The problem is whether it is a useful strategy to carry on rigorously treating more and more complicated phenomena of language structure in this way or to try to incorporate forms of flexibility into a tool which was intended to exclude it. It is certainly true that complication and flexibility can be approximated to any desired degree, but the price to be paid by the resulting complexity of the rigid system may be rather high. The strategy may be ill-guided, because the extent and the flexibility of these systems does not follow naturally from an insight into the character of actual language use and ordinary (sometimes erroneous) reasoning, but is imposed secondarily on a system of rigid ideas about language as an interpreted calculus functioning independently of situative perception and action, habits, large frameworks of presuppositions, and imagination—a system of ideas correctly motivated by a completely different aim, i.e. the control of scientific language.

However, language is not a device for securing rigorous judgement, but serves flexibly in normal but highly structured contexts. In such contexts, language develops in children in speech-acts closely connected with acts of perception and action. It seems that the ordinary use of language never becomes completely independent of this context, although in situation-independent language uses, such as in reading, situation context is being substituted by situative imagination. Intuitive lines of quick reasoning are inculcated by early experience and by society and are spontaneously applied in appropriate situations. The pay-off for spontaneity and flexibility in ordinary circumstances is error in situations which require more sophisticated argumentation, e.g., argumentation in an intellectual philosophical, situation-independent context prompted the development of logic and the rigorous control of the form and function of language. In short, it is rather doubtful that we can incorporate a flexibility and a formally secured rigour of argument by the same kind of mechanism. The concept of a self-sufficient language consisting of expressions which are composed of words with literal meanings and whose interpretation is wholly computable from the meanings of the words, their forms of composition and a general framework of interpretation, is an ingenious construct for controlling the rigour of scientific language but it does not seem to have much to do with ordinary language and reasoning. The attempts to specify natural logic and natural languages as special cases of interpreted calculi seem to be misguided *in this context*.

If our aim is the understanding of flexible language use in concrete situations and not only textual understanding we need a new starting point which may differ in some respects from approaches guided by the analyses of more or less formal languages and calculi of reasoning. Do we know how to start?

First, how are we to express our descriptions? Do we have a theoretical descriptive basis apart from formal logic? The answer is yes, the new paradigm of connectionism provides such a basis. Connectionism is essentially similar to the methods for the definition and analysis of dynamical systems already well known from the natural sciences. After all, physics is not defined in terms of logical calculi but it is still sufficiently rigorous. Why should similar descriptive methods be excluded from the analyses of mental/biological systems?

Secondly, the new start should not only be determined by the new descriptive method. Part of its motivation was the insight that certain features were lacking in formal calculi and this insight must therefore be capitalised upon. The systems to be described should consist of:

1. *Massively parallel (intuitive) processing* (in place of sequential rule application).
2. *Situational determination of meanings* (in place of merely contextual determination in a framework of formal expressions).
3. *Stepwise build-up of complicated natural systems from simple deeply situation-determined language use* (in place of trying to determine all levels of complication by a single system).

We thus need to enter into careful studies of the build up of languages in situational contexts, based on processing methods characteristic of the input systems of intuitive perception and the output systems of skilled action (such as parallel processing and learning in the context of parallel processing). We need a *new starting point with careful studies on multi-modal language use and reasoning*. This is particularly important in the context of spoken language.

The crucial role of multi-modal systems has also been acknowledged in attempts to achieve more flexible natural language systems within the established paradigm. It has been clearly specified, for instance, by Wahlster (Chapter 7), where multi-modality appears as a desirable development; for the new start just outlined it is not merely desirable, but absolutely essential.

It is clear from what has been said that the *established paradigm* of formal logic and linguistics together implemented on computers provide *an excellent basis for the development of natural language systems with practical importance and for flexible knowledge base management in limited and well-defined contexts.* They need strong support for more concentrated development. At the same time, the *new start* must be vigorously developed *by combining studies of massive parallelism and connectionism in logic and linguistics, situational language use and a stepwise build-up of system-complication related to processes of language learning and reasoning.*

However, the extension of existing systems and the development of new ones require a very systematic framework for the organisation of research. I shall try to give an outline of such a framework.

3. FIELDS OF RESEARCH

From a scientific viewpoint, the world is a structured and organised system. There are various ways of representing this structure scientifically. One is the method of Leibniz: Describe the world as if it were constructed on the basis of an architectural plan proceeding "top-down" from aggregates (or groups) of individuals to single individuals and from single individuals to their parts, parts of parts, etc., down to infinitesimal components. (Today, we would say down to the quantum-physical units.) Each whole and each part which can be clearly characterised functionally, i.e. each group, each individual, each of the individual's organs, cells, cell membranes, etc., has, if the characterisation is adequate, an essential unity, which Leibniz calls a monad. It is this unity which determines the specific functioning of a physical entity. This holds for whole organisms as well as for all of their parts right down to the smallest ones. The organism is thus a hierarchy of functional units, such that the higher units determine functionally (not physically) the lower ones whose operations and cooperations serve to realise the function of the higher unit.

On the other hand, each functional unit (the monad) corresponds physically to a (usually highly complicated) configuration of quantum-physical units, which constitutes the spatio-temporal extension of the unit, its functioning principle. Corresponding to the hierarchy of functional unit-specifications we thus have a hierarchy of the bodily constitution of wholes from their parts.

Leibniz refers to all of this under the term architecture. Today, the same principles are applied in the *structured designs* of programs or circuits. It seems fruitful to describe the domain of tasks in cognitive science in general and in cognitive linguistics in particular in following these principles.

Our starting point for a top-down analysis in linguistics is an interactive system of cognitive organisms having non-cognitive mechanisms (things, creatures) in their environment. The essential facts can already be specified by considering just two *cognitive organisms*, communicating in an environment, such as in Bühler's diagram (Fig.1; cf. Bühler, 1934). It contains two mental/biological systems A and B, relating

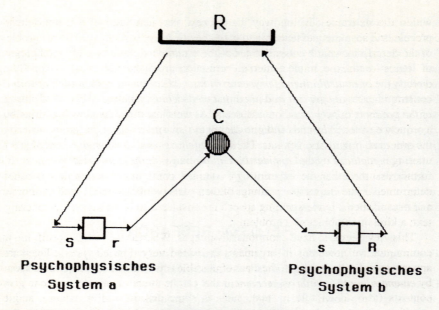

FIG. 1. Communication schema for cognitive organisms.

to an environment R and being related through a system C of communicative channels (acoustic, visual, etc.) for signal transmission. The specification of the environment may be thought of as given in ordinary or in scientific language. The properties of the transmission channels could be described in terms of the various sciences for signal transmission processes. The essential problems for further analysis are posed by the analysis of the functioning and structure of the bio-mental units A and B.

Ordinary language specifies the functioning of persons as bio-mental units by referring to the external functional characteristics of action (e.g. by speech-act verbs). It thus disregards the internal biological structures and mechanisms which form the basis for these abilities.

Particular examples are the abilities of speaking and understanding in some languages. These abilities presuppose the more concrete abilities, such as intentional causation of articulatory movements, auditory attention, and linguistic and conceptual understanding. Being able to understand means being able to repeat what can be said in a language and knowing why it was said. It seems that a scientific description of these processes in speakers and hearers would have to specify these various facts both individually and in relation to each other.

This is not, however, the way in which the grammatico-linguistic tradition approaches the problem. The enormous cultural importance of writing led to the assumption that speaking is just like producing a sequence of letters and hearing like following it with the eye, and that these sequences can be clearly separated into subunits, i.e. words and sentences, which identifiably reoccur at appropriate places within the sequences. In this way, the original problem to explain the bio-mental processes in speakers and hearers and in their environments is replaced by the problem of the description of the controlled production and recognition of sequential patterns of letters—or of the sound patterns corresponding to them. *Instead of* specifying directly the *internal bio-mental processes* or the external visual or acoustic phenomena constituting acts of speaking and hearing, one considers regularised forms of *patterns of the products of such acts*, i.e. one describes words and sentences as identifiable in a sequence of letters/sounds and one describes their order and organisation instead of the order and organisation of acts. The *study of the communicative functions* of acts of uttering is *replaced by the consideration of meanings of the words and sentences*. It is further assumed that the meanings of complex configurations (sentences) can be determined if one knows the meanings of their parts (words) together with their orders and organisations. Understanding speech is considered to be similar to deciphering a text, a kind of combinatorial problem.

This view seems to have enormous advantages. Whereas the task of specifying the communicative processes in organisms is indeed very difficult, this reduced task appears to be fairly tractable. The class of possible acts could be specified, so it seems, by *enumerating the words and sentences* that can be uttered in that language in given contexts (also specifiable by text, such as stage descriptions in drama), and by specifying in each case which *meaning* is communicated in each context. There are methodological requirements which determine the adequacy of description. First, one requires that the units of a language be correctly enumerated (this requirement is sometimes called "observational adequacy"). Secondly, one requires that sentences be correctly related to their meanings (this is the requirement of "descriptive adequacy"). Both of these terms are taken with respect to the reduced task of linguistics and not in the sense of observational or descriptive adequacy with respect to the actual bio-mental processes.

The core problem, however, still remains: the specification of the internal communicative dynamics of the bio-mental processes giving rise to sentences and texts. Modern grammarians have tackled this problem with a method of symbolic representation—they introduce terms for grammatical categories, grammatical features, and symbols for ordering (brackets of various forms) and represent internal structures by sequences and sets of sequences of such terms. Sentences and words are thus connected with sets of grammatical representations (in the form of symbol sequences) and the whole complex of sets is to be taken as a highly abstract representation intended to correspond to the actual occurring bio-mental patterns in the organism.

Moreover, these representations have internal structures cased in terms of algebraically specifiable operations and transformations, i.e. a combinatoric or formal syntax of symbols. Clearly, as a consequence, the combinatoric or syntax of symbols becomes the core discipline for theoretical linguistic analysis for specifying expressions as well as their grammatical structures. (We shall come back to this aspect.) In any case, the assumption underlying all specifications is that somehow—nobody knows as yet just how—the bio-mental patterns in the organism will correspond to these reduced patterns if they are observationally and descriptively adequate at least in the reduced sense.

The results of linguistic research carried out on this basis have been impressive and have proved that it is indeed a fruitful working hypothesis to consider an act of utterance as the ordered production of sequences of identifiable units and acts of hearing similar to deciphering a text.

The enormous advantages of this approach seem to be obvious. Representations of words and sentences, of their syntactically combinatorial structure and of formal patterns of meanings, all of them formally tractable in terms of written sequences, take the place of whatever the actual bio-mental facts in us may be. This substitution seems to be recommendable since, first, we do not yet have sufficiently adequate biological evidence, and, secondly, other representations are less tractable.

Some psycholinguists and linguists have recently come to disagree with this evaluation, arguing that though we do not yet know much about the actual bio-mental set-up we know enough to derive certain structural insights which contradict the assumption that there are rigorous combinatorial processes in our brains which combine and transform strings. The structures seem rather to emerge as patterns in a field of interactive units similar to the wave patterns on the surface of a lake. In applying various methods from discrete systems theory, such as the structured design of logical nets, signal flow graph networks (applied, for example, in linear filter design), and formal nerve nets, formally and theoretically adequate representations are possible. The argument of greater tractability advanced in favour of symbolic formalisms is valid at best only for scientists used to formal symbolic analysis (abstract algebra, formal logic, formal linguistics) but not for researchers of the natural sciences in general. Clearly, it is extremely important to evaluate the new approaches advocated by these psycholinguists and linguists and to study the basic questions of representation and appropriateness which are involved.

However, given the overwhelming and impressive mass of results obtained in formal linguistics on the basis of the simplifying assumptions discussed, it would certainly be irrational not to continue research based on these established idealisations.

The linguistic idealisations described had other consequences—the abstraction from the ways in which the understanding of words and sentences depend on the environment in which they are uttered. While it is generally true of texts that they are understandable independently from the environment in which one perceives them, this is not true of most of everyday speech, which is rather highly dependent on the situation, as can be seen from the dominant use of words like *I, you, this, now, come here*, etc. Moreover, it is doubtful that one can speak of an understanding of activity verbs abstractly, i.e. without specifying the concrete processes the organism experiences in situations in which these verbs apply. In any case, the full specification of linguistic form and content will necessarily be complicated in cases of language use in concrete situations. It then involves structure *and* concrete context simultaneously, i.e. activities such as *perceiving, acting, thinking, imagining, memorising*, etc., *concurrent to* the activities of the appropriate *articulation and identification of the words, sentences and texts.*

Thus we see that the abstraction leading from situation-determined language use to textual language use requires several intermediate steps. In analysing the speakers and hearers A and B (Fig.1), we must first separate the linguistic processes from the concurrent processes, such as vision and movement. This leads us back to the Leibnizean idea of construction: we must assign these different processes to different sub-units of the bio-mental units of A and B. Understanding sentences and texts would then be realised through the *cooperation of sub-units.* Each sub-unit would have a specialised task but, being able to interact with other sub-units, it would contribute to their activities whenever needed.

The sub-units would form a small society with a cooperative division of labour. The importance of elaborating this idea has been expressed on several occasions (e.g. Minsky, Hofstadter). It seems, however, that there is an essential difference between a society of interactive individuals and a system of interactive units in the organism: The latter do not move around to contact their colleagues, but sit at fixed positions, having fixed channels with their neighbours; this is the position of connectionism.

It is difficult to tell exactly, at present, what the essential sub-units should be. A possible suggestion might be the one presented in Fig.2. This is certainly not yet the

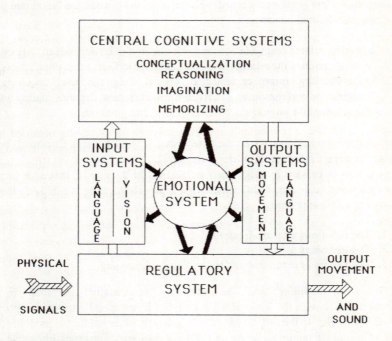

FIG. 2. Components of a cognitive system.

full system, but it relates important sub-units, such as vision and movement, conceptualisation and imagination, to language perception and language production, all in the context both of regulatory processes which stabilise the organic existence and of the emotional system which regulates attention and memorising.

This representation is an adaptation of one proposed by Norman and it seems that it has some biological plausibility as well as being functionally motivated. The sub-units may turn out to correlate with separate regions in the brain.

Functionally, the system also relates roughly to the four competencies enumerated in our report on *Cognitive Science in Europe: Analysis and Survey* (Imbert et al., 1987):

1. Perception (vision).
2. Language.
3. Reasoning.
4. Action (by movements of limbs, head, and trunk).

The report explained how these competencies can be studied with regard to the forms which they typically have in adults (referred to in the report under "ii. final state of development") or with regard to the various forms that can be found in the developing organism ("i. ontogenetic analysis of development").

An important topic which can be analysed at this level is *the multi-modal analysis of language*. Here we are concerned with the relation between the functional parts or modules just defined, because:

1. Situation-related language use (in particular in deixis) depends mainly on a clarification of the relation between Language to Perception plus Action.
2. Understanding more complicated textual language use, requiring imagination and reasoning and its conceptual frames, depends mainly on the relation of Language to Reasoning plus Imagination.

There has been much research on the latter area (see van Benthem, Chapter 8) but little research on the former (cf. Wahlster, Chapter 7).

It is now necessary to subdivide the field of the faculty of language (language perception and language production). A first approach might be to subdivide it into the following sub-components:

1. The *input-output transduction.*
2. The *grammatical-system*
3. The *system of discourse understanding and planning.*

Discourse planning and understanding is usually described in close correspondence with the logic of reasoning, but it has specific functional properties which are foreign to the ordinary logic of reasoning, in particular the modelling of the user of linguistic communication and of his pragmatic characteristics (cf. Wahlster, Chapter 7).

As regards their methods of description, the two fields—logic and discourse analysis—are, however, identical in that both define their systems in terms of rules for symbol manipulation. Discourse appears as a rationally conceived tool for transmitting information about states of affairs effectively (cf. Guenthner, Chapter 5). Some scientists see problems here, however, agreeing that the account given may be appropriate for written discourse, but they find it quite doubtful that the concept should apply naturally to discourse which is strictly situated by ongoing non-linguistic acts of perception and action, or small talk, etc.

The descriptive situation is quite different in the case of *input–output transduction*. The peripheral processes are usually described in terms of both real functions of time, i.e. temporal *signals*, and the differential equations which determine their generation in the articulating organ and their transformation in the cochlea. They can also be described by systems of integral transformations (such as Fourier transformations) which lead to the acoustic representation of sounds and to the definition of some of their *characteristic properties* (such as the formants which are characteristic for vowels).

The typical signals and properties are usually analysed and explained in the field of phonetics. The problems of *phonetics* are particularly important for linguistics in the present situation, because phonetics provides a wealth of insights into the *differences and correlations of modelling in terms of signal processes on the one hand and of symbol manipulation (phonemes and feature matrices) on the other*. We can even find models trying to relate the two in a mathematically precise way (e.g. Lindblom, 1986; Petitot, 1985).

Apart from the importance of phonetics deriving from reasons of principle, the results hold much promise for practical systems of speech production and recognition (cf. Laver, Chapter 2).

4. THE GRAMMATICAL SYSTEM AS THE CORE OF LINGUISTIC RESEARCH

We will now return to the grammatical issues mentioned on pp.8–10, because of the longstanding tradition of linguistic concern with writing and texts. It was this orientation which established the firm belief that the analyses and definitions of terminological, categorial and symbolic grammatical systems form the core of linguistic research.

Today, it is widely agreed by linguists that grammatical research was given a truly scientific status through the work of N. Chomsky, even if they vigorously disagree with some or all of the specific proposals made by him. Quite a number of basic methodological assumptions are usually accepted without question, often without awareness of the fact that they are far from obvious. I shall now discuss some of Chomsky's considerations about the scientific status of grammatical research.

Chomsky's approaches led to an analytical position according to which the basis of a science can be found in the form of its theories analysable as a system of formal representations and statements. Concern with the form of representations led to the dominance of combinations and transformations of symbol strings as the descriptive basis for strictly scientific theories in general and for linguistic theory in particular. The consequences of this for linguistics have already been presented on pp.8–10. Let us summarise the following points. Possible communicative acts, by speakers or hearers, should be specified by *enumerating formally the words and sentences* that can be uttered by them, and by specifying in each case which *meaning* is communicated in each context. As already has been mentioned above, the requirement to enumerate the units of a language correctly is called "observational adequacy" and the requirement to relate correctly sentences and their meanings "descriptive adequacy", both terms taken with respect to the reduced task of linguistics and not in the sense of observational or descriptive adequacy with respect to the actual bio-mental processes. The descriptive adequacy understood in this way implies that the relation between sound and meaning is mediated by appropriate structural descriptions, given in terms of symbol configurations of grammatical categories, features, feature values, etc., i.e. a formal system for deriving grammatical representations.

That *highest precision and rigour* could be achieved by concentrating on studying strings of symbols with the standard form known from print has been clear from the beginning—ever, since Leibniz' studies of logical calculi. That a corresponding approach allowed rigorous studies of linguistic expressions and their grammatical structures has been clear since Chomsky's proposals for formally rigorous generative grammars and his general theory of such grammars. As Chomsky stated:

> A [general] theory of generative grammar is concerned with the human language faculty as such. A grammar constructed in accordance with the principles postulated in such a theory gives an explicit characterization of a language and its structure—and within the broader semiotic theory envisioned but not developed here, an explicit characterization as well of the meaning and reference of expressions [acts of expressing] and conditions of appropriate use. So construed the theory can be accurately described as a study of one aspect of human intelligence, and thus constitutes a particular sub-branch of cognitive psychology. (Chomsky, 1975: 9).

Upon comparison of what has been said in the previous paragraphs, the words "but not developed here" stand out quite characteristically, as neither Chomsky nor his followers became concerned with this broader semiotic theory, i.e. in the context outlined in the previous paragraphs. On the contrary, the content was always restricted to questions of the form of expressions, as was traditional among grammarians. In this tradition, it was taken for granted that formal constraints of grammar can be studied and defined separately from questions of situational reference and conditions of use. Thus words like "there", "this", "now", "who", "do" and "no" are at best grammatically related to ordinary content words or expressions. Their special operative role in language use and language acquisition is completely neglected and moved out of focus, with the almost perfect agreement of grammarians (and logicians).

However, this has not been done without careful reflection. Chomsky explicitly stated that:

the study of meaning ... is unquestionably central to the general theory of language and a major goal of [my] approach is to advance it by showing how a sufficiently rich theory of *linguistic form* can provide structural descriptions that provide *the basis for* the fruitful investigation of *semantic questions* (Chomsky, 1975: 21).

The position is obviously the one which also prevails in formal logic and in logic applied to linguistics: the syntactic form is the basis for the semantic interpretation, or *Semantics presupposes Syntax.*

In a similar way, Chomsky argues for another position known from formal logic according to which the reason for "this self-imposed formality requirement [is that] there seems to be no other basis that will yield a rigorous, effective and 'revealing' theory of linguistic structure." (Chomsky, 1975: 18). As I have argued elsewhere (both in this Chapter and Chapter 6) this "reason" is today rather ill-founded.

For Chomsky then, it is obvious that the linguistic sub-branch of cognitive psychology should only be defined in terms of the forms of words and sentences. The linguist introduces various elements of form (phonemes, morphemes, lexemes, sentences and sentence constituents), and rules for their combination and relational correspondence.

The grammar of [language] *L* is a theory of *L*, incorporating the linguist's hypotheses concerning the elements and rules of L.... The theory of transformational generative grammar (or some other general linguistic theory) expresses a hypothesis concerning the "essence of language", the defining properties of human language (Chomsky, 1975: 9).

With a view to the development of a general cognitive science, Chomsky requires a corresponding theory for each human cognitive faculty:

Were such theories available for various cognitive systems, we might proceed to investigate the general structure of human intelligence. That is we might inquire into the interaction and relations of various cognitive systems, the general principles (if there are such) by which they operate, the relative independence of one system from the other, and so on (Chomsky, 1975: 10).

Chomsky considers it as obvious,

that the user of a language is a finitely specifiable organism and that language can be described by a discrete temporal process. But from these truisms it does not follow that the grammar represented in the mind of the speaker-hearer is a 'device' of this character [i.e. of a finite state source] and observations of the facts of language show clearly that it is not (Chomsky, 1975: 7).

These statements make it quite clear that Chomsky does not merely want to specify the cognitive faculties by a system of hypotheses about the abstract properties underlying intelligent behaviour but also aims at specifications of bio-mental properties, i.e. constraints on the structure of the organism which shows up language competence as a species of the organic faculties determining intelligent behaviour. More specifically, he thinks that this aim should be approached on two levels. First, a grammar should specify constraints on the adult organism which has acquired competence in a language and, secondly, the general theory of grammar should specify that particular endowment of a newborn child which enables her/him to acquire a specific competence in any language:

> General linguistic theory can appropriately be regarded as an explanatory theory, in that it seeks to explain how a child in a speech community comes to know the language of this community, and to know innumerable particular facts with regard to the form and meaning of particular expressions, and much else (Chomsky, 1975: 7).

The core of this explanation being the development of the knowledge of form as represented by sequences of symbols, of course!

The terms "knowledge" and "know the language" seem to refer to both the conscious conceptual knowing-that and the intuitive know-how, i.e. two aspects separated in other languages (e.g. German). This also applies to language competence: What we acquired naturally and without the aid of teaching in schools, is more similar to a skill than to a type of conceptual knowledge. This skill does indeed manifest itself in very regular forms, but this is typical for many special skills and does not constitute proof that one has to know something conceptually about what one is able to do. Regularity on its own does not show that its manifestations are controlled by some underlying conceptual knowledge.

My remark is not a mere quibble about words or definitions. Knowledge of a particular domain is naturally expressed by statements and rules. A skill is better characterised by the special organisation and control of the interacting organs. Hence the different terms suggest different ways of theorising! Since there are presently reasons to try new ways of theorising deviating from those commonly accepted among grammarians, we should be careful in our choice of basic terms.

But let us for the moment continue to present the common approach to formal grammar theory. An appropriate definition of the form or of the linguistic units of a language—such as the sentences of a language—requires characterisations under various different aspects. The formal specification of these different aspects is made on various descriptive "levels". Chomsky (1975) writes:

> we define, in general linguistic theory, a system of levels of representation. A level of representation consists of elementary units (primes), an operation of concatenation by which strings of primes can be constructed, and various relations defined on primes, strings of primes and sets and sequences of these strings.

On the basis of these operations and relations, abstract objects (in the sense of abstract algebra) are constructed:

Among the abstract objects constructed on the level L are L-markers that are associated with sentences. The L-marker of the sentence S is the representation of S on the level L. A grammar of a language, then, will characterize the set of L-markers for each level L and will determine the assignment of L-markers to sentences (Chomsky, 1975: 6).

Most approaches to linguistics agree with this view, both in form and content. In the same sense, Klein (Chapter 3) states that:

we claim that there are a number of levels of linguistic description which need to be taken into account; these may include phonetic, phonological, morphological, syntactic and semantic levels. In order to characterise a linguistic level, we need to define a set of primes (e.g. phones, morphemes, categories, etc.) and a set of operations on the primes; we also need to define possible relations between levels.

With respect to the syntactic level it is said that "syntactic structure determines how a complex expression is systematically composed out of parts" (ibid.). Klein explains how three different theories of grammar (Transformational Grammar, Lexical Function Grammar, Generalised Phrase Structure Grammar and Unification Based Grammar as an extension of these) provide differing formal contents to this common conception.

There are alternatives to this approach. The alternative which I advocate agrees also with the conception of levels but disagrees with the conception that structure is determined by combinatorial operations and relations defined over sets of primes. In my view, a level should be conceived as a spatio-temporal region in which activities develop and are momentarily represented. Activity configurations at the sensory periphery may represent the presence of a speech signal and start a process (represented by evolving internal activities) which ends with a configuration which codes L-markers of the sentence embodied in the speech signal. The resulting configurations of states may then be understood as one of the momentary sentence representations possible in the spatio-temporal region (e.g. an idealised part of a brain region). The activity configurations do not result from combinatorial operations (such as concatenations, structural combinations and transformations) but rather from processes of interaction relating local units of symbol occurrences (each of which may also be understood as a linguistic hypothesis about what is momentarily present in the environment). The formal character of a level is that of *signal processing dynamics* (specifiable in ways similar to systems known from spatio-temporal dynamics, e.g. in terms of inhomogenous difference equations) and *not that of an abstract algebra*. This is a brief indication of a formal alternative to the currently prevailing conception of the specification of linguistic levels.

There is thus general agreement among linguists with respect to the following: *Grammar can (and must) be subdivided* into a system of *levels*. According to this view, each structurally unambiguous sentence (a possible expression in a language) receives a *representation of its structure on each level*. The assignment of the structures is determined by a *formal system of conditions*. We shall return later to the question of how the representations and the system of conditions could be described formally or mathematically.

In ordinary systems of linguistic analysis the dynamic nature of the processes of generation or interpretation is not yet determined directly by the rule specifications assigned to the units of expressions at the different levels, but must be specified by *procedures which implement the rule systems*. The processes which actually provide a structure for a given utterance are called *parsing procedures*. The system can thus be separated into two parts:

1. The processor with its procedures (acting as an *active control* system).
2. The stored rules and symbol structures (constituting the passive *data* structures).

The system thus reflects the well-known structure of rational processing. The results of processing seem to come about through the cooperation of two distinct systems: an *active system* (symbol manipulator) and a *passive system* (store).

A careful analysis of the cognitive processing going on in the human organism must bring us, however, to an *important modification* of such a conception. We find that the passive system must be more than an inactive store. Even if the system is called passive—as it is in Husserl, 1939/1972—it is only passive in so far as the processors which determine consciousness are not involved. It is not passive in the sense of not changing its states. On the contrary, the passive system itself processes and stores information.

We have a cooperation of two systems which is similar to that between a Turing machines "head" and a "tape" or memory space which is not inactive but is itself a connectionist network (see Schnelle, 1981a; 1981b). A similar suggestion has been made by Fodor:

> If we start with anything like Turing machines as models of cognitive psychology, we must think of them as embedded in a matrix of subsidiary systems which affect their computations in ways that are responsive to the flow of environmental events (Fodor, 1983: 39; cf. Schnelle, 1983: 1).

Quite recently, this idea was introduced as a suggestion for the further development of parallel distributed processing concepts by Norman (1986: 543) where the active system is called DCC (deliberate conscious control). Essentially, it has the properties which I also enumerated, following Husserl. Norman's suggestion was accepted as a major task for future PDP research (McClelland et al., 1986: 549). The editors mention that "a slight variant of this approach is to embed calls to parallel modules inside a conventional sequential processing scheme". A more detailed specification of the model has been presented by Smolensky (1988).

This idea appears to be exactly what is suggested for a parsing system by Tanenhaus, Carlson, and Seidenberg (1985). There we have a *general cognitive system* which consists of as many modules as there are linguistic levels, all of them operating in parallel. The general cognitive system has access to the output of each of the modules.

It has also access to the knowledge base stored in the cognitive system in what psychologists commonly refer to as the episodic and semantic memory (Tanenhaus et al., 1985: 365). There is, however, a contrast between what Fodor and Tanenhaus et. al. suggested and my proposals. For me the modules are not "impenetrable" by direct conscious control. Instead, their operation can be brought under conscious control, at least partly when the tasks they have to solve become too difficult. In this case the operation of an interactive tape unit is substituted by controlled operation of the reading and writing head. If, however, the situation is simple, unambiguous, and straightforward, the active system (the deliberate conscious control, in Norman's terms) will not interfere. There is another aspect of the model by Tanenhaus et. al. with which I disagree. In their model the information cannot flow from one module to the other without the interference of the general cognitive system. Here again I believe that in the case of relatively simple sentences which are understood automatically (in a psychological sense), the general cognitive system does not interfere. It only interferes when the situation becomes too difficult, ambiguities have to be resolved by thought, etc.

These clarifications out of the way, we can present the grammatical system with an input transducer as in Fig.3. This is an adaptation of that given by Tanenhaus et al. (1985: 380).

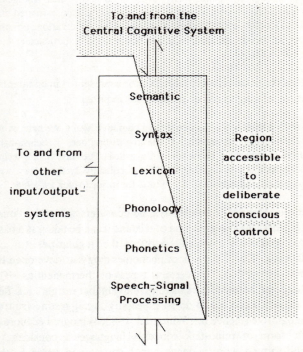

FIG. 3. Levels of a linguistic input/output system.

LL—C

5. DIMENSIONS OF CONCEPTUAL ANALYSIS

The fact that the disciplines of logic and linguistics are not to be considered in themselves but in the context of cognitive science and research on artificial intelligence requires, to my mind, a careful analysis of the aspects involved to locate problems and to organise interdisciplinary cooperation.

The scientists of each discipline must have a global knowledge of how their colleagues approach their problems empirically and conceptually, on the one hand, and mathematically on the other. Having now discussed the sub-division of the problem areas of linguistics, I shall turn to the dimensions of conceptualisation and then the aspects of mathematical modelling. In the former, we distinguish aspects of the phenomenologically motivated fixing of levels, aspects of learning, and dimensions of abstraction.

In our discussion of the fields of linguistics we referred to different levels in a Leibnizean spirit. The criteria were, however, mainly structural and must be distinguished from the phenomenological criteria which also lead to a fixing of levels in the approaches. In this connection, MacKay wrote:

> Man as a phenomenon requires many levels to do him justice. The science of man inevitably provides us with a whole spectrum of accounts framed in categories appropriate to its own level. The key question is how these various possible scientific accounts are related to one another and to our personal experience as human beings (MacKay, 1980: 27).

For MacKay the personal experience is to be represented in an intentional language of human action relating to our own conscious experience:

> We know at first hand what it is like to be a cognitive agent. We bear witness to these facts in first-person statements: I see-this-as-brighter; I hear-a-car-coming; I feel-a-pain-in-my-tooth; I know-(or believe-)it-is-Tuesday; I am-trying-to-decide -on-a-holiday-spot; and so on. Let us call these, collectively, the *I story*, where I stands for the first personal pronoun, or, if you like, for inside (MacKay, 1984: 293).

As the title of MacKay's article says, he considers this to be "mind-talk". It is, however, an intuitive, unanalysed kind of talk and it can be taken as a basis for analysis in "conscious givenness", which uncovers the regularities (in consciousness) underlying this talk. This is the task of phenomenology, as developed by Husserl and his followers, as well as in certain types of hermeneutics. The results of phenomenology and hermeneutics have given valuable insights (cf. Schnelle 1981a, 1981b) and may be expected to do so especially in suggesting fruitful explanatory schemata in cognitive science (cf. Winograd, 1983: Winograd & Flores, 1986).

A specific form of mind-talk concerns language: I consider " ..." to be a well-formed/ill-formed word/sentence and I am sure to agree in this with other speakers of my language. Judgements of this type form a wealth of empirical data in linguistics which require systematic analysis and explanation in terms of underlying grammatical structure.

MacKay confronts "I-stories" and their analysis results ("mind-talk") with scientific accounts—"O-stories" where O stands for *intersubjectively observable* or *"outside"*:

> As an observer you would have a large choice of stories [levels] each of which could claim to be complete in its own terms. You might choose to talk about a man out in front of you scratching his head and scribbling [or mumbling some words] in English; alternatively you might talk about a living organism engineered in protoplasm, having a certain mass, volume, temperature and the like, wiggling some of its limbs to and fro (MacKay, 1980: 17).

"Of particular interest are those levels of brain science at which, among other things, we can in principle hope to find a correlate of the I-story in physiological categories . ... Let us call these collectively the *brain story*" (MacKay, 1984: 223). Below the levels of brain stories:

> a molecular physicist might have still another story to tell in terms of the coordinated motions of billions of organic molecules. In other words, what we are referring to as the O-story [observer's story] is really a whole hierarchy of stories .... Whether we study a human being scientifically or in other less sophisticated ways, what we see—the kind of points we recognize, and the kind we will miss—may depend crucially on the relationship we adopt, and the categories we choose to employ. No single O-story, however complete at its own level, can say all that needs to be said about man. If we do not choose the right logical level at which to give our description, important points may be totally missed. Understanding, as distinct from mere cataloguing, requires the choice of an appropriate level of description for the aspect that we want to understand (MacKay, 1980: 17–18).

Essentially the differences between stories depend on the objects and properties at different orders of magnitude. Each order of magnitude requires, as a matter of course, a particular system of concepts and terms and the systems for different orders of magnitude relate to each other as "micro" and "macro"; in fact each level is "micro" with respect to some levels and "macro" with respect to others.

It is a general and important insight that in the description of complicated phenomena different levels have to be taken into account:

> If one hopes to achieve a full understanding of a system as complicated as a nervous system, a developing embryo, a set of metabolic path ways, a bottle of gas, or even a large computer program, then one must be prepared to contemplate different kinds of explanation at different levels of description that are linked, at least in principle, into a cohesive whole, even if linking the levels in complete detail is unpracticable (Marr, 1982: 20).

In this context, we must certainly also acknowledge the possibility of taking an even broader perspective of description, in which, in addition to the levels referring to an individual organism and its parts, we also have levels referring to aggregates, a pair of communicating organisms, an organism and its environment including its cultural environment, a group of organisms, etc. This would be in the spirit of *ecological approaches* to psychology (von Uexküll, Gibson) or of anthropology.

The cognitive abilities of human beings are acquired during developmental processes. This is particularly important for language. *Principled considerations of the formal conditions on language learning* (Wexler, 1979), may provide a first guideline for our discussion.

According to Wexler, we should characterise development as a process of learning based on the existence of some *learning mechanism* in the organism. There are two positions that may be distinguished:

1. The mechanism in the organism is a *general learning mechanism* "sufficient to account for the learning of any kind of human capacity" (Wexler, 1979: 295). Many approaches in theoretical psychology are based on this assumption, among them associationism, and neural network learning processes (Hebb, 1949), right up to the latest suggestions of the PDP group (Rumelhart et al. 1986: 41, 152f., 159f.), Kohonen (1977, 1984), and Palm (1982), or various proposals from physics, mainly synergetic processes.

2. According to the other position it is assumed that the organism has *specific learning mechanisms* based on *specific capacities* (second-order abilities) allowing the organism to *learn specific* (first order) *abilities* such as the ones mentioned above. Language learning would thus be the outcome of a specific language-learning mechanism different from the mechanism which is responsible for learning the visual representation of the environment.

The first position usually prevails among theoreticians of peripheric perception and physiological transduction. Theoreticians analysing more complicated human capacities such as language, visual understanding of scenarios, imagination, reasoning etc. have usually been sceptical about the possibility of a general mechanism. They typically assume that "very little that is characteristic and fundamental in human cognition is learnable in this sense" (Wexler, 1979: 296). These theoreticians prefer the second position of specific learning mechanisms.

For language, the specific learning mechanism may be developed on the basis of the following principles:

1. *Principle I (Learnability)*: Language *is* learned, that is every normal child *can* learn any natural language. This principle is "firmly grounded in experience" (Wexler, 1979: 291).

   • *Principle Ia (Easy or natural learnability)*: Language is learnable in a natural way. This "condition demands that language learning take place in the apparently easy and quick manner in which children do the learning. Not only is convergence demanded, but we must also have quick and simple convergence" (Wexler, 1979: 292).

- *Principle Ib (Learnability in stages)*: Language learning passes through various intermediate and identifiable stages and leads to a final (stable) stage.

2. *Principle II (Correlation of learning and linguistic theory)*: The representation of the final state of the learning process (the adult representation) is to be given by the "representation reached by linguistic theory [or, more generally, the theory accounting for the developed capacity, whose learnability is to be accounted for]" (Wexler, 1979: 291).

- *Principle IIa (Correlation of learning and linguistic theory of stages)*: Not only the final state but also the intermediate states are to be given by the representations specified by a linguistic theory for linguistic subsystems, markedness relations, etc.

Most linguists would usually take principle II for granted, some also principle IIa. They would assume that a clear theoretical understanding of the complexities, structures, and types of uses at the various stages (but in particular at the final stage) would be a precondition for the specification of natural learning mechanisms. They would specify the tasks of the "theory of language acquisition to include:

prediction of the stages of language acquisition (the time course) and a theory of how the child can construct his grammar (over time) under empirically true conditions concerning data (input to the child), memory, and so on. Given the limited kind of data available to developmental psycholinguistics, it is difficult to see how an adequate explanatory theory could be constructed without taking into account the final state of the learner (Wexler, 1979: 295).

On the basis of these assumptions an interesting learning theory has been developed for language, in particular by Osherson and Weinstein (1984) and Osherson et al. (1984), which concerns the specification of a learning function whose application generates a sequence of conjectures of grammars from utterances presented. The application of the function has the following properties:

1. It is not disturbed by a limited amount of noise.
2. It has a certain locality property, i.e. the next conjecture (about grammatical structure) is only based on the current conjecture and memory of recent sentences).
3. It presupposes an ordering of the space of accessible hypotheses (of grammatical structure) in "increasing complexity" in such a way that the learning procedure never has to take too large a leap in forming its next conjecture. (Berwick, 1985).

The arguments given by Wexler, Osherson et. al., and Berwick are primarily directed against views which hold that language learning is possible without innate structure in the organism. They are able to show that this assumption is not cogent: we need to assume an innate language acquisition device (LAD). There are quite a number of psychologists and some linguists who would agree with this general point but would be *very* dissatisfied by the restriction of the argumentation to questions of syntactic form and by the exclusion of functional semantic context and communicative interaction. Some researchers, myself included, would believe that:

1. We have in addition *innate endowments for communicative competence and for referential attention and that the activation of all three competencies are innately interdependent.*

2. The innate mechanism may presuppose another device in adults, a device called a *Language Acquisition Support System* (LASS; Bruner, 1983), such that *only both systems*, LAD and LASS, *together are sufficient to produce language learning.* Syntactic competence is a necessary but by no means sufficient component of the innate endowments for language learning.

Even with respect to the learning of language form, the possibility of accepting or rejecting principle II depends on which linguistic theory is assumed. If the linguistic theory assumes that adult language is adequately described by only one system of rules—as most linguists do—and that the stages of language learning are just stepwise approximations to this system, one may have grave doubts. Some linguists (Wegener, Brugmann, Bühler) hold that language learning is a process of fundamental change of language structure, leading from a language completely determined by concurrent sensory motor processes (a dominantly deictic language), over intermediate stages of intuitively elaborated conceptual determination (cf. McNeill, 1979), to a stage at which language form and analytic thinking become interdependent (cf.Bruner, 1975). The effect of this last step is to change language from its intuitive use, "in which one deals in concrete events in a logic that is *ad hoc*, local rather than universal, probabilistic, and not based on propositions related to each other by a principle of logical necessity" (ibid.:70), into an elaborated language form which allows the transmission of information independently of situation or conceptualisation. This is, finally, the stage of the autonomy of language structure which is often wrongly supposed to characterise language in general. If the linguistic theory mentioned in Wexler's principle II refers only to the elaborated syntactic devices characteristic of this phase, this principle is wrong. As Bühler put it, we overestimate the degree to which our current language use is independent from the situation and the degree in which hypotactical devices of sentence structure dominate over more paratactic chaining (cf. Schnelle, 1984). What we put to use is a mixture of the devices learned at different stages (one built on the top of the other) and still available and applied whenever appropriate and "ready-to-hand". It is essential to note that the spontaneous deictic stage is *multi-modal*, or better embedded *in the sensory motor system form of language.*

Let me re-emphasise this last point: it is only a form of language! The sentence "Put this there!" is only well-formed when there are gestures accompanying the words "this" and "there". Deictic terms function only in connection with acts of orientation and deixis is not a peripheral phenomenon of language as the logician and the formal linguist would like it to be. As Bühler made quite clear, classifying these small words as pronouns is a perspective taken by the grammarian interested in the classification of words according to their possible positions within sentences in fully developed autonomous language. But in their concrete use, these words do not *stand for* nouns but they function referentially. This example should be sufficient in the present context to illustrate the incorrect perspectives taken by the monosystemic grammarians, which judge words merely as to their formal roles in complicated sentence constructions.

Which are the consequences to be drawn from research in the context of cognitive science and artificial intelligence? I think that some remarks by Bruner are very relevant in this context:

> language acquisition begins...when mother and infant create a predictable format of interaction that can serve as a microcosm for communicating and for constituting a shared reality (Bruner, 1983: 18).

Furthermore, it has been established by psychologists that:

> much of early infant action takes place in constrained, familiar situations and shows a surprisingly high degree of order and "systematicity" (ibid.: 28).

It seems to me that these phenomena need further theoretical analysis in the context of information processing, and that it is quite feasible to create appropriate information processing environments. A first approximation would be a computer or information processing system supplied with a video-camera and microphones as input channels, a (possibly simple) arm/hand-system as an output channel and programs for the analysis of vision and the analysis and production of speech and gesture as a basis for creating "a predictable format of interaction that can serve as a microcosm for communicating and for constituting a shared reality". We may thus obtain simple *transactional formats for a sort of quasi-natural language learning*. In this way we would *provide the information processing system with a very concrete knowledge of language and conceptualisation* which would be a much better base for the understanding of orders given by human beings in concrete situations than if the information processing system had only been given an abstract internal knowledge base.

Many phenomena which have been studied in human language learning could be reproduced in similar ways. The role of speech intonation for the binaurally determined orientation of the hearer to an attentional target enabling the vision intended by the speaker is an important early phenomenon in language learning to be realised in situational communication with artificial systems (cf. Lyons, 1975; Bruner, 1983: 72–3).

6. ASPECTS OF MATHEMATICAL MODELLING

It can be easily appreciated that this wealth of conceptual and formal levels and categorial systems can lead to misunderstandings between specialists and to apparent incompatibilities of approach even where in fact merely different aspects of the same phenomenon are involved. The basis for agreement should always be sought in those domains in which a common orientation is most easily achieved, namely in:

1. The *careful clarification* of common conceptual schemata.
2. The development and application of *mathematically oriented structural definitions of models*.
3. The *detailed mathematical analysis* of descriptive theories.

It seems that the *essential level of comparison* is, in fact, the second one, i.e. the level of formal explanation through mathematically oriented definitions of models: *Conceptual clarifications should be oriented by the types of mathematical modellings chosen and the detailed mathematical analysis should be determined by these models.*

At the level of formal explanatory modelling we are confronted with conceptual frameworks which seem to be fundamentally different:

1. The frames of *modelling in terms of symbol manipulation.*
2. The frames of *modelling in terms of signal processes* (discrete or continuous).

Mathematically, the former framework is based on abstract algebra (which is in turn inspired by group theoretical analysis). The primary concept is an associative two-argument operation, often interpreted as concatenation, and the secondary concept is the replacement operation. These algebraic models are particularly popular in logic and linguistics, and in program-theoretic computer science (in contrast to hardware design).

The signal systems are analytic. Their primary notions are one-argument functions which assign values to entities of a given domain and relate different functional assignments. The functions are usually interpreted as measurable quantities assigning numerical values to objects or space-time points. Difference equations or differential equations define the interdependencies of neighbouring value assignments, i.e. constraints defined on possible value assignments for a given domain. These methods of mathematical description are popular in phonetic, associationist, distributionist, connectionist, psychological, electro-acoustic and concrete parts of hardware design.

The former disciplines have generated their conceptual framework around the central notions of (constructive) *representation* (or symbolic information) and *computation* (change of representation) and claim that the *essential features* of cognitive processes are to be explained with reference to them. This position postulates a logical and methodological priority for modelling based on *symbol manipulations* specified either more abstractly in terms of *rule systems* (calculi), or more concretely in terms of *algorithms* and *computer programs* (usually for current so-called von Neumann computers).

In many cases, the proponents of this position go even further, saying that we should not only specify our theories by means of (formal) representations and computations (that is obvious), but we should also assume that the representations and computations described really *exist* in the organism *in the form of particular stored marks and memory manipulations* whose form is structurally equivalent to the formal symbolic description. In this view, symbols and symbol substitutions are not merely units which the theorist uses on paper, they really *exist in* the organism. Thus, a structural correspondence between the descriptive apparatus and the desired phenomena is postulated—both are representations and computations which change representations—in contrast to most other sciences. In so far as cognitive science is based on this conception, it is obvious that formal logic, formal linguistics and information processing will form the methodological and theoretical core of cognitive science.

Pinker and Prince (1988) even called it a:

'central dogma' of modern cognitive science ...that intelligence is the result of manipulation of symbolic expressions. To understand language and cognition, according to this view, one must break them up into two aspects: the rules or symbol-manipulating processes capable of generating a domain of intelligent human performance, to be discovered by examining systematicities in people's perception and behavior, and the elementary symbol-manipulating mechanisms made available by the information-processing capabilities of neural tissue, out of which the rules or symbol-manipulating processes would be composed.

As Pinker and Prince continue:

the strategy has remained compelling [because] it has given us precise, revealing, and predictive models of cognitive domains that have required few assumptions about the underlying hardware other than that it makes available some very general elementary processes of comparing and transforming symbolic expressions (Pinker & Prince, 1988: 2).

In their mathematical structure, we are thus only concerned with elements of algebraic semi-groups (strings) and the systematic mappings defining constraints on them, i.e. the specific structure embodied in the domain of cognitive phenomena for which the mathematical model is defined.

This position may well enhance the challenge for the formally oriented disciplines, but from the point of view of interdisciplinary organisation it brings with it a *serious danger*—the danger of methodological one-sidedness—precisely because of its restricted type of modelling. The natural sciences also use formalisms and it is difficult to understand why these formalisms should be ruled out in cognitive science. It is certainly true that in very abstract investigations of quantum-theory, algebraic methods also play an important role for organising systems of field-theoretic equations. The difference is, however, that this discipline knows how to relate the conditions of algebraic abstraction to the concrete dynamic facts which constitute the processes to be explained. This is not the case for linguistic abstraction, where possible relations to dynamic processes are not merely abstracted away—this would be understandable—but are not even understood in principle.

In arguing against this one-sidedness, one might perhaps come to agree with MacKay that:

> although an abstract theory of 'ideal' cognitive processes can doubtless be developed in ignorance of all neuroscience, this enterprise should be sharply distinguished from the effort to understand human cognitive experience, which I maintain cannot be divorced from the study of neural processes ... one natural way to make neuroscience helpfully relevant to cognitive science, and vice versa, is to develop information engineering specifications for the tasks performed by the nervous system and (conversely) for the information-processing repertoire offered by its components (MacKay, 1984: 305).

There are some positions which accept the requirement to understand the relation between cognitive processes defined by systems of symbol manipulation and the descriptions of the possible embodiments of the latter in neural networks or similar networks of elementary operational units. Marr has made a proposal as to how this relation could be clarified. We should distinguish according to him:

1. The analysis and definition of *what* the goal of a particular task to be described is and why it is appropriate.
2. The analysis and definition of *how* the task can be implemented by an algorithm (which can be executed by a universal computer).
3. The analysis and definition of an *embodiment*, i.e. a neural (or electronic) net of simple interactive units realising the task.

For the first level we may distinguish an intuitive conceptual clarification of the task from a formal definition. Marr calls the latter the *computational* analysis, referring in this connection to the work of Chomsky, and implying thereby that the best way for it to be defined is cognitive analysis in terms of symbol manipulation. As algorithms are also defined in terms of symbol manipulations the relation between symbol manipulation and signal processing seems to be that between the second and third levels.

This is probably the prevailing view. I do not find it, however, very fruitful. It seems to me that, from a sufficiently abstract point of view, the relations expressed by sequential replacements in strings (or trees or whatsoever) should also be representable as changes of states in configurations (e.g. sequences) of interactive units which take place automatically (as contrasted with replacements caused by an agent following rules) whenever certain contextual situations are present. This suggestion certainly needs some detailed underpinning, but the principle should at least be clear. If this

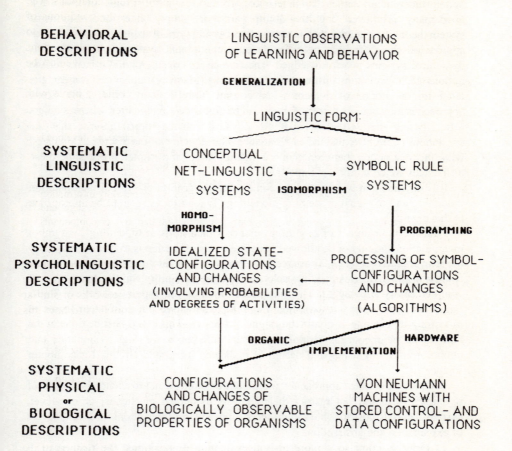

FIG. 4.   Levels of explanation and formal representation in linguistics.

suggestion is feasible, we could correlate rule systems directly with structurally equivalent networks. These networks could then be enriched on another level by using continuous, instead of discrete, information (yielding a counterpart to an algorithm), and then further refined to take into account the details of the physical embodiment. The relations among the different conceptual levels are given in Fig. 4.

The theoretical position illustrated to the left of Fig. 4 is different from positions which maintain that one level of analysis, namely the physical, is enough, though it is similar to them in assuming that the same methods (those of system theoretic analysis) can be applied on each level. The position thus agrees with the physicalist positions in so far as it also recognises the importance of studying alternative approaches to the formal approaches of mainstream cognitive science; simply understood in terms of system-theoretic principles than in terms of processing symbol strings. I believe that a good many 'privileged' cognitive abilities are more simply understood in terms of system theoretic principles than in terms of processing symbol strings. In some of these approaches the difference between discrete operational systems and continuous dynamical systems is acknowledged. The former are considered to be basic for the notions of information, information engineering (MacKay) and measurement, the latter for the notion of dynamics and control (Carello et al. 1984: 238). Some approaches may believe that the former can be embedded in the latter, whereas others (often basing themselves on quantum physical considerations) assume that the continuous could be explained as a statistical consequence of the discrete. Compared with the distinction between symbol manipulation and signal processing these differences are certainly less important.

It is obvious that we must try to come to an integration of symbol manipulation modelling and of signal processing modelling. Two attitudes seem to be appropriate in this regard.

First the mainstream of cognitive science which aims at modelling by symbol manipulation should not be allowed to define on its own what is to be understood by the term cognitive science. Those research groups which continue their research in the context of the mainstream should acknowledge the possibility and the desirability of complementary approaches. The disciplines based on this type of modelling (logic, linguistics, computer science) should develop alternative but equivalent forms of modelling by discrete or continuous signal processes. This could best be done at the borders of neighbouring disciplines (visual inferences for logic, phonetics and phonology for linguistics and design of dedicated integrated circuits for computer science).

Secondly, the other approaches (dominant in biology, neuroscience and parts of psychology) should not restrict their analysis to radical physicalist or one-level, system-theoretic positions but should accept and develop descriptions on several levels of explanation and abstraction.

In order to come to a more neutral evaluation of positions, the mathematical structures underlying the approaches should be specified and the *levels of descriptive complexity* should be evaluated. The levels of descriptive complexity are determined by the complexity of the space of possible *attributes or values* assigned to real or idealised *units*. We should not just count numbers but also more complicated entities, vectors, strings, trees or other configurations as value configurations (marks) on squares on a tape or "sheet" (corresponding to Turing's proposal). Whether the values or marks are changed by an agent or automatically when appropriate neighbourhood values obtain should be considered as irrelevant to the kind of descriptive complexity.

There is certainly not yet an established theory on these matters, but the problem as such should be clear enough to set an *excellent research goal*. A start should perhaps be made by classifying the complexities of the values assignable to the different units described above. The most simple cases are those whose states may be characterised by two values (the *Boolean* value set). The next level of complexity is the one usually found in physics. There one assumes units whose status can be described by *numbers* (natural, real, imaginary) or *vectors, matrices, arrays*, etc., with numerical values. In removing the restriction of limited lengths for vectors and accepting *sets of symbols as values* for the vector components, we gradually move to the notions of *strings, configurations*, and then to sets of the latter, i.e. *formal languages* and even *representations of structure descriptions*. It is usually understood that more complicated values can only be assigned to more complicated units; thus languages (more exactly the individual knowledge of language) can only be assigned to whole areas of the brain which realise language production and understanding. Vectors of finite length are usually assigned to registers in a computer, i.e. units more complicated than a simple bit-store.

In referring in this way to the underlying mathematical structures of processing, many misunderstandings or controversies could be resolved and theoretical positions which were described in purely conceptual terms, and which appear to be fully incompatible, could be related as being more or less specific descriptions of the same facts.

It should thus be clear, after these indications, that it is in the last analysis very difficult to understand the intuitively deeply felt difference between a system-theoretic state description, a Turing machine or a Post-type calculus. After all, we are in each case confronted with certain changes of configurations of marks which are defined by functions. What is the formal difference between a rule for the change of symbol configurations on a tape and a law for the change of vector values assigned to locations or particles? To me the essential point is that we need several levels of formal descriptions. But as Marr remarked, this is characteristic for any complicated phenomenon—it is as Leibniz saw quite clearly—a sign of the complication which is typically found in organisms. What this calls for is architectural insight into how the complexity characterised on a coarse-grained level of analysis is related to complexes of simpler units on a finer-grained level of analysis (cf. Shaw et al., 1982: 194–195; Fowler & Turvey, 1982: 3, 10–15).

The insight (originating from the formal analysis of effective computation) that the same complicated behaviour (specified as a calculable function) can result from different functional architectures is, of course, correct. But instead of taking this as an argument not to become concerned with functional architecture at all, we could also take it as a challenge to find out those architectures compatible with as much *data about the internal organism* to be modelled as possible. Separating our problem into analysis on different levels, and with coarse- or fine-grained analysis, it becomes clear that interdisciplinary research should proceed at all levels simultaneously, all the time trying to relate them.

7. RESEARCH TASKS

What are the promising research areas that linguistics in the context of research into artificial intelligence and cognitive science should be concerned with? As Klein points out, the promising research areas should be considered to be those which (a) involve central concerns of linguistic theory, (b) offer some hope of significant progress in the next 5 years, and, in most cases, (c) raise research problems of an interdisciplinary nature, with a view to achieving a unified cognitive model. We should distinguish:

1. Research in *the well-established core areas (words–sentences–texts) using standard methods* such as representation by symbol-structures and implementations on ordinary computers (the core areas of linguistics and logic).

2. Research in *fundamentally related areas (speech processing, visual perception of scenes, gestures, and facial expressions)* which necessarily require the application of non-symbolic methods and which may lead to *integrated systems of speech and vision* applicable to concrete situations.

3. Research into *new methods of description in the core areas of linguistics*, such as methods representing linguistic structure and structure of linguistic behaviour in terms of the *connectivities of parallel interactive units*, rather than by the connectivities of the combinatorially defined symbolic configurations known from standard approaches.

Let me summarise some specific challenges in these three research areas:

1. Current systems are usually only developed for small and limited domains and applications. It is of very considerable importance, whether a language system comprises 100 or whether it comprises tens of thousands of words, whether it is able to act according to a few standard rules or whether it is a complicated system of flexible rules. We have experience with quite a number of promising models of the first type. We are now faced with the formidable problem of *projecting the insight* gained in studying small models on *to large-scale language systems* (using large grammars, or large dictionaries). We will need much experience with methods which extend a system without disturbing its established properties. (cf. p.4; also Klein, Chapter 3).

The problem cannot merely be solved theoretically. On the contrary, very practical steps must be taken: *specialised software tools for speeding up the development of large dictionaries and grammars and for ensuring their well-formedness and consistency* must be developed (cf. Wahlster, Chapter 7).

The various grammatical properties of different languages have been studied to quite different depths. There are some important features (e.g. free word order, disjunct constituents) which present problems which are not yet as clear as others. We thus need *deeper grammatical and lexicological insight* (cf. Klein, Chapter 3).

Grammatical and semantical analyses have traditionally stopped at the borders of sentences. Sentences in texts, however, are of course understood by dependence on previous sentences and their meaning. The conditions for understanding change gradually as the text unfolds. This has been very extensively studied in recent years under the heading of *language and discourse* with regard to both its syntactic and semantic characters. In the latter context modifications of processes of formal logic are involved (cf. Klein, Chapter 3; Guenthner, Chapter 5; van Benthem, Chapter 8).

Much theoretical research has addressed problems of one level only and has also presupposed unproblematic combinations with other levels (e.g. the relation between the syntactic and morphological levels). We need many more *studies* about structuring and defining *different levels and their composition* (cf. Klein, Chapter 3).

Another very important research area is the *relation of well-formed and semantically well-determined expressions to ill-formed or ill-determined expressions*, which are nevertheless understood by human listeners. Could we specify systems for automatic correction of spelling errors, errors of grammatical or logical structure, etc.? It is obvious that the flexibility and applicability of automatic language processing will heavily depend on the solution to this problem.(cf. Wahlster, Chapter 7).

The previous considerations have mainly been concerned with linguistic knowledge. As Wahlster points out, the development of practical natural language systems must overcome the *problems of integrating the linguistic system with other areas of knowledge, such as conceptual knowledge, inferential knowledge*, etc. These different types of knowledge are usually defined by the same methods as linguistic knowledge, that is, by symbol-structures and rule systems (in contrast to integrated speech and vision systems or non-standard specifications of linguistic skills).

A rather particular example is the very important *problem of text generation*, which involves translating the knowledge represented in a formal language into natural language text (cf. Wahlster, Chapter 7).

2. The central concern is the development of a unified cognitive model (cf. Laver, Chapter 2). It is connected with some very *fundamental problems* and a number of *specific ones*. The fundamental problems concern:

(a) *Relating the results obtained from different research areas*, such as speech and vision, and the results obtained in *direct development of integrated systems* involving more than one area.

(b) *Relating high-level cognitive studies* (linguistic structures and high-level vision) *to low-level, neuro-muscular and neurosensory studies*, bridging simultaneously the *gap between symbol-oriented methods and signal processing methods* (cf. Laver, Chapter 2).

The analysis and definition of systems for speech production and speech recognition provide clear insight into the fundamental issue of the *link between (high-level) linguistic form and (low-level) speech substance*. Linguistic form is realised in terms of sequences of units. In speech production we are faced with the problem of appropriately specifying the various durational and rhythmic activities, the synchronisation of the various articulators and the determination of their coarticulatory interdependencies, etc. (cf. Laver, Chapter 2). In speech recognition the main problem is the separation of the acoustic information, allowing the identification of a linguistic expression, from those factors which merely signal the voice characteristics of speakers and the specifics of their momentary style of speech. The problem is particularly difficult because the acoustic signal is not usually sufficiently distinct on its own and can only be decoded in context. A human speaker understands everything that is said in the context of the situation and previous utterances quite naturally. The definition of contextual understanding and its implementation pose formidable problems.

The corresponding problems between high-level and low-level vision are not directly the concern of linguistics. They must, however, be considered when *the interaction of speech, the production perception of gesture (e.g. pointing) and the perceptual understanding of a visual scene* are at stake. The time is ripe for the study of at least small models of *integrated multi-modal systems (in particular for speech and vision)*, especially in connection with pointing (cf. pp. 6 and 25; Wahlster, Chapter 7).

Another, completely high-level problem is the *integration of the language system with the system for communicative motivation and tactic adaptation*. In treating this problem involved in the development of transmutable systems, researchers have been led to study the knowledge bases and the systems for specifying intended dialogue behaviour, associated conversational tactics and capability of adaptation to diverse communicative settings (cf. Wahlster, Chapter 7).

3. *New methods* for the description of linguistic processing in terms of interactive connectivities have been developed in recent years *under the names of connectionism, parallel-distributed processing or net-linguistic* (cf. Schnelle, Chapter 6). They are powerful and flexible and show a strong similarity to the signal-processing methods applied in low-level analyses. Their application is particularly promising where flexiblity of use, learning and other specific aspects of cognitive modelling are the goals. It seems that more complex cases of language understanding, vision, etc., can only be solved when definitions of parallel processing along these lines become available; purely sequential processing in ordinary computers will never provide real-time speech understanding or speech production. These new methods are, however, not yet widely known or used. *Extensive studies of these methods and of their connection with insight gained in neuro-computing* are necessary.

These studies should also keep in view the *long-term perspective* of specifying the *architectural constraints* on neural nets which would allow the modelling of simple and *straightforward language learning*.

REFERENCES

Berwick, R.C. (1985). *The acquisition of syntactic knowledge*. Cambridge, Mass.: MIT Press
Bühler, K. (1934). *Sprachtheorie*. Jena: Fischer (2nd edn, 1965, Stuttgart: Fischer).
Bruner, J. (1975). Language as an instrument of thought. In A. Davies (Ed.), *Problems of Language and Learning*, pp.61–88, 148. London: Heinemann
Bruner, J. (1983). *Child's talk: Learning to use language*. Oxford: Oxford University Press.
Carello, C., Turvey, M.T., Kugler, P.N., & Shaw R.E. (1984). Indadequacy of the computer metaphor. In M.S. Gazzaniga (Ed.), *Handbook of Cognitive Neuroscience*, pp. 229–248. New York: Plenum Press.
Chomsky, N. (1986). *Knowledge of language*. New York: Praeger.

Chomsky, N. (1975). *The logical structure of linguistic theory*. New York: Plenum Press.

Fodor, J.A. (1983). *Modularity of mind*. Cambridge, Mass.: MIT Press.

Fowler, C.A. & Turvey, M.T. (1982). Observational perspective and descriptive level in percveiving and acting. In W.D. Weimer & D.S. Palermo (Eds), *Cognition and the symbolic processes*, pp.1–29. New York: John Wiley.

Hebb, D. (1949). *The organization of behavior*. New York: John Wiley.

Husserl, E. (1939/1972). *Erfahrung und Urteil*. Hamburg: F. Meiner.

Imbert, M., Bertelson, P., Kempson, R., Osherson, D., Schnelle, H., Streitz, N., Thomassen, A., & Vivani, P. (1982). *Cognitive science in Europe*. Berlin: Springer.

Kohonen, T. (1977). *Associative memory*. Berlin: Springer.

Kohonen, T. (1984). *Self-organization and associative memory*. Berlin: Springer.

Lindblom, B. (1986). Phonetic universals in vowel systems. In J.J.Ohala (Ed.), *Experimental Phonology*, pp.13–44. London and San Diego: Academic Press.

Lyons, J. (1975). Deixis as the source of reference. In E.L. Keenan (Ed.), *Formal semantics of natural language*. Cambridge: Cambridge University Press.

MacKay, D.M. (1980). *Brains, machines and persons*. London: Collins.

MacKay, D.M. (1984). Mind talk and brain talk. In M.S. Gazzaniga (Ed.), *Handbook of cognitive neuroscience*, pp.293–317. New York: Plenum Press.

Marr, D. (1982). *Vision*. Cambridge, Mass.: MIT Press.

McClelland, J.L., Rumelhart, D.E., & the PDP Research Group (Eds) (1986). *Parallel distributed processing: Explorations in the microstructure of cognition, Vol. II: Psychological and biological models*. Cambridge, Mass.: MIT Press.

McNeill, D. (1979). *The conceptual basis of language*. Hillsdale, N.J.: Lawrence Erlbaum Associates Inc.

Norman, D.A. (1986). Reflections on cognition and parallel distributed processing. In J.M. McClelland, D.E. Rumelhart, & PDP Research Group (Eds), *Parallel distributed processing: Explorations in the microstructure of cognition Vol II: Psychological and biological models*, pp.531–546. Cambridge, Mass.: MIT Press.

Osherson, D. & Weinstein, S. (1984). Formal learning theory. In M.S. Gazzaniga (Ed.), *Handbook of cognitive neuroscience* pp.275-292. New York: Plenum Press.

Palm, G. (1982). *Neural assemblies*. Berlin: Springer.

Petitot, J. (1985). Paradigme catastrophique et perception categorielle. *Recherches Semiotiques/Semiotic Inquiry* 207-246.

Pinker, S. & Prince, A. (1988). On language and connectionism: Analysis of a parallel distributed processing model of language acquisition. *Cognition, 28*, 73-193.

Rumelhart, D.E., McClelland, J.L. & the PDP Research Group (Eds) (1986). *Parallel distributed processing: Explorations in the microstructure of cognition, Vol. 1: Foundations*. Cambridge, Mass.: MIT Press.

Schnelle, H. (1981a). Phenomenological analysis of language and its application to time and tense. In H. Parret & M. Sbisa (Eds), *Possibilites and limitations of pragmatics*. pp.631–656. Amsterdam: Benjamins.

Schnelle, H. (1981b). Introspection and the description of language use. In F. Coulmas (Ed.), *A festschrift for native speaker*, pp.105–126. The Hague: Mouton.

Schnelle, H. (1983). Some preliminary remarks on net linguistic semantics. In G.Rickheit & M.Bock (Eds), *Psycho-linguistic studies in language processing*, pp.82–98. Berlin: de Gruyter.

Schnelle, H. (1984). Von der situationsgebundenen zur situationsentbundenen Sprache. In A. Eschbach (Ed.), *Karl Bühlers theory of language*. Amsterdam: Benjamins.

Shaw, R., Turvey, M.T., & Mace, W. (1982). Ecological psychology. In W.D. Weimer & D.S. Palermo (Eds), *Cognition and the symbolic processes*, pp. 159–223. New York: John Wiley.

Smolensky, P. (1988). On the proper treatment of connectionism, (to appear in: *The Behavioral and Brain Sciences, 11*, 1-74).

Tanenhaus, M.K., Carlson, G.N., & Seidenberg, M.S. (1985). Do listeners compute linguistic

LL—D

representations? In D. Dowty et al. (Eds), *Natural language processing*, pp. 359–408. Cambridge: Cambridge University Press.

Wexler, K. (1979). A possible theory for language acquisition. In E. Wanner & L.R. Gleitman (Eds), *Language acquisition*, pp. 288–315. Cambridge: Cambridge University Press.

Winograd, T. (1983). *Language as a cognitive process*. Reading, Mass.: Addison-Wesley.

Winograd, T. & Flores, F. (1986). *Understanding computers and cognition*. Norwood, N.J.: Ablex.

CHAPTER 2

Cognitive Science and Speech: A Framework for Research

John Laver

Centre for Speech Technology Research,
University of Edinburgh, Edinburgh, U.K.

1. INTRODUCTION

The objective of this chapter is to offer a framework within which the contribution to the cognitive sciences of research on fundamental aspects of speech can be placed, and to identify some major strategic research problems within a cognitive approach to speech. Companion chapters in this volume cover higher-order aspects of language relevant to speech such as syntax and morphology (Klein), semantics (van Benthem), discourse (Guenthner), linguistics and parallel processing (Schnelle), and applied aspects of natural language processing (Wahlster). Chapters in other volumes also cover other interests which are directly relevant to the study of speech, such as psycholinguistics (Noordman) and auditory processing and recognition of speech (Patterson and Cutler). The choice is therefore made in this chapter to focus chiefly on questions of speech production, with some brief discussion of phonology, and some more extended comments on the use of speech technology as a test-bed for theories about speech production, perception, and understanding.

The long-term goal of cognitive science is to understand the integrated nature of the complex of neural, muscular, and sensory systems that mediate our cognitive interpretation of the physical and social world. Spoken communication, with its three elements of production, perception, and understanding, offers one of the most accessible examples of the workings of this complex of systems. Furthermore, it seems reasonable to insist that a comprehensive view of the human cognitive system would be radically incomplete without an accompanying understanding of the relationships between the production, perception, and understanding of speech. Spoken communication thus deserves the concentrated attention of the cognitive sciences.

The subsystems integrated in the overall process of spoken communication range

37

from the ideational creation of the message to be transmitted, through the neurolinguistic, neuromuscular, and neurosensory mechanisms of the speaker, through the acoustic characteristics of the transmission phase, to the sensory, perceptual, and interpretive mechanisms exploited by the listener to reach an understanding of the content of the message transmitted. The integrated subparts can be thought of as making up a cognitive, biological, and physical chain that links the speaker's mind to the hearer's mind. (A similar integrated approach is applicable to the cognitive, biological, and physical systems for achieving linguistic communication through writing and reading.) An adequate description of the production, perception, and understanding of speech is thus obliged to invoke strata at very many levels, from ideation to production, through acoustic transmission, and on through perception to semantic interpretation of the message. Some parts of this continuum of levels are normally considered primarily from a cognitive perspective, others from a biological or a physical perspective. A full appreciation of the task faced by the cognitive functions involved in planning, executing, decoding, and understanding speech will come only from a clear understanding of the biological and physical machinery with which the cognitive system has to mesh. I shall therefore refer from now onwards to an integrated cognitive, biological, and physical model of the human communication system as a "unified cognitive model".

There can be no doubt that we are at present a very long way from any such unified cognitive model for language performance in either the spoken or the written medium. The gap which is currently visible between high-level cognitive psychology and the lower-level neuromuscular and neurosensory systems is a very broad chasm across which all the different disciplines concerned must somehow build a scientific bridge. The necessary continuity of the bridge does not mean, nevertheless, that each different discipline should expect all collaborators to use a common set of methodological tools. This problem has been elegantly characterised by Smolensky, in his discussion of the potential contribution to cognitive science of the parallel distributed processing (PDP) paradigm applied to perceptual processing :

> The vast majority of cognitive processing lies between the highest cognitive levels of explicit logical reasoning and the lowest levels of sensory processing. Descriptions of processing at the extremes are relatively well-informed—on the high end by formal logic and on the low end by natural science. In the middle lies a conceptual abyss. How are we to conceptualize cognitive processing in this abyss?

> The strategy of the symbolic paradigm is to conceptualize processing in the intermediate levels as symbol manipulation. Other kinds of processing are viewed as limited to extremely low levels of sensory and motor processing. Thus symbolic theorists climb down into the abyss, clutching a rope of symbolic logic anchored at the top, hoping it will stretch all the way to the bottom of the abyss

> The subsymbolic paradigm takes the opposite view, that intermediate processing mechanisms are of the same kind as perceptual processing mechanisms. Logic and

symbol manipulation are viewed as appropriate descriptions only of the few cognitive processes that explicitly involve logical reasoning. Subsymbolic theorists climb up into the abyss on a perceptual ladder anchored at the bottom, hoping it will extend all the way to the top of the abyss (Smolensky, 1986: 197).

The relevance for a unified cognitive model of these comments on what we might call the "Smolensky Gap" is not that identical mechanisms and modes of description must be proposed for every stratum of the model, but rather that a multilayered, unified, cognitive model must display a proposed continuity from the lowest to the highest layer (and vice versa), with explicit connectibility between adjacent layers. Each stratum will have mechanisms and modes of description whose nature may in principle be unique to the stratum. But the essence of a unified model involving mutiple strata is that the methodology particular to the description and explanation of a given stratum must be compatible with the methodologies of at least its neighbouring strata. The search for commonalities thus has to be given priority, here as in all science, as a standard objective of scientific method. Given that the cognitive sciences currently have only a very tenuous understanding of many of the intermediate strata in the overall model, a comprehensive understanding of the continuities throughout the model is bound to take many years and much fundamental research to be achieved.

More immediately, practicable goals might consist of putting theories of subparts of the overall system to effective test in working simulations. In the case of speech and natural language processing, these simulations could be incorporated and tested in the computer-based systems for natural language synthesis, generation, recognition, and understanding of the next 15 years.

The structure of the chapter will be to look first at three perspectives on the human system for speech production and perception—a semiotic perspective, a biological perspective, and a physical perspective. Then some recent developments in phonological theory will be briefly discussed. The chapter concludes with a discussion of the ways in which knowledge of functional characteristics of the human speech production and perception system, and about the acoustic characteristics of speech transmission, can offer design principles for machines which can produce and recognise speech, and which in their turn can act as test-beds for the theories they embody.

2. PERSPECTIVES ON THE HUMAN SYSTEM FOR SPEECH PRODUCTION AND PERCEPTION

2.1 The Semiotic Perspective

The first perspective on speech to be discussed is the semiotic perspective, where the process of communication is analysed in terms of the information conveyed between speaker and listener. This perspective comes from the general theory of signs, and an important distinction here is that between two types of semiotic function in speech—the *symbolic* function (which serves the communication of semantic information, and which is sufficiently familiar that further explanation can perhaps be dispensed with), and what we shall call (in the spirit of C.S. Peirce, the nineteenth-century American pragmaticist philosopher) the *evidential* function. In order to explain the evidential function, some brief preliminary comments should be made.

It is convenient within a semiotic approach to linguistic theory to draw a distinction between language and the medium exploited by the producer of linguistic acts of communication: language lies in the patterns formed by the medium, and not in the physical events as such, or the artefacts, of the medium (Abercrombie, 1967). A linguistic pattern is said to be distinct from its material embodiment (or manifestation, or implementation) so that where language is *form*, the medium is *substance*. Formal aspects are of two types: phonological and grammatical. These two aspects combine to show a dual patterning of structure in the speech code, which has variously been called "double structure", "double articulation", or "dual structure" (e.g. Lyons, 1968: 45). The relatively small number of phonological units (including, but not only, consonant and vowel phonemes) have the sole linguistic function of being combinable and permutable, within narrowly defined structural constraints of sequence, to give distinctive shape to the very large number of grammatical units (words) whose identity and sequence in their turn make up the lexical and syntactic patterns of the language. The meaning of these lexical and syntactic patterns constitutes the semantic level of language, which is of prime cognitive relevance.

However, it deserves emphasis that insisting on the differences between form and substance offers the risk of blurring an important issue in cognitive science—the bridging of the Smolensky Gap between high-level, abstract, formal, cognitive categories and the substantial events of the observable, manifestatory surface. The major issue in cognitive science, in the concerns of this chapter, is the nature of this link between cognitive form and manifestatory substance.

Although it is essential that the spoken medium is capable of being formed into abstract symbolic patterns which carry language and have semantic meaning, the medium has other properties as well. Because the substance of the medium is an artefact, such artefacts inevitably carry evidence of the handiwork of the artisan who created them. This then is an evidential property of the medium. Among the different evidential properties of the medium, it is possible to distinguish social, psychological, and physical markers of identity of the speaker (Laver and Trudgill, 1979). The cognitive perceptual work of the hearer, on listening to speech, is thus not only to register the formal, symbolic content of what was said, but also to reach conclusions about the identity and attitudinal state of the speaker. The continuing registration of the speaker's changing attitudinal state is a skill that is extremely important to the due conduct of a conversational interaction, and involves no little cognitive effort.

A further semiotic distinction can be drawn between "communicative" and "informative" aspects of vocal signals. A signal is communicative if "it is intended by the sender to make the receiver aware of something of which he was not previously aware". A signal is informative if "(regardless of the intentions of the sender) it makes the receiver aware of something of which he was not previously aware" (Lyons, 1977: 33). A unified cognitive model will need to give a comprehensive account of both communicative and informative traffic between speakers and listeners.

Finally, we should distinguish between three sorts of information carried by speech: *linguistic*, *paralinguistic*, and *extralinguistic* information. Symbolic linguistic information in speech is fully communicative, in the terms offered above, and is coded by the segmental and suprasegmental (metric and prosodic) elements of phonology. It is important to note, however, that artefactual aspects of the speech substance used to convey communicative, symbolic contrasts also have evidential properties of accent which serve an informative role in marking regional or social affiliation.

Paralinguistic information is conveyed by what is generally called tone of voice. An example would be the whispery phonation adopted in English when the communication is intended to be conspiratorially confidential. Paralinguistic communication tends to exploit phonetic features which have a longer time-base (such as a whole phrase, or whole utterances) than the use of those same features for linguistic communication, and is a psychological marker of the speaker's attitude or mood. Such features are *para*linguistic in the sense that they form a communicative code subject to cultural convention for its interpretation; but they are not fully linguistic in that paralinguistic communication involves no possibility of the creation of meaningful sequential structures. Unlike language, where the semantic interpretability of the messages communicated relies in part on the structural sequence of the phonological and grammatical units involved, the sequence in which particular paralinguistic features are expressed carries with it no superordinate value of interpretability. Paralinguistic communication has only a vocabulary, as it were, and no syntax. The semiotic function of paralinguistic features is hence more evidential than symbolic.

Extralinguistic features in speech are those properties of vocal artefacts, such as the habitual quality of the speaker's voice, which carry neither linguistic nor paralinguistic communicative functions. They are solely informative, and solely evidential. They often have a powerful role as physical and social markers of individual identity (Laver, 1980; Nolan, 1983). They arise from such physical origins as the length and geometry of the individual speaker's vocal tract and larynx, and from phonetic, learnable origins (acquired through a lifetime's experience of speaking), such as the linguistically irrelevant aspects of detailed pronunciation that mark a speaker's accent as personally idiosyncratic.

Much work on speech has historically concerned itself with an idealised speaker, choosing to ignore as irrelevant the wide range of anatomical and physiological differences between speakers. An acceptance of the responsibility for accounting for extralinguistic facts about speakers would mean that a broader scope would have to be pursued. Failure to provide an adequate theoretical model for such extralinguistic facts as inter-speaker variability of acoustic output would mean, for example, that ambitious automatic speech recognition systems would be deprived of the possibility of effective knowledge-based speaker adaptation components.

The comments offered above about paralinguistic and extralinguistic features in speech concentrate on the surface realisations of such features. But obviously very many such features are the consequence of both high-level and low-level neurophysiological actions which are not very different in complexity from those that underpin linguistic communication. Indeed, there is a more immediate relationship in some cases where it becomes possible to say that paralinguistic and extralinguistic evidential features are themselves directly relevant to symbolic linguistic interests. This is because many of the same manifestatory phonetic features are exploited in all three cases, typically differing chiefly in their time-base. They constitute a background, or baseline, against which the linguistic articulations can achieve their perceptual prominence. An example would be the medium-term paralinguistic action of smiling, where the phonetic perception of linguistic events has to allow for the systematic phonetic distortion introduced by the spreading of the lips. If such perceptual adjustment is thought of as a normalising process, something of the same type of normalisation is necessary to recover the intended linguistic communication from longer-term extralinguistic perturbations, such as habitual nasalisation as a speaker-identifying feature.

A unified cognitive model should therefore account for the generation, transmission, reception, and interpretation of all informative and communicative aspects of speech, and should thus address all three types of features—linguistic, paralinguistic, and extralinguistic.

2.2 The Biological Perspective

The second perspective to be explored is the biological perspective, where the speaker and the listener are regarded as organic entities to be described in terms of anatomy, physiology, and neurology. There are three planes of study that intersect in this perspective: the study of the normal, adult system for producing, perceiving, and understanding speech and language; the study of the acquisition of speech and language by the child; and the study of speech and language "in dissolution", or the study of speech and language pathology.

One of the benefits of studying acquisition and pathology is that while the details of the operational design and function of the normal, established adult system tend to be very opaque, an examination of the errors which are characteristic of the system during acquisition and breakdown tends to be much more revealing of functional design principles. The study of pathology, valuable in its own right, is particularly profitable, potentially, for its contribution to knowledge about the normal, adult system at the neurolinguistic and neurophysiological levels.

Caplan's (1987) recent book, which explores neurolinguistics and linguistic aphasiology, is relevant for a unified cognitive model. Caplan characterises the chief goal of these two subjects as:

a study of the relationship between two theories: that of language structure and processing, and that of neural tissue and its functioning. Linguistic aphasiology is partly a domain of its own, and partly a source of data on which neurolinguistic theories are constructed (Caplan, 1987: 15).

He suggests that three basic theoretical questions in neurolinguistics and linguistic aphasiology are as follows (Caplan, 1987: 12-14) :

1. Is language breakdown related in natural ways to the structure of normal language?
2. Does language disorder parallel language development in reverse?
3. Can the brain support language in many different ways, or can it do so only in one or in a limited number of forms?

This last question is especially important for a unified model, in that, while the discovery of what

> neural elements and organizational features are responsible for language (is highly problematic), ... the existence of regular patterns of breakdown—if they exist— would indicate that the ways in which neural tissue supports language are restricted, even when neural tissue is incomplete, damaged, and partially self-repaired (Caplan, 1987: 14).

The remaining comments in this section will be addressed chiefly to the study of the normal process itself.

One of the underlying issues in a complete model of the role of speech in cognitive performance is the question of whether the brain integrates the performance of a plurality of biologically more primitive functions to serve the singular purposes of speech, or whether it is more valid to propose that speech (and, more generally, language), has its own biology.

Alvin Liberman (1984), the distinguished American experimental phonetician, characterises his earlier work on speech synthesis and the perception of speech as espousing the non-specialised view, for which he suggests the metaphor of a "horizontal" organisation:

> As applied to language, the metaphor is intended to convey that the underlying processes are arranged in layers, none of them specific to language. On that horizontal orientation, language is accounted for by reference to whatever combination of processes it happens to engage. Hence our assumption, in the attempt to find a substitute for speech, that perception of phonological segments is normally accomplished, presumably in the first layer, by processes of a generally auditory sort, by processes no different from those that bring us the rustle of leaves in the wind or the rattle of a snake in the grass. To the extent that we were concerned with the rest of language, we must have supposed, in like manner, that syntactic structures are managed by using the most general resources of cognition or intelligence. ... But all the processes we might have invoked had in common that none was specialized for language. We were not prepared to give language a biology of its own, but only to treat it as an epiphenomenon, a biologically arbitrary assemblage of processes that were not themselves linguistic (Liberman, 1984: 171).

In his more recent work, Liberman has abandoned the epiphenomenal view, in favour of an approach to speech and language as a specialised biological system:

> The opposite view—one toward which I now incline —is, by contrast, vertical. Seen this way, language does have its own biology. It is a coherent system, like echolocation in the bat, comprising distinctive processes adapted to a distinctive function. The distinctive processes are those that underlie the grammatical codes of syntax and phonology; their distinctive function is to overcome the limitations of communication by agrammatic means. ... What the processes of syntax and phonology do for us ... is to encode an unlimited number of messages into a very limited number of signals. In so doing, they match our message-generating capabilities to the restricted resources of our signal-producing vocal tracts and our signal-perceiving ears. As for the phonetic part of the phonological domain ... I suggest that it, too, partakes of the distinctive function of grammatical codes, and that it is, accordingly, also special (ibid.).

Liberman's current view that speech is supported by integrated, specialised biological subsystems is shared by many (perhaps most) workers in the field today. But the extract from Liberman is quoted here at some length to allow me to offer the following major reservation about the issue of biological specialisation of speech: such specialisation as might exist does not lie notably at the periphery of the system.

We can consider first the vocal apparatus for the production of speech. In talking about the vocal apparatus, we make an arguable assumption. It already implies that the organs used for the production of speech can be thought of as biologically specialised for this purpose. It could be argued, for instance, that the evolution of the physiological capacity for speech gave mankind a biological advantage that promoted our social and cognitive development to such an extent that the very nature of this sociocognitive organisation is a biologically unique characteristic of the species. Against such a view, however, is the opinion that not one anatomical aspect of the so-called "vocal" apparatus can be singled out as specialised for the purposes of producing speech as such, apart perhaps from some aspects of the neuroanatomy of the brain. Every action of the apparatus that is involved in speaking could be claimed to exploit the physiological capabilities (neural and muscular) of an architecture whose primary biological functions are other than articulate speech—breathing, sucking, biting, chewing, swallowing, licking, spitting, sniffing, clearing the throat, coughing, yawning, lifting and straining, and phonating while laughing, crying, threatening, and shouting (Laver, forthcoming).

There thus seems to be no evidence yet that the peripheral apparatus for speech production is specialised for speech. It is true that the capacity of the peripheral speech production apparatus to generate signals is limited, and it may well be true that spoken language evolved in such a way as to take account of this limitation. Considering now the perception of speech, there seems to be no corresponding limitation of the peripheral auditory system that is governed by criteria relevant to speech as such. Playback of speech recordings can be accelerated to a rate well beyond the maximum articulatory rate without losing its intelligibility, for example.

The specialisation of the biological systems supporting speech, to the extent that such specialisation exists, is better thought of as located upstream from the peripheral apparatus, in the stages of neural processing. This argument becomes clearer if we examine the analogy that Liberman himself invokes as a parallel in the perceptual domain—that of echolocation in the bat.

As Roy Patterson pointed out to me in a review of a draft of this chapter, it is true that the bat's echolocation system is a coherent biological system, as one might concede speech to be. But there the parallel ends, in that the bat is an animal which once "learned", in a cognitive sense, to make some rudimentary use of reflected sound, and which then progressively evolved a peripheral physiological structure to take over the responsibility for this cognitive processing, reducing the load on neural processing. There seems to be no evidence that the peripheral auditory system in man has been evolutionarily modified to reduce the cognitive burden of speech processing. The more apt analogy would have been the dolphin and other cetaceans, where elaborate echolocation systems exist with a minimum of peripheral specialisation and a maximum of specialisation at the level of neural processing.

2.2.1 The Production of Speech

The anatomy of the vocal apparatus is an intricate assembly of different physical materials. The materials include a number of cartilages and bones, motor nerves carrying control messages from the brain, sensory nerves carrying information back to the brain, and a fairly large number of muscles, together with associated tendons, ligaments, and membranes. The muscles are mostly rather small and fast-acting, and their dynamic, interlinked actions give rise to the continually changing patterns of articulation. They contract in obedience to neural commands and change the configuration of the vocal apparatus. In order for the vocal apparatus to take up a given configurational state, the different muscles have to be made to collaborate with each other in an appropriately cooperative way.

A slightly extended account of the scale of the neuromuscular control problem, for the solution of which a comprehensive unified cognitive model will have to be able to offer an explanatory account, is appropriate here. A convenient assumption is that the anatomy and physiology of the vocal apparatus can be described as if the muscles of the vocal apparatus acted in cooperative groups, or muscle systems (Laver, forthcoming). The benefit of making this assumption is that it allows attention to be focussed on the strategic targets of cooperative muscular action, and the notion of a muscle system will therefore be discussed as if the muscles which made up the system were members of a conspiracy to achieve the articulatory, phonatory, or respiratory objectives attributed to the system. Eight functional groupings of muscles into major muscle systems can be suggested. These make up the respiratory, phonatory, hyoid, pharyngeal, velopharyngeal, lingual, mandibular, and labial systems. It is further possible to isolate a number of smaller functional subsystems within these major systems. It is also possible for a given muscle to participate in more than one muscle system or subsystem.

Another assumption, closely related to the previous one, is that the consequence of the contraction of a single muscle for the configuration of the vocal apparatus can usefully be discussed in isolation, when considering the contribution of these individual muscles to their muscle systems. In reality, of course, the muscular fabric of the vocal apparatus is densely interwoven. Any change in the length of one muscle will inevitably change the degree of passive tension in all other muscles to which it is anatomically connected. This holds true not only for the other muscles in the same muscle system, but for all other muscle systems to which a pathway of physical connection exists. The states of such passive tension, and the consequent geometry of the vocal apparatus, are then variables that the brain has to take into account in designing and executing a program of neural commands to control the contraction patterns of the active muscles, to reach a given target configuration.

In performing any movement of the human body, some muscles play a primary, protagonist role. When the protagonist role is played by multiple muscles, the primary contributors are sometimes called the prime movers, with the assisting muscles being called synergists. But two other potentially active roles can also make a crucial contribution to the success of the overall performance. The first of these is a permissive role, played by muscles acting in an opposing, antagonist function. Antagonist muscles can be either passive or active. When passive, they are inhibited from actively opposing the effort of the protagonists. When active, their part in the performance is to offer exactly the amount of checking resistance that will allow the protagonist muscles to bring the vocal apparatus to the planned configuration and no further. Reaching an articulatory target is hence often a finely graded balancing of the opposition between protagonist and antagonist forces, with collaborative action of this sort facilitating the delicately controlled precision of the overall performance. Other muscles can play a more minor role, giving support by fixating and bracing the structures on which the protagonists and antagonists are operating. From an analytic point of view, a given muscle may simultaneously be called on to play different roles, e.g. as a protagonist in the actions of one muscle system, while also performing a bracing role in the actions of another muscle system of which it is recruited as a member, and an antagonist role in another.

A general word of caution is necessary here. Many textbooks on the anatomy and physiology of speech describe the functions of individual muscles as if they were clearly understood and widely agreed. This is perhaps acceptable when relatively simple manoeuvres are being described, and to the extent that the given muscle can be thought of as acting in isolation. But as the discussion above emphasises, muscular action is typically collaborative, with complex mechanical consequences throughout the network of linked muscle systems. The detailed repercussive nature of such collaborative action in speech is still not well understood, and constitutes a major potential research area, especially in the context of synchronised inter-articulator programming.

There are nearly 80 different muscles in the vocal apparatus, most of them arranged in pairs, which can plausibly be thought of as being directly involved in the different neuromuscular strands of speech production. The process of speaking requires virtually continuous changes of tension and position of all of these muscles, with the result that the configurational state of the vocal organs is constantly in transition. One can view the changes of muscular tension and position as trajectories through the possible space of such configurations. The navigational course of every such trajectory through this space has to be planned and monitored, and the actual muscular performance that takes place has to fulfil, within acceptable limits, an intricately detailed timetable. The scale of the navigatory and co-ordinatory problem of physiological control that the brain has somehow to deal with in producing speech is thus immense. The gap between our present understanding and a comprehensive model is difficult to exaggerate, and the importance for a unified cognitive model of closing the gap difficult to over-emphasise.

An important debate on the nature of physiological control in speech is that between the approach that has been dubbed "Translation Theory", and its critics who support "Action Theory". This debate has been succinctly and effectively reviewed by Nolan (1982). The essence of the Translation Theory approach, according to Nolan, is that :

> a translation theory is one in which a representation in terms of discrete primes, taken usually from linguistic theory, is considered as input to the speech mechanism; the problem is then defined as how these primes (abstract in that they are discrete, invariant, and lacking a time dimension) are implemented as, or TRANSLATED into, the continuously varying flow of speech articulation taking place in time. ...
> Two separate questions can be distinguished which arise in work in the translation theory mould: first, what are the primes, the "building blocks" out of which utterances are constructed? And second, what are the organisational structures within which the primes are concatenated? (Nolan, 1982: 289).

Translation Theory of the sort described above is overwhelmingly the most common type of theory of the study of speech production to date. Many primes have been postulated, almost all familiar from linguistic theory. They include the individual consonant and vowel phoneme, the syllable, the rhythmic unit called the foot, and prosodic intonational units. Many investigations have found evidence that such postulated primes indeed appear to be concerned in the organisation and control of speech: For example, Boomer and Laver (1968) found that all the above-mentioned primes play a statable role in the empirical data of speech errors, such that prosodic and metrical units to do with intonational, rhythmic, and syllabic structure appear to act as organising constructs in the neuromuscular planning and execution of the performance of individual vowel and consonant phoneme segments. Unfortunately, a vicious degree of circularity is involved (probably inevitably) in arguments in favour of such "discoveries": Given that the search for organising entities is conducted with the help of these primes as basic descriptive tools, it is hardly surprising that the entities discovered might then be describable in terms of those *a priori* units of description. At the limit, the best that one could say on the basis of such work would be that the proposed primes were not inconsistent with the cognitive structure being investigated.

A further problem has been that the involvement of the major primes has not been able to be demonstrated on a simple, straightforward, and unequivocal basis, without somewhat debilitating qualifications and assumptions almost always having to be made.

One of the most general research problems in the area of the control and co-ordination of speech is that of the variability of speech. This is a problem that has exercised translation theorists for many years, and it may be helpful here to give a brief account of the four main types of variability that normally occur within the speech of a single speaker.

No two repetitions by a single speaker of a given phrase spoken at the same tempo are ever fully identical, at the level of articulatory and temporal microstructure. There is a type and degree of articulatory and temporal microvariability which seems to be describable only on a stochastic, quasi-random basis. This is observable, particularly in fast speech, in the area of the synchronisation of inter-articulator programming, where the movements of one articulator relative to those of another are not precisely time-locked, even though their co-ordination has to satisfy some necessary and demanding acoustic and auditory temporal constraints. As Kent comments:

> ... in the case of speech, fluent motor execution and a high event rate may depend on overlapping of movements rather than synchronization of movements. I do not mean to imply that synchronized movements are unnecessary or undesirable, but only that exclusive reliance on the principle of "everything moves at once" does not seem to be the plan of speech articulation. Synchronous patterning may be a default principle that is over-ridden by phonetic and motor learning to yield the highly overlapping patterns that characterize rapid, fluent motor execution (Kent, 1983: 70).

An example of this would be the observable variability of timing of movement of the soft palate with respect to the tongue in the production of a nasalised vowel in repetitions of the same word at a standard rate.

Secondly, the articulatory and temporal phonetic manifestation of a given (supposedly invariant) phonological prime varies according to the phonological context in which it finds itself. Two sets of factors contribute to this contextually conditioned variability, whose articulatory aspects are usually given the label of "co-articulation" (Kent, 1983). The first is the complex of biomechanical factors, which by definition lie beyond the possibility of control, that constrain the physical realisation of the articulation as part of a continuous muscular performance—factors of inertia, elasticity, and muscle geometry. The second is the complex of phonetic factors of volitional control that the speaker has learned to prefer, as part of his habitual accent, for the pronunciation of the given phonological element in the particular sequence in which it finds itself. The co-articulatory influence of one phonological element over another adjacent or nearby element tends to be more powerful when the direction of influence is anticipatory—that is, the influence of elements yet to be pronounced on those currently being articulated tends to be more powerful than the perseveratory influence of elements pronounced earlier in the string. In English, the span of co-articulatory influence in a phrase of informal, continuous speech such as "they strewed flowers in her path", shows itself more powerfully in the way in which the rounded lip-position for the /uu/ vowel in "strewed" is anticipated as early as the initial /s/ of the word, while its influence typically disappears during the /f/ or the /l/ of "flowers". Such anticipatory influence on current muscular contraction patterns by events that have at that moment only a neural representation is a pivotal piece of data to be accounted for by neurophysiological models of speech control.

The third type of articulatory variability lies in the changes in speech patterns that characterise different rates of speaking. Speaking faster is not simply a matter of a linear acceleration of a standard chain of muscular activities. First, the formal phonological content of the message typically changes, with the structure of individual syllables changing (usually tending to reduce in complexity at faster rates by deleting individual consonants and/or vowels). In addition, unstressed peripheral vowels have the option of changing to a more central vowel phoneme. Examples of both a structural and a vowel change of this sort would be the reorganisation of the phrase "Do you know a good solicitor" from the slow, careful pronunciation represented in (1) (in the machine-readable transcription of British English developed at CSTR Edinburgh for work on speech technology, where the symbol "*" means a word boundary, and the symbol "@" stands for a central, schwa vowel) to the more informal, faster pronunciation shown in (2):

(1) /d uu * y uu * n ou * @ * g u d * s @ l i s i t @ * /
(2) /d * y @ * n ou * @ * g u d * s l i s t @ * /

In such circumstances, unstressed vowels in English tend also to reduce both their duration and their peripherality in vowel space, as a phonetic phenomenon without change of phonemic identity, selecting more central locations. As an aspect of the time-course of articulatory events, vowel reduction of this sort can be envisaged as an undershooting device to minimise articulatory effort (Lindblom, 1983). Undershoot of navigatory targets can thus be seen as a smoothing device, allowing the tongue (and jaw and lips) to economise on the range of articulatory displacement needed to achieve the vowel performances. However, Lindblom points out that undershoot of this sort is not simply an inevitable mechanical consequence of shorter duration. He cites Kuehn and Moll (1976) as interpreting the results of their cineradiographic work on articulatory velocities at rapid speaking rates to mean that "'speakers have the option of either increasing velocity of movement or decreasing articulatory displacement'. In other words, undershoot can be, and sometimes is, avoided by making more rapid approaches to targets" (Lindblom, 1983: 229). This emphasises that adjustments of articulatory velocities for rate are not able to be described simply as linear adjustments (Kuehn, 1973).

The fourth type of variability is at the phonological level, where the sequence of phonological primes that represent the lexical items of the phrase may differ according to the choice of formal versus informal style made by the speaker. Vowel reduction, at both the phonological and the phonetic levels, also applies as a typical process in moving from a more formal to a more informal style. There are thus obvious correlations between rapid and informal speech, and between slow and formal speech. The example of syllabic reorganisation given immediately above in fact included some phenomena of style-change, in that the pronunciation of "solicitor", characterised above as /s l i s t @/, is much more typical, for example, of an informal style than a formal style. A similar example would be the word "actually", which a British English speaker with an educated accent from the South of England speaking in the most formal possible style might pronounce as :

/a k t y u @ l i/

However, if the speaker's pronunciation becomes more informal, the forms of this word could vary from the still quite formal:

/a k ch u @ l i/

through

/a k ch u l i/
/a k ch @ l i/
/a k ch l i/
/a k sh l i/

to the most informal possible pronunciation

/ a sh l i /.

On average, English words have between two and three reorganised forms of this sort for informal pronunciations, though some can have very many more alternatives. However, there are other reorganisational phenomena that are typical of informal speech in addition to syllabic reorganisation. These include assimilatory phenomena, where the segments at the margins of adjacent words can optionally change in type to become more similar in some phonological respect to their neighbour. The formal pronunciation of the phrase "Horse shoes can bring you luck" is:

/ h oo s * sh uu z * k a n * b r i ng * y uu * l uh k/

A more informal pronunciation of the same phrase would be:

/ h oo sh * sh uu z * k @ m * b r i ng * y u * l uh k/

where assimilatory influence has worked (anticipatorily) on both the /s/ of "horse" and the /n/ of "can", to make them more like their immediately following neighbour, in terms of a feature-copying process involving the contextually controlled revision of the specification of their place of articulation. In addition, the /a/ of the formal pronunciation of "can" has been reduced to the more central vowel /@/, as has the /uu/ of "you" to /u/.

The phenomena of variability are thus far from explainable simply at a relatively peripheral level of phonetic processing, making appeal solely to ideas of articulatory economy of implementation. They involve some of the most central aspects of phonological planning and execution. It is, however, the more phonetic aspects of variability such as co-articulation and rate-related phenomena that have given the translation theorists the most trouble, and which Action Theory claims to be able to handle better. Nolan leads in to his discussion of Action Theory with the following comments:

> The failure of the [translation theory] models ... to uncover simple regularities underlying speech production has led a number of researchers to question not (merely) the elements of such models—the primes, and the organisational structures—but also the fundamental concept of the translation of abstract representations into physical articulations which is the presupposition behind these models. It is this duality—between phonetic plan and execution—which critics see as misguided, and the origin of problems which may turn out to be merely artefacts of the models (Nolan, 1982: 291-292).

Action Theory is a model that has been extended to speech from its sources in the general physiological study of the muscular control of cyclic events such as walking. Its main proponents are associated with Haskins Laboratories in New Haven, Connecticut (e.g. Fowler et al., 1980; Kugler et al., 1980; Scott Kelso, Holt, Kugler, & Turvey, 1980; Scott Kelso, Tuller, & Harris, 1983; Scott Kelso & Tuller, 1984; Tuller, Harris & Scott Kelso, 1982; Tuller, Scott Kelso & Harris, 1982). It is a more neurophysiologically informed approach than that taken by most translation theorists, and it attempts to provide an action-oriented, physiological description of speech which expresses intentions and muscular actions in compatible vocabulary. One of the most characteristic constructs of this approach is that of the "co-ordinative structure", which consists of a "group of muscles marshalled to act together, the degrees of freedom of the group being constrained so that together they produce activity of a specific type" (Nolan, 1982: 300). This development of the notion of a co-ordinative structure gives more precise shape to the general concept described earlier in this chapter of a "muscle system" or "subsystem".

The idea of a co-ordinative structure derives from earlier concepts of neuromuscular co-ordination in neurophysiology, such as a "synergy", from the Soviet school influenced by Bernstein (1967), a "collective" (Gel'fand, Gurfinkel, Tstetlin, & Shik, 1971), or a "linkage" (Boylls, 1975). Boylls, cited by Scott Kelso and Tuller (1984: 322), defined a linkage as being "a group of muscles whose activities covary" as a result of shared efferent and/or afferent signals, deployed as a unit in a motor task. Synergistic linking of individual muscles into cooperative systems was proposed by Bernstein (1967) as a solution to one of the basic problems of control and co-ordination, to which Nolan alludes in the comment quoted directly above, namely that of the multiplicity of potential degrees of freedom enjoyed by the skeletomuscular apparatus. Given that volitional muscular actions seem typically to be designed to reach relatively standard goals from innumerably different starting positions (the "motor equivalence" or "equifinality" problem), the linking of different parts of the apparatus in such a way that the collective degrees of freedom are minimised by mutual compensation results in a reduction of the number of control decisions needed (Scott Kelso and Tuller, 1984: 325).

The concept of a co-ordinative structure of linked muscles is very helpful, for example, in providing the explanatory basis for the tendency of many speakers to put a consistent bias on their articulatory activities, as a recurrent aspect of their characteristic voice quality, such as a tendency to keep their lips in a rounded position throughout speech, or to use a habitually whispery mode of phonation (Laver, 1980).

One property of a co-ordinative structure is said to be that it is "modulable", to support changes of rate. However, while the notion of a co-ordinative structure is of relevance in considerations of cyclic, automated activities such as walking, where rate-changes can perhaps plausibly be seen as open to modulation of the overall structure, the complex and non-linear physiological changes in the organisation of speech at different rates are much less clearly captured by such notions. Furthermore, since a given muscle must necessarily be able to be marshalled to participate in different co-ordinative structures for different activities, it is hard to see how the concept of control of such marshalling is not subject to unconstrained theoretical regress to ever-higher levels in the neurophysiological system, eventually obliging the analyst to make appeal to a type of translation theory. Given that eventual appeal to a concept of an interface between symbolic representation and neuromuscular implementation is necessary, even though Action Theory as applied to speech developed out of discontent with a Translation Theory approach, it could be argued that the two approaches are complementary rather than incompatible. The competitive issue between the two approaches then reduces to the question of the location in the unified cognitive model of the interface between the symbolic and the implementational components of the model. It also has to be said that the Translation Theory approach has been made much more explicit and systematic than has the Action Theory approach, where discussion is still focussed more on mechanisms than on a complete model.

Action Theory depends heavily (and not unreasonably) on the notion that general (non-speech) mechanisms of physiological control can be extended to explain the modes of speech control. To the extent that Action Theory adopts this approach of invoking general mechanisms of physiological control to explain the physiology of speech, it commits itself to the view that speech and language do not have their own biology. While this is a parsimonious approach, it also deserves saying that speech is by far the most complex muscular skill that human beings ever achieve, and that the scale of the co-ordinatory task is almost certainly more demanding in precision and variety than is the case in other spheres of skilled neuromuscular activity. If Liberman, cited earlier, is correct in believing that speech and language have their own biology, then the modes of neuromuscular co-ordination observable in speech may not be able to be accounted for simply by generalisation from the control of other activities.

Of the current models of speech production, Action Theory is nevertheless among the more immediately appealing for integration in a unified cognitive approach, not least because of its close attention to neurophysiological underpinnings. It is potentially compatible, for example, with the neural network simulations of the parallel distributed processing paradigm promoted by Rumelhart and McClelland and their colleagues (1986). A Translation Theory approach, on the other hand, is eminently suitable for the representation of phonetic, phonological, and linguistic knowledge in machine systems for speech synthesis and recognition, not least because virtually all the explicit rules that have been written by phoneticians, phonologists, and linguists about spoken language are couched in a Translation Theory framework. Its explicitness lends itself well to current efforts to find suitable modes of knowledge representation in computer-usable form for speech technology purposes.

2.2.2 The Perception of Speech

If we turn briefly now to the perception of speech, it is useful to distinguish between the peripheral auditory apparatus that accomplishes the transformation of the incoming acoustic signal into neural signals, and the more central recognition system that processes this neural product. The more peripheral element of this chain is relatively well understood, and is well described (e.g. Carlson & Granstrøm, 1982; Dickson & Maue-Dickson, 1982; Møller, 1983; Pickles, 1982; Schroeder, 1975). The peripheral auditory system consists of a complex biological series of mechanical and transducing elements, elegantly and simply described by Allen (1985) and Cooke (1985). In addition to its transducing function, the peripheral auditory system supplies data to achieve the functions of sound-source localisation and reverberation echo compensation. A more detailed account of the psychophysics of the peripheral auditory system is given by Patterson and Cutler (Volume 1, Chapter 3).

The more central element of speech perception (from the transduced neural signal to the symbolic phonological level of representation) is much less well understood at present. The identity of the individual auditory features that are exploited in speech recognition by human listeners, and the neurocomputational strategies whereby they are treated as evidence of phonological features, is the subject of a good deal of current research (Moore, 1982). It is far from clear, for example, that different listeners typically exploit the same set of temporal and spectral features, or even that a given speaker habitually relies on a standard set of features for listening to different speakers, or even to the same speaker in different ambient noise conditions. One of the topics that cognitive research will have to address is the variability of perceptual strategies both within a single listener, and between a wide range of listeners.

The general psycholinguistic issues of speech perception at the phonological level are discussed by Patterson and Cutler (Volume 1, Chapter 3). The higher psycholinguistic levels of morphological, lexical, syntactic, and semantic processing, are beyond the scope of this chapter. A detailed discussion is offered by Noordman (Volume 1, Chapter 6). An outline is also offered in Myers, Laver, and Anderson (1981).

A general point about the relationship between speaking and listening is relevant at this stage. Accepting a translation model as a framework, and leaving aside the question about the nature of the units in which speech perception is centrally represented, it is interesting to consider the relation between units of perception and units of production. Are listeners' abilities to decode and recognise the speech of other speakers based in part on knowledge about transformations which map their own articulatory activities onto auditory space? And, conversely, do speakers organise and control their speech on directly auditory criteria? It is notable that human languages exploit only part of the articulatory space potentially available to the vocal apparatus (Maddieson, 1984); have these constraints developed, as Stevens (1972) suggested in his "quantal" model of speech, in response to the differential ability of the vocal apparatus in different articulatory zones to make auditorily noticeable changes?

2.3 The Physical Perspective

In the third perspective, the speaker/hearer is modelled as a physical system, and appeal is made to a biocybernetic point of view. The speech production system can be described in terms of physical properties of the apparatus such as its three-dimensional geometry, its inertial parameters, the elasticity of muscles, the interdigitation of the muscles of the vocal apparatus and the complex mechanical consequences of contraction of a given muscle or muscle system for the other muscle systems to which it is physically connected, and limitations on the type and rate of mechanical adjustments. Also included in this approach is the cybernetic modelling of feedback and feed-forward as elements of a control system.

The physical properties of the speech perception system have to take into account the biomechanical properties of the peripheral auditory system, particularly in terms of limitation of perceptual acuity by phenomena such as masking, and of enhancement processes such as lateral inhibition, and of difference thresholds for spectral and temporal resolution.

The physical perspective also addresses the acoustic link through which speech is transmitted from the speaker to the listener. The acoustics of the transmission phase, very comprehensively covered by Fant (1960; 1973) and the wealth of texts in speech signal processing, such as Oppenheim and Schafer (1975) and Rabiner and Schafer (1978), serve as the public, manifestatory link between the biological and the semiotic perspectives.

The generally accepted model of speech acoustics, for whose development Fant himself deserves much of the credit, is the so-called "source-filter" model. This seeks to separate excitatory source phenomena from resonant filter phenomena, so that a basic analytic task in speech acoustics is how to deconvolve the relative contributions of these two components from the fully convolved time/amplitude speech waveform. The analytic theory of their deconvolution is reasonably well understood, but a major problem that speech technology has inherited from this theoretical work is that a model of speech acoustics has been worked out in great detail only for an idealised vocal apparatus which corresponds to a notional adult male speaker with a vocal tract length of 17.5 cm. The typical vocal anatomy of adult female speakers is not simply a scaled-down version of the typical male vocal tract, being different in the length-ratio of the pharyngeal component to the mouth component. The vocal apparatus of children approximates more closely, on a scalar basis, to female adult geometry than to male geometry. So we know less than is useful, from an acoustic point of view, about both adult females and children, compared to our knowledge about adult males. On a more general basis, the concentration on an idealised vocal apparatus has left us relatively ignorant about the acoustic differences between speakers which are due to anatomy rather than to accent.

A particularly crucial aspect of the acoustic characteristics of speech, for the automatic recognition of speech, lies in their variability. As pointed out earlier, no two speech events, even from the same speaker pronouncing exactly the same phrase, are ever fully identical; apparently random variation, within a distribution whose characteristics are not yet fully established for any class of speech sounds in any language, ensures that there is never any one-to-one correspondence between any given phonological prime and its detailed acoustic manifestation. Variation due to context then creates even more variability in the signals corresponding to different messages. Hypothesising the invariant (symbolic) primes represented by the randomly and contextually variable signal is the main problem of speech recognition (Perkell & Klatt, 1986). The human perceptual system copes with this inter-speaker and intra-speaker variability very well indeed: in the speech technology world, acoustic variation between speakers is a problem that is of the same order as the recognition of spoken messages from continuous speech, and variation within a single speaker is itself a major part of the speech recognition task. It is almost certain that the problem of successful recognition of continuous speech from a single speaker using a large vocabulary will be solved long before the solution is found to the problem of adequate adaptation to new speakers of different accents.

3. RECENT DEVELOPMENTS IN PHONOLOGICAL THEORY

Phonology, whose function it is to define and relate phonetic events to the segmental, suprasegmental, morphological, lexical, syntactic, and semantic levels of language, is a very large and active field. General introductions to phonology can be found in Chomsky and Halle (1968) (for English), Anderson, (1974) and Fischer-Jørgensen (1975). Some recent developments, particularly in suprasegmental phonology, can be pursued in Aronoff and Oehrle (1984), Beckman (1986), Clements and Keyser (1983), van der Hulst and Smith (1982), Kiparsky (1982), Ladd (1980), Liberman (1975), Liberman and Prince (1977), and Selkirk (1984). An interesting account of psychological reality in phonology is Linell (1979), and a view of the relevance of phonology to the cognitive representation of speech can be found in Myers, Laver, and Anderson (1981). This section on recent developments in phonology will be limted to some brief comments on two modern theories—Autosegmental Phonology and Metrical Phonology.

One of the principal issues in a cognitively oriented view of phonology is that of integration of subordinate parts into their superordinate structures, and the way that this integrational relationship can be represented theoretically. Recent phonological theories have taken issue with traditional approaches to this question. Van der Hulst and Smith explain the inadequacy of what they call the "strict segmental theory" in the traditional approach in these terms:

> In the standard theory phonological representations consist, at every level, of a linear arrangement of segments and boundaries. Segments are conceived of as unordered sets of features (with a feature-specification). The boundaries interspersed between the segments are, with respect to their "nature" and location, dependent on morphological and syntactic structure. They partition the string of segments into substrings that constitute possible domains for phonological generalizations (van der Hulst & Smith, 1982: 3).

(For the purpose of this chapter, the notion of "segments" here corresponds more or less to the familiar concept of consonant and vowel phonemes.)

The standard view of generative phonology that van der Hulst and Smith are criticising is sometimes called a one-tiered approach. One recent development in phonological theory is autosegmental phonology, which proposes a multi-tiered approach, where individual tiers of organisation, consisting of linear arrangements of elements, are autonomous (Halle & Vergnaud, 1981; 1982; van der Hulst & Smith, 1982: 1-46). The benefit of proposing multiple tiers, where individual elements on different tiers are linked to each other by association lines subject to rule-governed "association principles", is that separation of types of elements into different tiers allows certain phonological generalisations to be more easily handled. An example of this facilitation is the case where the domain of a phonological rule applies to the internal substructure of an individual complex segment (not expressible in the standard theory where segments are indivisible entities). Another example is where the domain of a phonological (or morphological or syntactic) rule is a suprasegmental aspect of the speech stream, and where the suprasegmental phenomenon is separable from any direct notion of a fixed segmental "carrier".

Proposing a phonological representation which consists of independent segmental and suprasegmental tiers promotes the question of the nature of the neurolinguistic control mechanisms whereby these autosegmental tiers might be co-ordinated and synchronised (Halle & Vergnaud, 1982: 65). This question is relevant for a cognitive model, and would have been more difficult to pose in the standard generative theory of phonology.

Another recent development in phonological theory is metrical phonology, which has grown from original proposals by Mark Liberman (1975) and Liberman and Prince (1977). As its name suggests, metrical phonology is concerned chiefly with suprasegmental (or "prosodic") phonology. It proposes a hierarchy of phonological units in which segments are grouped into syllables, syllables into rhythmic "feet", and feet into phonological words. Metrical properties of interest include stress and length, and metrical phonology today is "a theory about this phonological hierarchy, its internal organization, its role in the application of phonological rules, and its relation to the morpho-syntactic hierarchy" (van der Hulst & Smith, 1982: 30). The morpho-syntactic hierarchy referred to here is the one where segments are composed into morphemes, morphemes into words, words into phrases, and so forth.

Metrical phonology, like autosegmental phonology, is designed partly to escape from the constraint of segmental unilinearity suffered by the standard theory of phonology. Both metrical phonology and autosegmental phonology are multi-level theories, and can be regarded as largely complementary, though recent work has sharpened the debate about apparent competition between them. Leben (1982: 189) suggests that in fact autosegmental phonology can be regarded as a special case of metrical phonology. Both have encouraged a surge of work on suprasegmental phenomena, and have brought the issue of integration of the different segmental and suprasegmental levels of phonological representation to the forefront of current research in phonology. A good introduction to metrical phonology is Hogg and McCully (1987).

4. PERSPECTIVES ON THE MACHINE SYSTEMS FOR AUTOMATIC SPEECH SYNTHESIS AND RECOGNITION

We can now return to the suggestion made in the introduction to this chapter—that the more practicable goals of research addressing a unified cognitive model of speech might consist of putting theories of subparts of the overall system to effective test in working simulations, in computer-based systems for natural language synthesis, generation, recognition, and understanding. The simulations would consist of models of the functionality of the human system, and an important practical question is whether we already know enough about speech to make the effort of simulation worthwhile from the point of view of speech technology. An important question here is whether the simulated speech functionality is better supported by explicit knowledge-based rules from a unified cognitive theory, or by tacit knowledge developed by allowing the computer system to learn the knowledge structures for itself through automatic learning algorithms.

Automatic learning of relevant knowledge is becoming possible in the parallel distributed processing paradigm, where systems simulating neural networks can learn the necessary weightings between the elements of the network by exposure to exemplar material (Rumelhart et al., 1986). However, the ceiling of achievement in such automatic learning, though impressive, is still quite low, and it seems likely that advances of a significant order in speech technology using such techniques will only be made when a method is found of injecting explicit rule-formulated knowledge into the performance of the learning algorithms. So the answer to the question, for many years ahead, is likely to be that even from the perspective of the usefulness of applying explicit phonetic and linguistic knowledge to speech technology, it is desirable and profitable to test a unified cognitive theory by machine simulation.

Benefit also flows in the other direction. Indeed, as Miller and Gazzaniga (1984:

8) insist, "the study of nervous systems promises to reveal important new design principles for artificial cognitive devices". In the interests of drawing connections between speech technology and cognitive processing, the discussion that follows of automatic speech recognition will concentrate on systems which attempt to implement what is known about human performance, rather than on the solely statistical model-based systems for Hidden Markov Modelling and the like which currently dominate the commercial marketplace, and which are relatively free from explicit knowledge about speech.

4.1 Automatic Speech Recognition Systems

The attempt to develop automatic large-vocabulary systems for phonetic feature-based speaker adaptive recognition of continuous speech is currently a major research effort in a number of institutions, in both the United States and in Europe. The process of trying to build such a system is mutually illuminating for both speech technology and cognitive science.

In phonetic feature-based automatic speech recognition, four serious problems exist. The first is straightforwardly the problem of how to extract enough information from the time/amplitude speech waveform to hypothesise plausible linguistic utterances, in the interpretive light of a rich knowledge-base of phonetic and linguistic rules. The second is the need to overcome the variability of speech patterns that has been described above as occurring within the same speaker and between different speakers. The third is the problem of how to reduce the contaminating effects of environmental and other sorts of noise. The fourth, because we are now beginning to deal with machines endowed with a certain amount of linguistic knowledge-based intelligence, is how to design a recognition system that fits as naturally as possible into the human user's cognitive world, without forcing the user into unnaturally constrained modes of cognitive behaviour. We can discuss each of these problems briefly in turn.

First, in automatic speech recognition, a distinction can be drawn between a *selective* approach, that seeks to extract conclusions about linguistic structure from the speech waveform in a bottom-up process, and an *instructional* approach, that compensates for the impoverished nature of the linguistic material represented in the speech waveform by inserting amplifying hypotheses based on top-down knowledge of linguistic expectations. A basic attitude in linguistic knowledge-based approaches to automatic speech recognition is that a solely selective method will never succeed in the objective of recognising large vocabularies of continuous speech from multiple speakers of different accents. The human listener brings a wealth of knowledge to bear on the interpretation of the speech signal. This allows the listener to generate hypotheses not simply in a selectional, detection mode based only on surface evidence, but also in a creative, instructional manner illuminated by the empathetic ability to predict what the speaker is most probably intending to say. It will be a very long time before we succeed in making machines with a capacity for automatic learning that will emulate the scale and richness of linguistic knowledge that the human listener brings to bear on the task of speech recognition.

Secondly, as well as incorporating the necessary linguistic knowledge to recognise speech, machines will have to deploy a capacity to compensate for differences within and between speakers. Differences within a single speaker form an inherent part of the main speech recognition task. This is because linguistic hypotheses can only be deployed efficiently by taking such variability into account, by exploiting knowledge about the distribution in acoustic space of the speaker's typical performance. A successful automatic recognition system will have to be able not only to compensate for intra-speaker variability of this sort, but will also have to become speaker-adaptive, progressively moulding its own performance over time to the analysed characteristics of the speaker to whom it is attending.

In order to deal with inter-speaker differences, techniques for speaker normalisation are necessary to reduce the more gross differences between speakers of the same accent that derive from such factors as differences of vocal tract length, especially between men and women, that have been commented on earlier. Such techniques are increasingly based on auditory modelling approaches.

Human listeners seem able to adjust to new accents fairly efficiently. For automatic speech recognition systems based on an explicit phonetic and linguistic rule-based approach, this constitutes one of the most severe problems in the whole domain. The worst problem of all for explicit linguistic knowledge-based systems is that the inventory of consonants and vowels differs in different accents and, therefore, the phonemic specification of pronunciation in a recognition system's dictionary has to be rewritten for every new accent, if possible on an automatic basis. It would not be so serious if the correspondences between accents were one-to-one, with every instance of one sound in one accent being able to be replaced with a different but standard pronunciation in the other. An example where this does happen is the case where speakers of an educated Southern English accent pronounce a diphthongal vowel of changing quality in words such as "day", whereas speakers from most parts of Scotland pronounce such words with a monophthongal vowel of unchanging quality. In most cases of comparison of two accents of English, however, the specification of vowels is chosen from a list (or "vowel-system") which varies in number between the two accents. This means that there are many cases where two distinct words in one accent cannot be distinguished in the other, and vice versa. An example of this is that where almost all accents of England distinguish between the words "tot" and "taught", Scots accents typically make no distinction. Similarly, "pull" and "pool" are not distinguished by many Scots accents. On the other hand, Scots distinguishes between "tide" and "tied", whereas many English accents do not. The mapping of the one accent onto the other is thus partly unpredictable, and the system dictionary's pronunciation element has to be written anew for each new accent.

A related problem of speaker-adaptation concerns the question of vocabulary size. Training of the recognition system by the new speaker on every single word of the vocabulary is impracticable once the vocabulary exceeds some 1500–2500 words (for reasons of sheer tedium for the user). Such systems therefore have to be constructed to be intelligently adaptive to the style of pronunciation of the new speaker, often by extrapolating from partial information about one aspect of the speaker's pronunciation to a prediction of the anticipated pronunciation of another aspect. Some progress is being made in this area, but the issue of how to make knowledge-based speech recognition systems successfully speaker-adaptive is one of the most challenging problems in speech technology today.

Thirdly, to achieve practical success, a sophisticated automatic speech recognition system will have to be able to perform a number of tasks such as noise reduction, and spatial localisation of the speaker. Noise reduction relevant to machine (and human) recognition of speech is of three types: the cancellation of noise of relatively stationary spectral and temporal characteristics, such as the 50–60 Hz hum from fluorescent lights, or air-conditioning noise; the identification and filtering of more dynamic types of noise that contaminate the speech signal, such as passing traffic, doors slamming, or telephones ringing; and, most difficult of all, the compensation for the sound of competing speech from other speakers that the listener would prefer to ignore. This last is the "cocktail party" problem, and it is interesting to consider what resources the human listener requires to cope with the last and most severe of these types of noise.

Stereophonic exploitation of phase differences in the signal may allow the listener to localise the chosen speaker in space, in a horizontal plane (Blauert, 1983). This can be simulated in an automatic speech recognition system by means of a microphone array. Secondly, the ability to minimise the effects of competing voices (or of competing, dynamic non-human noise) depends on the listener's knowledge of the characteristic statistical properties of such signals. This is much harder to simulate on a machine, because a prerequisite is a typology of signals that distinguishes between human speech and non-speech, and even more challenging, a knowledge-base which would allow the listener or the machine to track an individual speaker's voice partly on the basis of statistical coherence of the data from that speaker's voice versus the data from the voices of other competing speakers.

Fourthly, there is the task of ensuring a comfortable fit between the machine's capabilities and the user's cognitive world. One of the problems that naive users are likely to have with apparently intelligent machines is that they are likely to over-estimate both the intelligence and the world-knowledge internalised within the machine. A lay user encountering for the first time a database query system using speech input and output for the human/computer interface may be misled into attributing to the system more world-knowledge than the machine actually has. The more fluent the working of the natural language interface, the more the lay user may have the impression that the human quality of the interface is matched by a human scale of understanding of the real world. One of the ergonomic problems in this area is, therefore, the education of the user-population about the limitations that currently remain on the capacity of machines to actually "know" about the world on any truly intelligent basis. Part of this education will have to focus on the efficient identification to the user of constraints on the domain of knowledge of the machine: how to offer the user an understandable and usable model of the machine's knowledge of the world is itself a difficult ergonomic research problem.

Other ergonomic problems that will have to be addressed are, first, the question of maintaining, in the face of restrictions of vocabulary size, some sensible and natural principles of vocabulary selection. Secondly, in the same vein, any attempt to constrain the grammatical characteristics of the speech material input to the system will be counter-ergonomic. Thirdly, it will be essential to develop mechanisms for the easy extension of the system's vocabulary, to the user's requirements. Finally, it is certain that the recognition systems of tomorrow will continue to make mistakes. Indeed, it is equally certain that they will always make mistakes, just as humans make perceptual mistakes. Only the scale of error, and perhaps the nature of error, will change. But it is going to be very important for the ergonomic acceptability of recognition systems that a simple, comfortable and effective method of error-correction is devised.

4.2 Text-to-Speech Synthesis Systems

In the area of speech synthesis and text-to-speech conversion systems, although the speech technology is perhaps somewhat more advanced than in the case of automatic recognition systems, it is noteworthy that no synthesis system yet exists which could be said to have a fully natural quality. This is a reflection of the fact that we do not yet know enough about the acoustics either of speech or of speakers. Similarly, no text-to-speech conversion system yet exists which knows enough about patterns of intonation and rhythm relevant to the discourse structure of the messages of the text to perform the task of reading aloud with a degree of discourse control comparable to that of a human reader. What this reflects is that we do not yet know enough about our cognitive strategies for understanding written language to be able to make a machine simulate our ability. Despite this idealistic criticism, it should be said that the most ambitious of the text-to-speech systems available today show considerable linguistic sophistication, and an impressive ability to generate continuous speech of a degree of intelligibility that is close to complete (Allen, Hunnicutt, & Klatt, 1987). The next phase of research will need to address two massive problems: how to make the systems sound more naturalistic, rather than simply intelligible, and how to give them the ability to make their prosodic performance relevant to the discourse structure of the messages they seek to communicate.

A valid criticism of modern research on synthesis is that, in the search for intelligibility, the pursuit of naturalness has been unduly overlooked. All commercial synthesis systems available today have voice qualities that are transparently mechanical, and not one would pass the test, over any length of time, of being taken for a genuine human voice. This is acceptable in some applications, provided that intelligibility is achieved. But to expand the field of applications of synthesis to its full potential range, it will be essential not only to guarantee intelligibility, but also to equip synthetic voices with substantially more natural, human-like qualities than is the case at present. The reason for this is not simply that in some applications it may be desirable for the synthetic voice to pass for human (though this is controversial), but that the unnatural quality of present synthesis is ill-designed for the human perceptual system to process efficiently.

Pisoni, Nusbaum, and Greene (1985) have shown that the perception of synthetic speech imposes a severe load on the cognitive processing capacity of listeners. This has many thoroughly undesirable consequences for the use of synthetic speech in the human/computer interface: synthetic speech loses full comprehensibility when listened to over any long period, with the attention of listeners tending to oscillate between "tuning in" and "fading out"; it is distinctly tiring to listen to for any length of time; it rapidly loses intelligibility in ambient noise or channel noise; and worst of all, because of the high cognitive loading, current synthetic speech is often unsuitable for use in applications where a competing demand for the listener's cognitive capacity exists. Pisoni et al. (1985: 1675) comment that "the presentation of a synthetic message might not be detected at all under very demanding or life-critical conditions in severe environments". The use of synthetic speech in current military aviation applications, or noise-contaminated factory applications, for example, is far from free of these problems.

One way to improve this situation is to enhance the naturalness of synthetic speech, and bring the attributes of the signal closer to those to which the human cognitive process is presumably evolutionarily optimised to attend with ease and efficiency. There are signs that research into synthetic speech is beginning to move in this direction.

Another enhancement of the perceived naturalness of synthetic speech, though this time in the area of prosodic control of intonation and rhythm, would be the ability to signal the discourse-structure of the message. To do this, a level of rule-based linguistic control is necessary which takes into account structural relations between phrases and sentences in the same paragraph, and preferably in the same overall text. Unfortunately, the very large majority of current text-to-speech systems are limited to controlling prosodic relations between linguistic units within the span of a single phrase or simple sentence.

Almost all state-of-the-art text-to-speech systems pronounce phrases and sentences as if they were isolated from their co-text, and as if knowledge about the grammatical and phonetic aspects alone of the individual words was sufficient. In many neutral instances, this is possibly satisfactory, and none of the intended sense of the message is lost. But even if it were simple (and it is not) to incorporate structural knowledge about items that have already been mentioned in the earlier co-text, some other types of knowledge about discourse are needed before a text-to-speech system could approach a human speaker's level of competence in this area. The prosodic structure of normal discourse often reflects knowledge about the semantic structure of the real world. In order to construct an appropriate prosodic structure for the pronunciation of the phrases and sentences which make up a given text, the system therefore sometimes has to know something about the semantic relationship between the objects and concepts mentioned in those phrases and sentences.

Few text-to-speech systems currently include any except the most rudimentary representation of semantic information. When the appropriate pronunciation of the sentence demands knowledge of such real-world semantics, then control of the relevant intonational and rhythmic performance is deficient. This can be seen in the following example. Almost all text-to-speech systems currently available would pronounce the sentence

These are VAXes, not microcomputers

wrongly, as

These are +VAXes, not microcom+puters

where the symbol "+" indicates the beginning of the syllable showing the auditorily most prominent intonational peak, by appeal to a standard rule which locates the prominence on the last lexical form of the phrase, on a syllable identified by the dictionary as the main accented syllable of the word concerned. A future system displaying appropriate knowledge of real-world semantics would place the intonational peak differently, as in

These are +VAXes, not +microcomputers

This pronunciation would reveal the fact that the system, like a human reader, knew the semantic fact that a VAX is a computer, but that its type is not that of a *micro*computer. In other words, it would be able to communicate the opposition that the writer had intended to convey, namely between a VAX as a type of minicomputer and smaller systems called microcomputers.

A further area where the design of text-to-speech systems could be much enhanced by adequate knowledge of a comprehensive model of the corresponding human domain is the extralinguistic and paralinguistic area of speaker attributes and voice-typing. A number of currently available text-to-speech systems provide a facility for changing the voice type of the system. The usual facility is to offer a range of voices from which to choose (male/female, same accent), and/or to allow the user to change the voice type of the given speaker, changing the apparent personality of the speaker. Tempo and pitch-range can also sometimes be altered by the user.

Options of this sort are the vestigial beginnings of a range of facilities that will become increasingly important as text-to-speech output becomes more natural. At the moment, guaranteed intelligibility is difficult enough to achieve. But as synthetic speech of an acceptably natural quality becomes accessible, there will be an increasing realisation that the voice type of a text-to-speech system needs to be able to be adjusted to suit the communicative and informative function to which it is being applied. The voice type needed for an application in a primary school teaching-support role is very different from that needed in an aircraft avionics emergency alert application. More subtly, the voice of persuasion is phonetically different from that of the voice of neutral reporting, even in the same speaker.

There are four layers of voice typing involved. The first concerns the vocal consequences of physical factors of sex, age, and individual anatomy. The second involves accent factors due to the regional and social milieu of the speaker. The third is to do with the reflection of a speaker's personality in the general quality of his voice, to the extent that such a connection exists. And the fourth is a matter of the more momentary changes in the individual speaker due to ephemeral variations of mood and attitude. All these factors are potentially capable of systematic description, and are thus candidates for inclusion in the sophisticated vocal engineering systems of the future. Because the voice is such a rich vehicle for evidence about the characteristics of its owner, any speech technology system that is able to control its presentation of vocal attributes of the apparent speaker in a way convincing to its human listeners, and appropriate to its intended communicative function, will be radically more plausible as an interlocutor in any conversational interaction.

Vocal engineering may look to phonetics and social psychology for a suitable descriptive model for different voice types, and for the link between given voice types and the perception of particular speaker attributes (in the terms mentioned above of the physical, social, and psychological attributes of speaker identity, as well as shorter-term attributes of mood and attitude). But, unfortunately, it will look largely in vain. Descriptive theories linking voice type and speaker attributes constitute a neglected area of research in both phonetics and social psychology. Some of the limited research that has been done in the last decade is reported in Laver (1980), Laver and Trudgill (1979), Laver and Hanson (1981), Scherer (1982), Scherer and Giles (1979), and van Bezooyen (1984). The requirements of speech technology might give this area some of the needed research impetus.

4.3 Basic Versus Pre-competitive Research

There are many technical problems that will have to be solved before speech technology can reach some of the ambitious goals for which it is striving. These technical problems often pose very serious challenges to the technical competence and imagination of the speech technology community. The recognition of continuous speech by the acoustic phonetic feature approach, for example, calls for an advanced and complex system design, particularly because the adequate representation and deployment of the necessary phonetic and linguistic knowledge-base in a computer-usable form still lies out in the twilight zone just beyond our present competence. Similarly, the generation entirely by rule of synthetic speech of a truly naturalistic human-equivalent quality is just beyond our present reach. But many of the future advances desired will only be possible if basic research into the characteristics of natural language and speech is vigorously pursued.

The discussion about the relationship between speech technology and cognitive research may be sharpened at this point by drawing a distinction between basic research and relatively shorter-term pre-competitive, industrially oriented research. The European programmes which currently support advanced research and development in information technology, such as the European Community's ESPRIT Programme, and the national programmes such as the United Kingdom's Alvey Programme, typically support pre-competitive research in speech and natural language processing which is aimed directly, if not necessarily in the shortest term, at industrial exploitation. As such, the major activity in such pre-competitive research is enabling current scientific knowledge to be expressed in a way that it is usable for computer-based speech technology purposes close to the potential marketplace. The research supported seldom addresses basic theoretical issues, and most often is limited, apart from issues of usability, to ones of comprehensiveness of coverage. The balance of emphasis has tended therefore to be more on the consolidation of present knowledge than on making the major theoretical advances which will constitute future knowledge: by definition, it has been concerned more with technology and engineering than with advancing science as such.

The speech and natural language processing technology that lies at the end of the present development cycle thus stands on a platform of current scientific understanding made available to industry by pre-competitive and enabling research. In the domain of the cognitive sciences, the range and degree of this scientific understanding is still rather limited. For future generations of speech and natural language processing products to continue to evolve, and to maintain economic competitiveness in an international market, it is clear that major advances in our basic understanding of the human processes of speech and language production, perception, and understanding are essential. Underlying this assertion, it has to be declared, is the assumption that the design of machines in this area is best illuminated by functional principles of human cognitive operation.

A stringent test of the adequacy of basic theoretical models of human cognition is an attempt to build working versions of such models through computer simulation, as indicated earlier. These simulations can be viewed not only as theoretical test-beds, but also as software prototypes of potential machines in speech and natural language processing technology. The effort to achieve a unified cognitive model and the effort to build advanced speech technology machines are hence mutually supportive, and mutually relevant. Each needs the other to succeed.

5. SUMMARY CONCLUSIONS: AVENUES FOR RESEARCH

It would seem appropriate to conclude this survey of the place of speech research in cognitive science by summarising some of the avenues along which promising and relevant advances may be made towards the goal of a unified cognitive model for speech.

The most fundamental issue in a cognitive approach to speech is the nature of the linkage between linguistic form and speech substance. This problem can be approached through an examination of the production, perception, and understanding of speech, during acquisition, normal use or pathology, and through the relation between these and speech acoustics.

In speech production, the most general issue is the nature of the central units of cognitive representation, and the strategic and tactical aspects of control. The issue surfaces in such areas as the control of sequence and serial order, the temporal control of durational and rhythmic activity, the control of inter-articulator synchronisation, the study of co-articulatory phenomena, the reorganisation of articulatory and acoustic performance in changes of rate and style, and the nature of compensatory strategies to reach relatively standard goals from contextually different starting points.

Over-arching questions in speech production concern the validity of generalisation from and to other motor skills than speech, and whether speech and language have a specialised biology. Another important avenue is the general issue of integration. This includes the general physiological question of how sensory feedback (of auditory, touch, contact pressure, muscle-tension, and joint-position information) participates in on-going control. It also includes the strategic question of how superordinate structures integrate their subordinate elements (e.g. how metrical units of rhythm in speech integrate their syllabic constituents, or how syllabic structures integrate their segmental elements).

In speech perception and understanding, a major issue is the question of how the listener exploits prosodic information in the stream of speech to reach a hypothesis about the pragmatic value and the relevance to discourse structure of the speaker's utterances. In order to do this, the listener has to call on knowledge about the context of the conversation, on the knowledge the speaker can be assumed to possess, and in particular on the knowledge that the speaker and the listener can be assumed to share. Perhaps the broadest of all the topics in this area is the problem of how a speaker and a listener successfully collude in the progressive development of the cognitive structure of a conversation.

The general topic of research methodology is itself an issue. Much valuable research can and has been done by studying the activities of the normal brain controlling the normal apparatus in normal speech production and perception. But it is worth reminding ourselves of the value of trying to penetrate an opaque system through an examination of its characteristic malfunctions. The study of neurolinguistics, aphasiology, and other topics in speech pathology, worthwhile for its own sake, offers some unusual opportunities for establishing the operational characteristics of the normal, healthy system. A similar argument can be made for the study of speech and language acquisition, as a window on otherwise hidden processes in the adult production, perception, and understanding of speech and language.

In keeping with the more comprehensive approach to semiotic behaviour that was urged earlier in this chapter, the value of paralinguistic research into cognitive aspects of affect and emotion is worth underlining. It may be plausible to assert that speech and language have their own biology, but it is unlikely in the extreme that such relatively young systems, phylogenetically speaking, are completely divorced from their antecedents in more ancient structures.

In the widest semiotic perspective on the study of speech and language, a necessary contribution to the creation of a cognitive model of speech and language that is fully general to human beings is the development of an adequate understanding of the extralinguistic factors specific to individual speakers and hearers. The aspect of speech and language production and perception that is idiosyncratic to the individual, and that which is general to the individual's speech community, are figure and ground to each other. Neither can be fully understood in the absence of an understanding of the other.

From the point of view of research on speech and language, a unified cognitive model should thus try to account for the generation, transmission, reception, and interpretation of all informative and communicative aspects of speech, and should therefore address all three types of semiotic features mentioned earlier—linguistic, paralinguistic, and extralinguistic features. Such a model is not only more comprehensive from a unified cognitive point of view, but is also of more general semiotic relevance than one which allows the inclusion of only linguistic features.

This chapter has argued that the aim of establishing a unified cognitive model, where there is an unbroken succession of links in the chain of implementation from ideation through to speech production and speech acoustics, and from auditory perception through to semantic interpretation, is no longer a wildly quixotic ambition. This is not to suggest that such an unbroken chain can be welded together in the near future; it will take generations of basic research before a convincingly integrated model is fully achieved. But a long-term drive towards a unified cognitive model now seems more practicable, in the sense of a growing readiness on the part of the disciplines concerned to accept an organising framework for research which is as wide as the cognitive sciences themselves, in which the individual subjects can pursue a unifying theme of mutual relevance.

REFERENCES

Abercrombie, D. (1967). *Elements of general phonetics*. Edinburgh: Edinburgh University Press.

Allen, J.B. (1985). Cochlear modelling. *IEEE ASSP Magazine* (January), 3-29.

Allen, J., Hunnicutt, M.S., & Klatt, D. (1987). *From text to speech: The MITalk System*. Cambridge: Cambridge University Press.

Anderson, S.R. (1974). *The organization of phonology*.London and San Diego: Academic Press.

Aronoff, M. & Oehrle, R.T. (Eds) (1984). *Language sound structure: Studies in phonology presented to Morris Halle by his teacher and students*. Cambridge, Mass.: MIT Press.

Beckman, M.E. (1986). *Stress and non-stress accent*. Dordrecht: Foris Publications.

Bernstein, N.A. (1967). *The coordination and regulation of movement*. London: Pergamon Press.

Bezooyen, R. van (1984). *Characteristics and recognizability of vocal expressions of emotion*. Dordrecht: Foris Publications.

Blauert, J. (1983). *Spatial hearing*. Cambridge, Mass.: MIT Press.

Boomer, D.S. & Laver, J. (1968). Slips of the tongue *British Journal of Disorders of Communication*, 3, 2-12.

Boylls, C.C. (1975). A Theory of Cerebellar Function with Applications to Locomotion: II. The Relation of Anterior Lobe Climbing Fiber Function to Locomotor Behavior in the Cat. *COINS Technical Report 76-1*, Department of Computer and Information Science, University of Massachusetts.

Caplan, D. (1987). *Neurolinguistics and linguistic aphasiology: An introduction*. Cambridge: Cambridge University Press.

Carlson, R. & Granstrøm, B. (Eds) (1982). *The representation of speech in the peripheral auditory system*. Amsterdam: Elsevier Biomedical Press.

Chomsky, N. & Halle, M. (1968). *The sound pattern of English*. New York: Harper and Row.

Clements, G. N. & Keyser, S.J. (1983). *CV phonology: A generative theory of the syllable*. Cambridge, Mass.: MIT Press.

Cooke, M.P. (1985). A computer model of peripheral auditory processing. *National Physical Laboratory Report*, Division of Information Technology and Computing, No. 58/85. England: Teddington.

Dickson, D.R. & Maue-Dickson, W. (1982). *Anatomical and physiological bases of speech*. Boston: Little, Brown and Company.

Fant, G. (1960). *Acoustic theory of speech production*. The Hague: Mouton.

Fant, G. (1973). *Speech sounds and features*. Cambridge, Mass.: MIT Press.

Fischer-Jørgensen, E. (1975). *Trends in phonological theory*. Copenhagen: Akademisk Forlag.

Fowler, C., Rubin, P., Remez, R.E., & Turvey, M.T. (1980). Implications for speech production of a general theory of action. In B. Butterworth (Ed.), *Language production*, Vol.1. London and San Diego: Academic Press.

Gel'fand, I.M., Gurfinkel, V.S., Tstetlin, M.L., & Shik, M.L. (1971). Some problems in the analysis of movement. In I.M. Gel'fand, V.S. Gurfinkel, S.V. Fomin, & M.L. Tstetlin (Eds), *Models of the structural-functional organization of certain biological systems*. Cambridge, Mass.: MIT Press.

Halle, M. & Vergnaud, J.R. (1981). Harmony processes. In W. Klein & W. Levelt (Eds), *Crossing the boundaries in linguistics*, pp. 1-23. Dordrecht: Reidel.

Halle, M. & Vergnaud, J.R. (1982). On the framework of autosegmental phonology. In H.G.van der Hulst & N. Smith, (Eds) *The structure of phonological representations* (2 Vols), pp. 65-82. Dordrecht: Foris Publications.

Hogg, R. & McCully, C.B. (1987). *Metrical phonology: A coursebook*. Cambridge: Cambridge University Press.

Hulst, H.G. van der & Smith N. (1982). An overview of autosegmental and metrical phonology. In H.G. van der Hulst & N. Smith (Eds), *The structure of phonological representations* (2 Vols), pp. 1-46. Dordrecht: Foris Publications.

Kent, R.D. (1983). The segmental organisation of speech. In P.F. MacNeilage (Ed.), *The production of speech*, pp.57-90. New York: Springer-Verlag.

Kiparsky, P. (1982). From cyclic phonology to lexical phonology. In H. van der Hulst, & N. Smith (Eds), *The structure of phonological representations* (2 Vols), pp.131-176. Dordrecht: Foris Publications.

Kuehn, D.P. (1973). A cinefluorographic investigation of articulatory velocities. Unpublished doctoral dissertation, University of Iowa.

Kuehn, D.P. & Moll, K.L. (1976). A cinefluorographic study of VC and CV articulatory velocities. *Journal of Phonetics*, *4*, 303-320.

Kugler, P.N., Scott Kelso, J.A., & Turvey, M.T. (1980). On the concept of co-ordinative structures as dissipative structures: I. Theoretical lines of convergence. In G.E. Stelmach & J. Requin (Eds), *Tutorials in motor behavior*, pp.3-47. Amsterdam: North-Holland.

Ladd, D.R. (1980). *The structure of intonational meaning: Evidence from English*. Bloomington: Indiana University Press.

Laver, J. (1980). *The phonetic description of voice quality*. Cambridge: Cambridge University Press.

Laver, J. (forthcoming). *Introduction to theoretical phonetics*. Cambridge: Cambridge University Press.

Laver, J. & Hanson, R. (1981). Describing the normal voice. In J. Darby (Ed.), *Speech evaluation in psychiatry*, pp.51-78. San Diego: Grune and Stratton.

Laver, J. & Trudgill, P. (1979). Phonetic and linguistic markers in speech. In K.R. Scherer & H. Giles (Eds), *Social markers in speech*, pp.1-32. Cambridge: Cambridge University Press.

Leben, W. (1982). Metrical or autosegmental. In H. van der Hulst & N. Smith (Eds), *The structure of phonological representations (2 Vols)*, pp.177-190. Dordrecht: Foris Publications.

Liberman, A.M. (1984). On finding that speech is special. In M.S. Gazzaniga (Ed.), *Handbook of cognitive neuroscience*, pp.169-198. New York: Plenum Press.

Liberman, M. (1975). The intonational system of English. Ph.D. dissertation, MIT, distributed by Indiana University Linguistics Club.

Liberman, M. & Prince, A. (1977). On stress and linguistic rhythm. *Linguistic Inquiry*, *8*, 249-336.

Lindblom, B. (1983). Economy of speech gestures. In P.F. MacNeilage (Ed.), *The production of speech*, pp.217-246. New York: Springer-Verlag.

Linell, P. (1979). *Psychological reality in phonology*. Cambridge: Cambridge University Press.

Lyons, J. (1968). *Introduction to theoretical linguistics*. Cambridge: Cambridge University Press.

Lyons, J. (1977). *Semantics* (2 Vols). Cambridge: Cambridge University Press.

Maddieson, I. (1984). *Patterns of sounds*. Cambridge: Cambridge University Press.

Miller, G.A. & Gazzaniga, M.S. (1984). The cognitive sciences. In M.S. Gazzaniga, (Ed.), *Handbook of cognitive neuroscience*, pp.3-14. New York: Plenum Press.

Møller, A.R. (1983). *Auditory physiology*. London and San Diego: Academic Press.

Moore, B.C.J. (1982). *An introduction to the psychology of hearing* (2nd Edition). London and San Diego: Academic Press.

Myers, T., Laver, J., & Anderson J. (Eds) (1981). *The cognitive representation of speech*. Amsterdam: North-Holland.

Nolan, F. (1982). The role of Action Theory in the description of speech production. *Linguistics, 20*, 287-308.

Nolan, F. (1983). *The phonetic bases of speaker recognition*. Cambridge: Cambridge University Press.

Oppenheim, A.V. & Schafer, R.W. (1975). *Digital signal processing*. Englewood Cliffs, N.J.: Prentice-Hall.

Perkell, J.S. & Klatt, D.H. (Eds) (1986). *Invariance and variability in speech processes*. Hillsdale, N.J.: Lawrence Erlbaum Associates Inc.

Pickles, J.O. (1982). *An introduction to the physiology of hearing*. London and San Diego: Academic Press.

Pisoni, D., Nusbaum, H.C., & Greene, B. (1985). Perception of synthetic speech generated by rule. *Proceedings of the IEEE, 73*, 1665-76.

Rabiner, L.R. & Schafer, R.W. (1978). *Digital processing of speech signals*. Englewood Cliffs, N.J.: Prentice-Hall.

Rumelhart, D.E., McClelland, J.L., & the PDP Research Group (Eds) (1986). *Parallel distributed processing: Explorations in the microstructure of cognition*, Vol.1: *Foundations*; Vol. 2: *Psychological and biological models*. Cambridge, Mass.: MIT Press.

Scherer, K.R. (1982). Methods of research on vocal communication: Paradigms and parameters. In K.R. Scherer & P. Ekman (Eds), *Handbook of methods in nonverbal behavior research*, pp.136-198. Cambridge: Cambridge University Press, and Paris: Editions de la Maison des Sciences de l'Homme.

Scherer, K.R. & Giles, H. (Eds) (1979). *Social markers in speech*. Cambridge: Cambridge University Press.

Schroeder, M.R. (1975). Models of hearing. *Proceedings of the IEEE, 63*, 1332-1350.

Scott Kelso, J.A. & Tuller, B. (1984). A dynamical basis for action systems. In M.S.Gazzaniga (Ed.), *Handbook of cognitive neuroscience*, pp.319-356. New York: Plenum Press.

Scott Kelso, J.A., Holt, K.G., Kugler, P.N., & Turvey, M.T. (1980). On the concept of co-ordinative structures as dissipative structures: II. Empirical lines of evidence. In G.E. Stelmach & J. Requin (Eds), *Tutorials in motor behavior*, pp.49-70. Amsterdam: North-Holland.

Scott Kelso, J.A., Tuller, B., & Harris, K.S. (1983). A dynamic pattern perspective on the control and co-ordination of movement. In P.F. MacNeilage (Ed.), *The production of speech*, pp.137-173. New York: Springer-Verlag.

Selkirk, E. (1984). *Phonology and syntax: The relation between sound and structure*. Cambridge, Mass.: MIT Press.

Smolensky, P. (1986). Information processing in dynamical systems: Foundations of harmony theory. In D.E. Rumelhart, J.L. McClelland, & the PDP Research Group, *Parallel distributed processing: Explorations in the microstructure of cognition*, Vol. 1, *Foundations*, pp.194-281. Cambridge, Mass.: MIT Press.

Stevens, K. N. (1972). The quantal nature of speech: Evidence from articulatory-acoustic data. In E.E. David & P.B. Denes (Eds), *Human communication: A unified view*, pp.51-66. New York: McGraw-Hill.

Tuller, B., Harris, K.S., & Scott Kelso, J.A. (1982). Stress and rate: Differential transformations of articulation. *Journal of the Acoustical Society of America, 71*, 1534-1543.

Tuller, B., Scott Kelso, J.A., Harris, K.S. (1982). Interarticulator phasing as an index of temporal regularity in speech. *Journal of Experimental Psychology: Human Perception and Performance, 8*, 460-472.

CHAPTER 3

Grammar Frameworks

Ewan Klein

Centre for Cognitive Science
University of Edinburgh
2 Buccleuch Place, Edinburgh EH8 9LW, U.K.

INTRODUCTION

Our ability to understand and produce natural language is undoubtedly one of the key problems of cognitive science. Linguists have generally adopted the view that the ability is founded on a knowledge of language, and that this knowledge is to be modelled in terms of a grammar. That is, a grammar is an explicit characterisation of the rules and representations which are held to play an essential role in language use. Of course, this is not to deny that many other factors may be crucial to explaining linguistic behaviour. However, the main goal of theoretical linguistics in recent years has been to elucidate the nature of specifically linguistic knowledge, and to develop accounts of the intricate and detailed regularities which are recognised by speakers. Moreover, linguists have attempted to discover not only the properties of individual languages, but also what is common to natural languages in general, on the hypothesis that this shared structure may provide the clue to how children come to acquire a first language with such apparent ease.

What is the relevance of linguistics to cognitive science? According to the view just sketched, theoretical linguistics just *is* one of the cognitive sciences. Because we adopt this perspective, the bulk of this chapter will be concerned with recent developments in formal grammar, particularly in the area of syntax. However, the place of "core" linguistics in cognitive science is also closely bound up with developments in two related subjects, namely computational linguistics and psycholinguistics. Although both these topics are dealt with in separate chapters of this volume, I shall also devote some space to the ways in which processing considerations —computational and psychological—have had an impact on theoretical linguistics.

Moreover, linguistics has had some technological impact; although we are still far from developing a comprehensive theory of natural language understanding, there has been significant success in using the results of research in this area to construct useful computational devices. In fact, over the last decade, work in computational linguistics has been perceived as increasingly germane to the interests of theoretical linguists, partly for the reasons just mentioned, but more importantly because the precise import of linguistic formalisms is much easier to gauge if they can be provided with a direct computational interpretation.

The major part of this chapter attempts first of all to give the reader some sense of what work is currently going on in the area of formal grammar, with most of the attention being directed towards syntax. This overview is intended to provide a background for the last section of the chapter, which points out directions for future research. I have tried to give fairly fully bibliographical references to enable the reader to follow up particular issues in greater depth.

MAJOR GRAMMATICAL APPROACHES

Research in linguistic theory over the last 15 years has been heavily influenced by two major figures, Noam Chomsky and Richard Montague. Chomsky's achievement was to establish much of the conceptual framework of linguistic theorising, and to propose an important agenda for research, based on the belief that the major problem in need of explanation was the relative ease and rapidity with which children acquire mastery of a natural language. Strong emphasis has been placed by Chomsky and his followers on the need to establish a theory of linguistic universals, founded on the belief that these constitute part of the innate endowment of the child.

Despite the fact that questions of semantic representation have always had an important place in generative grammar, much of the credit for establishing a rigorous and mathematically defensible theory of meaning in natural language rests with Montague, who established a firm bridge between the concerns of linguists and those of logicians. Montague's view of grammar has also had a subtle but pervasive influence on research towards designing linguistic formalisms which are computationally tractable.

One of the outstanding difficulties in linguistic research has been uncertainty about how to demarcate the domain of inquiry. It has been stressed by a number of authors that it is extremely hard, if not impossible, to find a set of identity criteria to define what counts as a language. Furthermore, even if there were some consensus as to what constitutes "English", different grammatical frameworks tend to focus on different sets of linguistic phenomena, and we lack any agreed methods for independently characterising and comparing such bodies of data. Consequently, in evaluating different theoretical proposals, it is difficult to know what to take as the basis of comparison, and a variety of considerations are brought to bear which are often of a methodological or metatheoretical nature. In the rest of this section, I give an extremely sketchy overview of the dominant linguistic frameworks which are currently under development, using this also as an opportunity to highlight certain research themes. However, I shall not attempt to draw any judgements about the empirical adequacy of the frameworks being presented. For more detailed overviews of the approaches discussed here, the reader might benefit from consulting Horrocks (1987), McCloskey (1988), Sells (1986) and Shieber (1986).

Transformational Approaches

Classical transformational grammar (i.e. the Standard Theory of Chomsky, 1965) starts from the premise that canonical sentence structure is determined by phrase structure rules which produce a parse tree of the traditional kind. Non-canonical structures, on the other hand, are derived by the operation of a set of tree-to-tree mappings. Simplifying somewhat, a sentence like *Hans put the car in the garage* would be produced solely by the phrase structure rules in (1), with the structure indicated in (2).

(1) S → NP VP
     VP → V NP PP
     NP → Det N
     PP → P NP

(2) [S [NP[Hans] [VP put [NP the car] [PP in the garage]]]

An additional component will be responsible for ensuring that the structures built by phrase structure rules terminate in lexical items; in effect, it will select appropriate words from the lexicon, and insert them into the tree. These lexical insertion rules are designed to place a verb, such as *put*, into the correct position in the VP; moreover, they must select a verb of the right subcategory, namely the subcategory which co-occurs with both an NP and a PP[loc] complement (PP[loc] stands for a locative prepositional phrase). For instance, the verb *disappeared* is not of this subcategory, as witnessed by the ungrammaticality of (3):

(3) *Hans disappeared the car into the garage.

More generally, lexical items such as verbs can be divided into subcategories according to the nature of the complements that they are grammatically required, or permitted, to co-occur with. A grammatical violation results if a verb is inserted into a structure where unlicensed complements are present, as in (3). Conversely, a violation also occurs if a verb appears in a structure where there are insufficient complements (cf. 4):

(4) *Hans put in the garage.

Thus, the verb *put* is subcategorised not only to permit an NP complement, but also to require it. In Chomsky (1965), the lexical entry for *put* will contain a subcategorisation frame of the form (5), which describes the structure of the VP subtree in which the verb can be inserted:

(5) +[__ NP PP[loc]]

Sentence (2) can be contrasted with the interrogative sentence (6), where it is held that the NP *which car* has been displaced from its canonical position as object of *put*:

(6)   [S [NP which car][S [V did] [NP[Hans] [VP put [PP in the garage]]]]

Sentence (6) is derived by the interaction of two distinct types of rule. Phrase structure rules generate a structure like (2), which we call D(eep)-structure, and a transformation maps this into the derived structure (6); we call the latter S(urface)-structure. Another transformation is responsible for inserting the auxiliary verb *did* in the appropriate position, but we ignore this detail here.

Notice that (6) contains the substring *Hans put in the garage*, which we just observed was ungrammatical as a sentence in its own right, since *put* is missing a complement. Transformational grammar explains the grammaticality of (6) by claiming that the subcategorisation requirements of the verb are in fact satisfied, but at D-structure rather than S-structure. It is also claimed that assignment of basic function-argument structure is determined as D-structure, e.g. the fact that *Hans* is assigned the "thematic role" of agent in a three-place relation, while *the car* is theme (the object that is moved), and *the garage* is the location. (The allusion to thematic roles here is anachronistic, in that they did not figure as such in mainstream transformational accounts until Chomsky (1981); however, this is mainly a matter of terminology.)

A further point worthy of note is that the transformation responsible for deriving (6) from (2) must be defined so as to be able to "move" into sentence-initial position an NP whose deep-structure position is indefinitely far away. Consider, for example, the series indicated in the following example:

(7)   Which car did Hans put in the garage?
       Which car do you think that Hans put in the garage?
       Which car do you think that Helen suspects that Hans put in the garage?
       Which car do you think that Helen suspects that you forgot that Hans
       put in the garage?

Although the acceptability of such examples decreases gradually in proportion to their length, there is no clear cut-off point where they become definitely bad. Consequently, linguists have generally preferred to adopt the position that the grammar places no upper limit on the distance between the canonical position of the displaced NP and its eventual sentence-initial position. Hence, the rule in question is termed an unbounded (or long-distance) movement rule. We shall also refer to sentences like those in (7) as unbounded dependency constructions.

A central tenet of classical transformational grammar is that syntactic generalisations should be stated on a purely structural basis. For example, the movement rule responsible for (6) might be defined as a function over syntactic trees which admit the analysis *X-NP-Y*, and whose value belongs to the set of trees with analysis NP-*X-Y*, where *X, Y* are variables over subtrees. The important point, for present purposes, is that no reference is made to the meaning or communicative function of the linguistic expressions involved in the transformational rule; only their tree structure is relevant. This contrasts with the functional view of language adopted by linguists such as Halliday (cf. Halliday, 1985, for a recent introduction).

Although the focus on formal properties of syntax attracted much criticism from non-generative grammarians, especially in the 1960s, it has proved to be of considerable heuristic value. It was soon noted that movement rules, if allowed to apply in a completely unconstrained fashion, led to a range of ungrammatical results. Contrast (6) with (8), (where the "gap" left by the movement rule is indicated with a *e*):

(8) a. *Which car do you know the man who put *e* in the garage?
     b. *Which car did you refute the claim that Hans put *e* in the garage?
     c. * Which car did you wonder who put *e* in the garage?

In (8a), the NP *the car* has been moved out of a relative clause (i.e. the clause starting *who put...*); in (8b), it has been moved out of the clausal complement of the noun *claim*; in (8c), it has been moved out of an embedded interrogative. The first systematic attempt to codify the grammatical constraints which are violated by such examples was due to Ross (1967). He proposed that certain syntactic configurations constituted "islands", out of which nothing could be extracted by an unbounded movement rule. Particular instances of islands included complex NPs, defined so as to cover NPs with relative clause modifiers and noun complements, and *wh*-complements such as the embedded interrogative in (8c). Another type of island for movement noted by Ross consisted of coordinate constructions, and the relevant restriction was dubbed the Coordinate Structure Constraint. Witness the contrasts in (9) and (10):

(9) a. Hans [VP removed the mower from the drive and put the car in the garage].
     b. *Which car did Hans [VP remove the mower from the drive and   put *e* in the garage]?
     c. Which car did Hans [VP remove *e* from the drive and put *e* in the garage]?

(10) a. Hans put [NP the mower and the car] in the garage.
     b. *Which car did Hans put [NP the mower and *e*] in the garage?
     c. *Which car did Hans put [NP *e* and *e*] in the garage.

Sentence (9a) illustrates a coordinate VP; (9b) shows that a violation occurs if an NP is extracted from one conjunct; (9c) shows that extraction out of a coordinate structure is nevertheless permissible when it applies "across-the-board" to both conjuncts. The examples in (10) show that the same restrictions hold for NP coordinate structures, with the additional constraint that across-the-board extraction is also ruled out if the whole of each conjunct is removed.

Ross (1967) formulated a battery of principles which were intended to be language-universal constraints on movement rules, and these turned out to be remarkably influential in subsequent linguistic theorising. It has generally been agreed that his proposals, important though they were, amounted to little more than a taxonomy, and the main thrust of subsequent research has been to seek a more explanatory account.

Chomsky's strategy starts by rejecting the idea that there should be a correspondence between construction types (such as interrogatives) and particular rules, since this tended to have the effect that increasingly complex conditions were placed on the applicability of individual transformations. Instead, he argues, grammatical patterns should emerge from the interaction of a set of broadly motivated, maximally simple, principles and rules. This is not the place to enter into a history of the diverse proposals that have been made within transformational grammar (Chomsky, 1986a, gives a useful overview of the main trends leading towards the Government-Binding theory). However, in order to convey the flavour of Chomsky's theorising, we will briefly indicate some of the current ideas.

We supposed earlier that the movement rule responsible for moving an NP into sentence-initial position operated in "one fell swoop". However, it is now generally assumed that the unbounded nature of movement rules results from a succession of strictly local movements. It has been proposed that what we have been calling "sentence-initial position" is structurally defined as the slot in which complementisers—subordinating conjunctions like *that* and *for*—are realised. Moreover, note that the recursive structure of a sentence like (11) is obtained by embedding a series of clausal complements, each with a complementiser position, beneath appropriate verbs:

(11) I wonder [s_3 who Hans claimed [s_2 that Helen thought [s_1 that Bill preferred [s_0 for Sam to see e]]]]

Each such clause is treated as domain for local movement into complementiser position. That is, the rule responsible for moving *who* from the position marked by *e* applies first to the most deeply embedded clause [s_0 *for Sam to see who*], and adjoins the *wh*-NP to the complementiser position marked by *for*. At the next stage, the rule reapplies to the domain s_1, moving *who* into a position adjoining s_1's complementiser, and so on until it reaches its eventual sentence-initial position.

The gap left in the object position of *see* is analysed as an empty category; that is, as a piece of syntactic structure (here, an NP) which dominates no lexical material. The movement transformation is formulated just as "Move-α", where α can be either a maximal constituent or a head, and left to itself will lead to the completely unconstrained generation of empty categories. However, an independent principle dictates that empty categories are only licensed if they are (properly) *governed*, which is given a disjunctive definition. One half invokes a traditional notion, according to which lexical categories such as verbs and nouns govern the complements for which they are subcategorised; the second half allows government of one empty category by another which occurs in the closest dominating complementiser position. The definition of government results in an analysis of (11) according to which all the empty categories produced by the successive application of Move-α are governed. However, it is also formulated so that certain constituent boundaries are classed as *barriers* to government. According to one formulation, γ is a barrier to the government of β by α in the configuration (12) just in case γ is a "projection" of a lexical head (i.e. just in case γ is a category of some particular type which dominates a lexical category of the same type):

(12)   ... α ... [γ ... β ...]

Although there is no space to enter into details here, plausible assumptions about the phrase structure of the NPs in (8a) and (8b) lead to the conclusion that two barriers to government intervene in the former, and one intervenes in the latter, which is held to account for slight differences in the degree of ungrammaticality involved.

Lexicalist and Monostratal Approaches

According to an early conception of generative grammar, the division between syntax and the lexicon corresponded to the distinction between regularities which can be stated by rule, and idiosyncratic information which can only be listed. This was replaced by a more sophisticated perspective in which it was appreciated that rule-governed regularities can be stated over words (or lexical items) as well as syntactically complex phrases. However, the new perspective brought with it new questions, as pointed out by Heny (1979); in particular, what criteria determine whether a particular linguistic phenomenon is to be accounted for by a lexical rule or a syntactic rule? Many linguists tended to the conclusion that as much information as possible should be localised in lexical representations and rules, thus significantly attenuating the role of syntactic rules. As part of this movement, it was also questioned whether the multiple syntactic analyses adopted by transformational grammar were indeed required; frameworks which make do with a single syntactic representation have been termed *monostratal*[1]

This point can be illustrated by considering passive constructions in English. Informally, the relationship between the two sentences in (13) hinges on two facts: (i) the direct object NP which *put* is subcategorised for is absent from (13b), the passive congener of (13a); and (ii), the subject NP of (13b) is interpreted as playing the same semantic role as the direct object of (13a).

(13)   a.   Hans put the car into the garage.
        b.   The car was put into the garage (by Hans).

The classical transformational account involved a rule which applied only to structures where the verb was followed by a complement NP, and which resulted in moving that NP into subject position. As we observed earlier, D-structure was held to be not only the representation at which subcategorisation requirements were satisfied, but also where logical function-argument structure was determined. Hence, the D-structure of (13b)—which is approximately the same as (13a)'s S-structure —dictates that it receives an interpretation in which *the car* is semantically the theme, and hence plays the same semantic role as it does in (13a).

We have already alluded to the proposal that part of the information associated with verbs in the lexicon is a subcategorisation frame, stating which complements they are permitted or required to co-occur with. Some illustrative entries are shown in (14).

(14)

	VERB	SUBCAT FRAME	EXAMPLE VERB PHRASE
a.	disappear	[_]	disappeared
b.	see	[_ NP]	saw [NP the cat]
c.	put	[_ NP PP]	put [NP the cat] [PP in the box]
d.	promise	[_ NP S]	promise [S Lee that it will rain]

Let us now reconsider the two facts which we took to be crucial to the passive construction. The first one can be restated as follows (for simplicity, we ignore the role of the optional *by*-phrase):

(15)   If an active verb α has a subcategorisation frame of the form [_NP-W] where W is a (possibly empty) string of categories, then there is a corresponding passive verb α' which has a subcategorisation frame of the form [_ W].

We assume, in addition, that a morphological operation assigns the correct inflected form to α'.

The lexical rule (15) would apply to the forms in (14) to yield (16):

(16)

	VERB	SUBCAT FRAME	EXAMPLE VERB PHRASE
a.	—	—	—
b.	seen	[_]	seen
c.	put	[_ PP]	put [PP in the box]
d.	promised	[_ S]	promised [S that it will rain]

The dashes in (16a) are intended to indicate that the rule fails to produce an output for intransitive verbs. Where a verb takes an NP complement, however, the rule predicts that it will have a passive counterpart which lacks that NP complement. Phrase structure rules then operate to generate (13b) in exactly the same way as they generate (13a).

The correct semantic interpretation of passives requires that their subject is assigned the same argument status as the object of the corresponding active. One mechanism for achieving this result is to define the meaning of a passive verb as a function f such that when g is the meaning of the active verb and a is the meaning of the subject argument, then $f(\alpha) = \exists\ [g(x, \alpha)]$. This, of course, is somewhat oversimplified, since it ignores the contribution of arguments other than subject and object; and alternative methods are possible. However, it is clear that the semantic regularity of passive constructions can be accounted for without invoking an underlying level of syntactic representation. When coupled with a lexical rule like (15), this observation undercuts the traditional motivation for a transformational account of passive. Proposals for lexical accounts of passive have a fairly long history; see, for example, Bresnan (1978, 1980, 1982), Freidin (1975), Hoekstra (1984), Hoekstra et al. (1980), Wasow (1977, 1980).

We saw earlier that constructions like *wh*-interrogatives and relative clauses have been characterised as unbounded dependencies. Constructions like passive are typologically distinct in that there is no appearance of unbounded movement, and correspondingly no pattern of island-constraints; instead, they are often classified as the result of rules which change grammatical relations (e.g. subject, object, etc.) within a clause—more succinctly, relation-changing rules. Some other such constructions in English are Dative Shift (17), Intransitivisation (18) and Middle Formation (19):

(17) a. Hans gave the book to Helen.
      b. Hans gave Helen the book.
(18) a. Hans ate the apricots.
      b. Hans ate.
(19) a. Helen sold the apples.
      b. The apples sold well.

Lexical approaches to these constructions have the advantage of accounting for the bounded character of the rules, since it is assumed that subcategorisation frames can only mention categorial information about sisters of the lexical head.

Lexical-functional Grammar

Lexical-functional grammar (LFG; Bresnan, 1982) represents one of the earliest systematic attempts to exploit a lexical characterisation of grammatical processes. Like transformational grammar, it assigns two distinct syntactic representations to each sentence. Roughly speaking, c(onstituent)-structure corresponds to transformational grammar's S-structure in that it provides an input to phonetic interpretation, while f(unctional)-structure corresponds to D-structure in determining the thematic assignments. However, there are a number of important differences. One is that c-structures are built directly by phrase structure rules, rather than being derived by transformations; moreover, c-structures contain no empty categories. Another distinction is that an f-structure is not a syntactic phrase marker, but a more abstract representation of function-argument structure in terms of grammatical relations. To briefly illustrate, the sentence *The baby was kissed by Kim* will have a c-structure like (20) and an f-structure like (21) (ignoring the contribution of the auxiliary verb):

(20) [S [NP the baby][VP was [VP kissed [PP by Kim]]]]

(21)

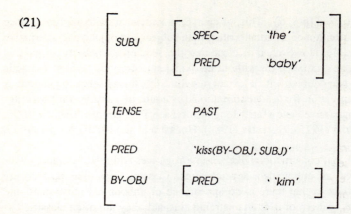

$$
\begin{bmatrix}
\text{SUBJ} & \begin{bmatrix} \text{SPEC} & \text{'the'} \\ \text{PRED} & \text{'baby'} \end{bmatrix} \\
\\
\text{TENSE} & \text{PAST} \\
\\
\text{PRED} & \text{'kiss(BY-OBJ, SUBJ)'} \\
\\
\text{BY-OBJ} & \begin{bmatrix} \text{PRED} & \text{'kim'} \end{bmatrix}
\end{bmatrix}
$$

F-structures are not themselves semantic representations, but can be converted into more or less standard logical formalisms (cf. Halvorsen, 1983; Fenstad et al., 1987). Adopting the convention that the first argument of KISS is the agent, and the second the patient, (21) expresses the claim that the value of *subj* is assigned the role of patient, while the value of BY OBJ has the role of agent.

The mapping between c-structure and f-structure is defined recursively. The basis of the recursion is given by lexical entries, and the inductive part is given by annotations on the phrase structure rules that build c- structure. We will not enter into details here. However, it will be useful to briefly look at a partial lexical entry for a transitive verb like *kiss*.

(22)   kiss: V, 'KISS((SUBJ), (OBJ))'
        kissed: V, 'KISS(\{(BY-OBJ),Ø\}, (OBJ))'

The first line of the entry specifies that the active form governs two grammatical functions, SUBJ and OBJ. Moreover, the SUBJ occupies the agent argument slot, whereas OBJ occupies the patient slot. Consequently, we gain the result that (20) makes the same thematic assignment as its active counterpart *Kim kissed the baby*; the latter's f-structure will contain a value for PRED of the form 'KISS((SUBJ), (OBJ))', and consequently the value of SUBJ, rather than BY-OBJ, will be linked to the agent argument place. The second line of the entry says that in the passive form, either the BY-OBJ is assigned agent role, or else that the thematic role of agent is omitted altogether; this is required for agentless passives such as *the baby was kissed*. The two parts of the entry are linked by a lexical rule, and the latter can be regarded as a language-particular instance of a more general, universal characterisation of passive which says, in effect, that the thematic argument position occupied by SUBJ in the active is either omitted or occupied by an OBLIQUE NP in the passive, while the position occupied by OBJ in the active is occupied by SUBJ in the passive.

LFG departs from classical transformational grammar in that the insertion of lexical items into phrase markers is not constrained by syntactic subcategorisation frames. As a result, the grammar will assign well-formed c-structures to strings like (3) and (4) above. However, they do not receive well-formed f-structures, and hence get filtered out. The reason is that f-structures are subject to two important conditions. One of these, *completeness*, requires that all the grammatical functions governed by the main predicate of an f-structure do in fact receive a value; the second, *coherence*, requires that all the governable grammatical functions in an f-structure are in fact governed by the main predicate.

Generalised Phrase Structure Grammar

Generalised phrase structure grammar (GPSG; Gazdar et al., 1985) is similar to LFG in avoiding the use of transformational rules; unlike LFG, it invokes only one level of syntactic representation. GPSG adopted the initial hypothesis that all grammatical structure is determined by context-free phrase structure rules, and tried to show that linguistically interesting generalisations can be defined over that set. The relative success of this enterprise in the early 1980s was unexpected, given the prevalent assumption that context-free phrase structure grammars were either incapable of describing certain central constructions of natural language (such as unbounded dependencies; cf. Pullum & Gazdar, 1982), or else could only do so at the cost of great redundancy and inelegance.

GPSG has employed a variety of mechanisms for succinctly defining large sets of phrase structure rules, including various kinds of schematisation, metarules (which play a role very similar to certain lexical rules in LFG), and devices for manipulating morpho-syntactic features: default rules, co-occurrence rules and distribution principles. We will briefly describe just two of these ideas, starting with the analysis of "across the board" phenomena.

In classical transformational grammar, the underlined string in (23a) is assigned the same category as that in (23b), i. e. both are S's:

(23) a. Which car did you say that *Hans put in the garage*?
      b. *Hans put the car in the garage.*

However, Gazdar (1981a, 1981b) argues that this is a mistake, and proposes to assign *Hans put in the garage* a distinct category S/NP; this is interpreted as a category which dominates the same constituents as S, except that somewhere inside they contain a gap of category NP. More generally, X/Y is the category of X constituents containing a Y gap. This information about the presence of a Y gap is initially licensed by allowing lexical heads which subcategorise for a Y to occur without such a complement, and the information then percolates up the phrase structure tree until it is discharged by the presence of a filler, also of category Y.

Gazdar observes that this leads to a natural explanation of Ross's Coordinate Structure Constraint discussed earlier. Assuming that there is a coordination schema which says that only constituents of the same category can be conjoined, the contrasts in (9) arise as follows. (9a) and (9c) are acceptable because they involve the coordination of two VPs, and two VP/NPs, respectively. But (9b) is prohibited because it involves the coordination of a VP/NP with a VP.

A second notable contribution from GPSG (made initially by Gazdar & Pullum, 1981; see also Gazdar et al., 1985) concerns the description of constituent order, and involves factoring out linear precedence relations from immediate dominance information in standard phrase structure rules. Thus, consider the set of rules in (24):

(24)   S → AdvP S
       S → S AdvP
       S → NP VP
       VP → V NP
       VP → V VP
       VP → V NP VP

These fail to express at least two generalisations: (a) V is always initial in its constituent, and (b) NPs precede VPs. We can make these generalisations explicit by replacing each context-free phrase structure rule by two more abstract kinds of rule. The first is called an immediate dominance (ID) rule, and is concerned solely with hierarchical information about mothers and daughters in a tree. To signal the distinct nature of ID rules, we use a comma to separate categories to the right of the arrow. The ID rules corresponding to (24) are listed in (25).

(24)   S → AdvP, S
       S → NP, VP
       VP → V, NP
       VP → V, VP
       VP → V, NP, VP

For example, the first rule in (24) is true of any tree in which a node labelled S immediately and exhaustively dominates nodes labelled AdvP and S; however, these daughters can be in either of the two possible orders. Thus, the same rule could equally well have been written as "S → S, AdvP." Similarly, the following rules in (24) are silent about the relative linear orderings of the categories to the right of the arrow. A second kind of rule, called a linear precedence (LP) statement, governs ordering constraints between sisters. We use "$A < B$" to mean that a node labelled B cannot appear to the left of a sister node labelled A in a tree. The ordering information contained in (23) is expressed in the linear precedence statements (25):

(25)   V < NP
       NP < VP

In combination, (24) and (25) hold true of just the set of trees admitted by (23), and are thus extensionally equivalent. However, the new format—dubbed ID/LP format—allows us to give direct expression to the two distinct sorts of constraint involved in (23), and hence represents a move towards the goal, advocated by Chomsky, of replacing individual rules by more abstract statements of linguistic generalisations. Notice, in this particular case, that we gain a more succinct characterisation of the fact that an adverbial phrase can either precede or follow the clause that it modifies; the relative economy of the notation increases dramatically when we consider rule sets for languages which have very free constituent order.

Categorial Grammar

Categorial grammar seems to have originated with the Polish logician Lésniewski, but was first brought to wider attention by Ajdukiewicz (1935). Interesting extensions were proposed by Bar-Hillel (1953, 1964), and Lambek (1958, 1961). Linguists in the 1960s displayed little interest, though Lyons (1966, 1968) gives a sympathetic overview.

The basic apparatus of categorial grammar involves syntactic categories and rules of combination. The essential ideas are (i) that categories are either basic or functors, and (ii) that syntactic combination involves functional application. Given two expressions α and β, if we can analyse α as a functor from B type expressions to A type expressions, and if we can analyse β as a B type expression, then α and β can combine to make an A type expression. The category of α is often notated as A/B. Thus, the combination rule which we have just described can be represented as follows:

(26) $A/B B \ll A$

It is now useful to introduce a corresponding rule in which the functor follows its argument:

(27) $B\ A\backslash B \gg A$

Notice that we use a backwards slanting slash to notate the new kind of functor (though many other notations have been proposed). (27) is interpreted as saying that $A\backslash B$ can combine with a B to its left to make an A.

The set of categories is defined inductively. First, we specify a set of B of basic categories, then give a recursive definition of the set B^* of all categories:

(28)   (i) B is included in B^*.
         (ii)   If A and B are in B^*, then so are A/B and A\B.

The recursion in (26) of course means that B^* is infinite, though we would expect that only a finite subset of categories in B^* will actually be used by a grammar. In fact, all that is required now for a simple grammar is to specify the set of lexical items, which gives us a pairing of basic expressions and categories. Just to illustrate a simple case, a transitive verb like *eat* will be assigned the category (S/NP)/NP, which we write as S\NP/NP, assuming that the slash is left-associative. By virtue of this category, it

LL—G

will combine first with an NP to its right, to make an S\NP, and then with an NP to its left, to make an S.

Although Bar-Hillel et al. (1960) showed that basic categorial grammar is weakly equivalent to (i.e. generates the same string set as) context-free phrase structure grammar, there are some interesting differences. Note, for example, that once a syntactic category has been assigned to an expression, we do not have to say anything further about the phrase structure rules which govern its behaviour. Categorial grammar, therefore, is one way of implementing the suggestion by Chomsky (1982) and Stowell (1981) that phrase structure information should be predictable from the subcategorisation frames of lexical items. A second feature of standard categorial grammar is that there is a tight relation between syntactic category and semantic type. In general, an expression of category A/B denotes a function f from B type objects to A type objects. The semantic value of the A constituents admitted by (24) and (25) are determined uniformly: if A/B denotes f, and B denotes b, then A denotes $f(b)$. Every syntactic rule application is accompanied by a corresponding semantic rule; the principle that such a correspondence holds is termed the rule-to-rule hypothesis by Bach (1976).

Various extensions of basic categorial grammar have been proposed. For example, Ades and Steedman (1982) and Steedman (1985, 1987) have argued that a comprehensive treatment of unbounded dependencies can be developed in categorial grammar by exploiting functional composition and type raising. One categorial version of composition takes the form (30):

(30) $A/B\ B/C \gg A/C$

Suppose, for example, that *think* has category VP/S, and that *you like* is analysed as S/NP (i.e. as in GPSG, a sentence that is still lacking an NP), then (30) allows us to analyse *think you like* as a VP/NP, where the information about the missing NP has been transmitted to the larger constituent containing the S/NP. Alternative approaches to handling unbounded dependencies within a categorial framework are proposed by Pollard (1985, 1988) and Morrill (1987). Recent work by van Benthem (1986a, 1988) develops the parallel between grammar rules and rules of logical deduction, particularly as proposed by Lambek (1958, 1961) and Geach (1972). Further linguistic applications of Lambek's calculus are explored by Moortgat (1987a, 1987b, 1988a, 1988b).

Montague's (1970) grammar fragment was an important factor in rekindling interest in categorial grammar. Rules in his grammar have the general form (31), and (32) illustrates a particular instance (i.e. essentially Montague's subject-predicate rule, S4).[2]

(31) $\langle F_i, \langle \text{CAT}_0, \text{CAT}_1, ..., \text{CAT}_{m-1} \rangle, \text{CAT}_m \rangle$, where F_i is an m-1 place structural operation.

(32) $\langle F_4, \langle S/NP, NP \rangle, S \rangle$, where $F_4(\alpha, \beta) = \alpha \cap \beta'$ and β' is the result of replacing the first verb in β by its third person singular present.

The first m-1 categories in (31) represent the input to the rule, and CAT_m is the result category. The format is useful for developing a taxonomy of categorial rules. Thus, basic categorial grammar imposes the following constraints on the structural operations F_i and CAT_0, CAT_1, ..., CAT_{m-1}, CAT_m:

(33) $<F_0, <A/B, B>, A>$, where $F_0(\alpha,\beta) = \alpha \cap \beta$
    $<F_1, <A\backslash B, B>, A>$, where $F_1(\alpha,\beta) = \beta \cap \alpha$

Systems which include metarules or combinators allow a looser relation between input and output categories; for example, composition allows the sequence $<<A/B, B/C>$, $A/C>$

Another option is to enrich the theory of categories. Zeevat et al. (1987) and Zeevat (1988) introduce unification over category variables in the object language which leads to polymorphic categories. It is also possible to assign an internal feature structure to categories, as suggested by Bach (1980, 1981).

A third possibility is to allow more powerful structural operations than just concatenation. For example, following Bach (1980) and Pollard (1984), we could define an operation $WRAP(\alpha, \beta)$ to be the result of inserting β after the head of α. Another option, proposed for Latin free word order by Dowty (1982a), is to to use set union in place of string concatenation.

A variety of studies have been carried out within the general framework of Montague grammar; notable contributions are made by Bach (1979, 1980, 1981, 1983), Dowty (1978, 1979, 1982a, 1982b), Flynn (1983), Janssen (1983), Partee (1975, 1979), and Thomason (1976a, 1976b).

Unification-based Grammar Formalisms

A number of recently developed grammatical formalisms—some of which have been alluded to above—exhibit a striking convergence in their use of unification as a basic operation on complex feature structures. The list includes functional unification grammar (Kay, 1979, 1985), generalised phrase structure grammar, head-driven phrase structure grammar (Pollard, 1985; Pollard & Sag, 1987), lexical-functional grammar, and the fragments written within the PATR-II framework (Pereira & Shieber, 1984, Shieber et al., 1983, Shieber, 1985, 1986). Closely related work by Cooper (1985) construes unification as an operation over the situation-theoretic objects which act as the interpretation of expressions on his approach.

Generalised phrase structure grammar (GPSG) might be regarded as belonging to a "first generation" of non-transformational grammars, and was one of the first linguistic theories to show that an appropriately specified context-free phrase structure grammar could achieve broad descriptive coverage in an elegant and perspicuous manner. Lexical-functional grammar also belongs to this first generation. There are two respects in which it differs strikingly from GPSG: it locates more information in the lexicon, and as we have seen it uses an extra level of syntactic representation, f-structure, as a filter on the structures derived by the phrase structure component of the grammar.

Head-driven phrase structure grammar and PATR-II fragments belong to the second generation of phrase structure formalisms. While sharing many of the useful design characteristics of GPSG, they exploit the resources of unification on feature complexes more fully, and, like LFG, embody a richer theory of lexical information. They also make use of important insights from categorial grammar, particularly with regard to verb subcategorisation.

A feature structure is a set of labels (or attributes) and values, where each label is associated with exactly one value. Thus, it has the following form:

(34)

$$\begin{bmatrix} Label_1: & Value_1 \\ Label_2: & Value_2 \\ ... & ... \\ Label_n: & Value_n \end{bmatrix}$$

A value consists of either an atom or another feature structure. Suppose, for example, that we have as labels *cat, number, person* and *agreement*. The first three of these labels take atomic values, and we can represent the appropriate set by means of a little grammar (cf. Gazdar & Pullum, 1982; Fenstad et al., 1987):

(35)   *cat* := {NP, VP}
     number := {*sing, plur*}
     person := {*first, second, third*}

As we mentioned before, not all values are atomic, however. Thus the label *agreement* takes as value a feature structure whose labels are *number* and *person*. We represent this by the following statement:

(36) *agreement* := [*number person*]

Finally, we might suppose that any root structure has the top-level labels *cat* and *agreement*. (37) illustrates the kind of structures admitted, using both matrix notation and an equivalent graph diagram:

(37) a.

$$\begin{bmatrix} cat: & NP \\ agreement: & \begin{bmatrix} number: & singular \\ person: & third \end{bmatrix} \end{bmatrix}$$

(37). b.

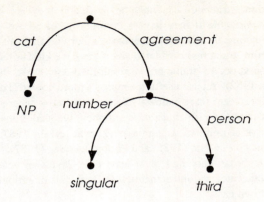

As the reader will presumably have gathered, this feature structure can be interpreted as the category of a third person singular nominal constituent.

We also allow feature structures to be incomplete, in the sense that any label–value pair can be omitted from a structure. For example, all of the following are possible structures:

(38) a.

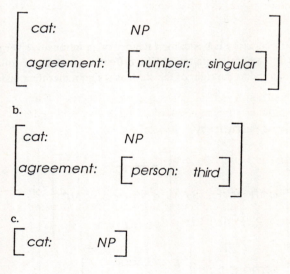

b.

c.

We turn now to unification. Given structures like the above, unification is essentially set-theoretic union. So, for example, the unification of (38a) and (38b) is (39). Similarly, the unification of (38b) and (38c) is (38b). Nevertheless, there is an additional condition: structures can only be unified if they are compatible. Two structures are *incompatible* if they have a common label whose values are either distinct atoms or incompatible feature structures; otherwise they are compatible.

So far, the feature structures considered are of the same kind as those employed by generalised phrase structure grammar; in graph-theoretic terms, they are trees (cf. Gazdar & Pullum, 1982). Yet it is useful to employ a more powerful device, according to which two labels can share values—feature structures where this occurs are sometimes called *reentrant*. To illustrate reentrancy, we shall consider an example drawn from categorial unification grammar (Zeevat, et al., 1987; Zeevat, 1988). Following proposals by Pollard (1985) and Pollard and Sag (1987), we take the basic grammar object to be an encoding of at least three levels of description, namely phonology, syntactic category, and semantics. Pollard calls this triple a sign, and (39) illustrates a simplified case.

(39)

$$
\begin{bmatrix}
phonology: & john \\
category: & NP \\
semantics: & j
\end{bmatrix}
$$

Notice that (39)'s category is basic; the category of an intransitive verb will be of the form S/NP, as in categorial grammar. The difference is that we follow Pollard in analysing the material to the right of the slash as a sign rather than just a category.

(40)

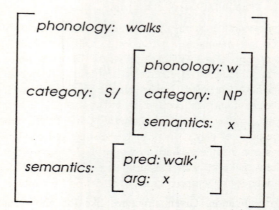

For present purposes, the important thing to note is that the label *semantics* to the right of the slash shares a (variable) value x with *semantic's arg*. The effect of this is to ensure that whenever we gain more information under unification about the value of one label, it will automatically lead to the same specification of the other label's value. Returning to graph theory for a moment, we require two arcs to be able to point to the same value, which means that the appropriate counterpart to (40) is not a tree, but a directed acyclic graph.

To see the effects of variable structure sharing, consider what happens when we carry out functional application of (40) to (39). First, we unify the sign to the right of the slash in (40). One consequence is that the variable x becomes specified as the constant j. Because of the reentrancy just observed, the effect of the unification is to also specify *semantic's arg's* value as j. We then discharge the sign to the right of the slash, just as in categorial grammar, and concatenate the argument's phonology with the functor's phonology. This leads to the following result sign:

(40')

$$\begin{bmatrix} phonology: & john\ walks \\ category: & S \\ semantics: & \begin{bmatrix} pred: walk' \\ arg: \quad j \end{bmatrix} \end{bmatrix}$$

SYNTAX AND SEMANTICS

An important area of research concerns the inter-relationship between different levels of linguistic analysis, for example, between syntax and (morpho)phonology, and between syntax and semantics, and it will be useful to devote a few words to this issue.

It is often easier, and frequently productive, to study natural language semantics in isolation from natural language syntax. Nevertheless, both linguists and logicians have devoted considerable attention—frequently in collaboration—to the way in which the meanings of linguistics expressions are hooked up to their syntactic structure.

From an intuitive point of view, it is plausible to suppose that individual lexical items have meanings, and that the meaning of phrases is determined by the meanings of the words and the way that they are put together. In fact, something very like this is known as the principle of compositionality (or Frege's principle): namely, the meaning of a complex expression is a function of the meaning of its parts. As Janssen (1986) observes, the principle is explicitly or implicitly adopted in a wide range of fields, including not only natural language semantics but also much philosophical literature, formal logic, and the semantics of programming languages. While it can be defended on purely technical grounds, compositionality is also highly attractive from a cognitive point of view, as it helps us to account for how humans can understand an infinity of linguistic expressions given only finite resources.

A strong form of compositionality is prominent in Montague's work on formalising grammar fragments for natural language: "a central working premise of Montague's theory ... is that the syntactic rules that determine how a sentence is built up out of smaller syntactic parts should correspond one-to-one with the semantic rules that tell how the meaning of a sentence is a function of the meanings of its parts" (Partee, 1975: 203). This systematic pairing of syntactic and semantic rules has been dubbed the rule-to-rule hypothesis (cf. Bach, 1976), and is adopted in a variety of grammatical frameworks, including GPSG (cf. also Klein & Sag 1985) and most versions of categorial grammar. It might be noted that a number of the unification-based formalisms, such as HPSG and UCG, also embody a version of the hypothesis, though differing from conventional categorial grammar in that the semantic structure is built up in parallel with the syntactic and phonological description. By contrast, work within the LFG framework has typically adopted a somewhat looser coupling of syntax and semantics, due to fact that the mapping from c-structure to semantic representation is mediated by a level of f-structure. A variety of approaches have been proposed; for example, see Fenstad et al. (1985), Frey (1985), Halvorsen (1983), Kaplan (1987), and Reyle (1988).

The exact status of compositionality has been energetically debated within recent years, and there is some question as to whether it is an empirical hypothesis, or a methodological programme; Partee (1984) gives a lucid overview of the issues. Particular attention has been paid to the way in which contextual factors, notably those concerned with anaphora and quantification, influence semantic interpretation; for some discussion, see also Barwise (1987), Cooper (1983), Groenendijk and Stokhof (1987), Heim (1982), Johnson and Klein (1986), Kamp (1981), Rooth (1987), and Zeevat (1988).

A closely related question is whether semantic representation should be regarded as a convenient but dispensable stage in the mapping from syntactic expressions to semantic objects (in the model-theoretic sense) or whether it constitutes an essential level of grammatical description, corresponding to a postulated level of mental representation. One of the main sources of evidence adduced for the latter view turns out to involve some of the same phenomena as are involved in the compositionality debate, namely anaphora and quantifier binding.

THE INTERPRETATION OF GRAMMAR FORMALISMS

Grammars effect a pairing between sounds and meanings. Modern linguistic theories all seem to essentially agree with Chomsky's (1965) contention that to do this, a generative grammar must assign structural descriptions to linguistic expressions. The theories that we have briefly reviewed have differed on the question of what constitutes an appropriate syntactic structural description (SD). In transformational grammar, it will be at least a pair of S-structure and D-structure; in lexical-functional grammar, a c-structure and an f-structure; in generalised phrase structure grammar, and certain categorial grammars, a single constituent structure tree; in Montague grammar, a derivation tree; in most unification grammars, a single complex feature structure with reentrancy. Thus, a theory of grammar determines a space of possible SDs, and the grammar of a particular language *L* characterises a subset of these as well-formed SDs of *L*.

Suppose we fix on a particular grammatical framework, and select some formalism or group of formalisms from the framework; and suppose in addition that we ask what the formalism "means". It seems reasonable to expect the answer to be couched in terms of the possible SDs determined by the grammar. Put slightly differently, every grammar formalism has both a syntax and a semantics, and the semantics is defined relative to the space of possible SDs. (Notice that we are not concerned here with the semantic interpretation of sentences which are analysed in the given formalism.) To take a trivial example, the rule in (41) has a familiar syntax, though we could equally have used the notation in (42):

(41) S $\rightarrow$ NP VP
(42) <S, NP VP >

Of course, the difference *is* merely notational, because we know that both rules have the same, well-defined interpretation: relative to a domain of constituent structure trees, they are true of a tree *t* at node *n* if *n* is labelled "S" and immediately dominates two nodes n_1 and n_2 such that node n_1 is labelled "NP" and node n_2 is labelled "VP".

The importance of providing grammar formalisms with a clear semantics was first brought into prominence by Pereira and Shieber (1984), where there is an extensive discussion of the interpretation of the equational language employed in PATR-II. Note, in particular, that it is difficult to make provable claims about the correctness of a proposed rule unless there is some independent characterisation of the objects which the rule is intended to be about. More recent work on the semantics of complex feature structures can be found in Johnson (1987), Kasper (1987a, 1987b), Kasper and Rounds (1986) Moshier and Rounds (1987), Rounds and Kasper (1986) and Smolka (1988), and the semantics of generalised phrase structure grammar is discussed in Shieber (1986, 1988) and Gazdar (1987).

By contrast, to date there seems to have been little corresponding attention paid to the interpretation of Government-Binding (GB) formalisms, a fact which has contributed to doubt whether the theory is adequately specified to be useful for formal investigations; cf. the complaint by Barton et al. (1987: x) that "we lack a complete, faithful formalisation of GB theory, and it is unclear what our complexity analysis would tell us if we had one". However, there is a growing interest in providing computational implementations for GB grammars, as illustrated by Berwick (1986), Correa (1988), Johnson (1988) and Stabler (1987), and it is to be hoped that more precise mathematical definitions will result.

MORPHOLOGY AND THE LEXICON

The internal structure of words, and the organisation of words in the lexicon, has become a topic of steadily increasing interest over the last decade, and we do not have space to do it justice here. Anderson (1988) provides an update of the main issues, and a useful overview can also be found in Scalise (1984).

We have already briefly looked at a lexical characterisation of passive, but we did not make precise the status of the lexical rule in question. Various options have been discussed in the literature. According to one view, we assume that what is involved is a redundancy rule which relates two lexical entries that are already listed; see, for example, Chomsky (1965) and Jackendoff (1975). In favour of this approach, we note that lexical processes tend to be only partially productive. A second view is that lexical processes are formulated as rules which generate new lexical entries; in this case, some system of diacritics are often employed to block overgeneration. A related issue which has received discussion is the extent to which the semantic interpretation of complex words is compositionally predictable from their parts, and it has been argued that idiosyncratic meanings result when a form is not derived by a productive rule but is simply listed (cf. Aronoff, 1976; Dowty, 1979).

Selkirk (1982), Lieber (1980), Williams (1981) and others have suggested that word-internal structure is determined by principles similar to those involved in phrase structure; that is, there are word-level context-free rules, subcategorisation frames associated with affixes, and feature percolation principles. (43) is an illustrative example taken from Selkirk (1984: 78), showing the structure of *nonpreparatory*:

(43)

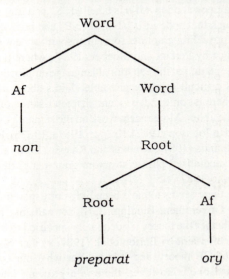

Somewhat problematic for this simple idea of word structure is the phenomenon of nonconcatenative morphology, typified by the verbal morphology of classical Arabic (McCarthy, 1981); the basic forms in a verb paradigm are consonantal roots, and inflections consist of interspersing different vowel patterns among the consonants.

Kiparsky (1982a, 1982b) and others have explored the idea that a certain class of phonological rules apply cyclically to the structure built by word-formation rules: the output of each morphological rule is processed by the set of phonological rules defined over that domain. Also of concern is the manner in which the semantic and relation-changing aspects of morphology are linked to the structural analysis. Baker (1985), for example, has argued that morphological structure mirrors the scope of the semantic/grammatical operations involved. Nevertheless, there are some well-known problems here, termed "bracketing paradoxes" (cf. Moortgat, 1988; Pesetsky, 1985; Sproat, 1984; Williams, 1981).

There has been continued debate about the extent to which morphological processes are isolated from syntax. Many researchers, partly under the impact of Chomsky (1970), have adopted the view that all morphology takes place in the lexicon (cf. di Sciullo & Williams, 1987; Jensen & Stong-Jensen, 1984; Lapointe, 1979, 1983; Lieber, 1980; Kiparsky, 1982a; Williams, 1981). However, it has also been proposed in the transformational literature that morphology can be fed to a certain extent by syntactic rules; see, for example, Anderson (1982), Baker (1987), and Fabb (1984).

The lexicon is, from a computational point of view, a large knowledge base, and it is not surprising that techniques from knowledge representation have begun to be applied. The notion of an inheritance hierarchy (e.g. Bobrow & Webber, 1980) appears to be particularly applicable, as we want transitive verbs to inherit the properties of verbs, and verbs to inherit the properties of words in general; interesting research along these lines has been carried out by Flickinger et al. (1985), Karttunen (1986b), Pollard and Sag (1987), and de Smedt (1984).

The investigation of most aspects of morphology and phonology from a computational perspective is less advanced than comparable work in syntax. An often-cited approach is that proposed by Koskenniemi (1983, 1984), in which rules mapping from lexical representations into surface phonological representations are formalised as finite state transducers. For an excellent summary and literature survey, see Gazdar (1985).

GRAMMAR AND COMPUTATION

Knowledge and Use

When viewed from the perspective of cognitive science, the question of how "knowledge of language" interacts with "use of language" naturally assumes a role of paramount importance. It is plausible to assume that the way in which information is organised in a competence model will crucially affect the organisation of a corresponding model of performance. On grounds of simplicity and economy, we might hypothesise that the mental processes involved in both parsing and production access a common store of linguistic knowledge (Kaplan & Bresnan, 1982: xix; though see Kay, 1985, for a dissenting view). The condition that there be a direct relationship between the rules and structures postulated by a formal grammar and those which are manipulated by a processing mechanism is called "the strong competence hypothesis" by Kaplan and Bresnan, and "type transparency" by Berwick and Weinberg (1984: 39). As the latter note, such a condition appears to provide a foundation for the hope that experimental psychological investigation will bear rather directly on the adequacy of linguistic theorising. It also bears on the extent to which computer implementations of grammars (for example, in natural language parsers or generators) can be viewed as potential models of human linguistic abilities.

Of the grammar frameworks surveyed earlier, Government-Binding has been least successful in inspiring processing models which achieve type transparency. This is illustrated by Berwick and Weinberg's (1984) discussion of the treatment of passive constructions in the Marcus (1980) parser. In Government-Binding theory, there is no rule which corresponds directly to the passive construction; rather, it results from the interaction of Move-α with a variety of principles: the Case filter, the θ-Criterion, and the Projection Principle (Chomsky, 1981). The Marcus parser produces the same surface structure as this analysis, but does not do so by invoking the relevant principles. Instead, it "precomputes" the effect of the principles into what is almost a lexicalist account of passive: after identifying a passive verb cluster, the parser postulates a trace immediately after the passive verb form, linking it to the subject NP that was encountered earlier in the parse. Given the considerable distance between the grammar formalism and the processing model, Berwick and Weinberg's (1984: 77) claim that "this system is still a 'realisation' of a transformational system" is less than convincing.

In defence of their general position, Berwick and Weinberg argue that our current lack of knowledge of the human processing mechanism makes it very hard to extrapolate from psycholinguistic results to claims about the kinds of algorithms and data structures involved. In particular, it is very difficult to determine whether current computational implementations of parsing models can be taken as supplying indirect evidence. Thus, although the Marcus parsing model runs counter to standard results on human sentence processing in taking longer to analyse passives than actives, it can achieve equal time if the architecture is modified so as to allow some parallel computation. However, it is not clear what significance to assign to the latter point, since the extra space resources required by the parallel algorithm might also be a processing load which should show up in reaction time probes.

It might also be disputed whether in fact there are no useful lessons to be drawn from psycholinguistic research in human language processing. On the contrary, there seems to be substantial support for the centrality of *incremental interpretation,* i.e. the piecemeal assembly of a meaning representation for an utterance during a left-to-right single-pass syntactic analysis. Introspective evidence that human beings carry out incremental interpretation derives from the ease with which we can make sense of sentence fragments, provided they occur in context. There is also growing experimental evidence that the mechanism by which people overcome the obstacle of proliferating local ambiguities while processing sentences is by comparing alternative interpretations of what they have encountered so far, even though these interpretations are necessarily incomplete. The impression that we "hear" what is said as it reaches us is apparently based on the very rapid use of context: Marslen-Wilson (1973) has found that subjects who are "shadowing" speech—repeating what they hear as fast as possible—will make semantically based "corrections" to items which would otherwise destroy the sense of the text, even when their speech is only about a syllable behind what they are hearing.

More generally, a reasonable range of results concerning the relationship between grammar formalisms, parsing models and computational complexity has been established; Perrault (1984) surveys the main mathematical results, and Briscoe (1988) provides an overview of the relation between human sentence processing and grammar formalisms.

Recently, Berwick (1986) has raised a number of interesting questions about "principle-based parsing". Although a large part of the discussion is oriented towards the problems of finding satisfactory parsing architectures for Government-Binding grammars, the issues are more general, as Berwick points out. For example, while it would be possible in theory to compile a GPSG into a set of context-free phrase structure rules, in practice the size of this set would be so vast as to be totally unmanageable. As a result, there has been ongoing debate about the extent to which it is desirable or possible to parse directly in terms of the more abstract constructs provided by the grammar. As a first example, one has a choice of applying metarules "on the fly" during parse time, or else precompiling them into phrase structure rules (see Thompson, 1982, for an argument in favour of the second strategy). As a second example, rules in ID/LP format can be converted into phrase structure rules, or the linear precedence statements can used as a constraint on possible analyses constructed on the basis of immediate dominance rules. The latter task turns out to be more subtle than might have been expected; for discussion, see Shieber (1983), Barton (1985a, 1985b), and Evans (1986).

Even if we decide to pose the issue as a question about the adequacy of theoretical frameworks for practical applications, the point can be inverted in an interesting way. For as generative grammars become increasingly sophisticated and highly developed, it becomes correspondingly difficult for theoreticians to assess the consequences of their proposals without the help of some computational tools. Some linguists seem to hold the view that there is no need to formalise linguistic proposals in a rigorous way, because their empirical inadequacy can often be determined by informal inspection. While this may be true, it still remains to be demonstrated that a given grammar fragment is empirically adequate for a particular set of data, and it is patently clear in many cases that hand computations fail to yield reliable results. (For a simple but revealing example of this, consider Janssen's (1980) discovery of an incorrect rule formulation in Montague's PTQ fragment, which still counts as one of the most precisely formalised grammars.) In fact, there is a growing body of implemented morphological analysers, parsers and generators which offer valuable grammar testing tools for the theoretician; see, for example, Briscoe et al. (1987), Byrd et al. (1987), Calder et al. (1988), Dalrymple et al. (1987), Evans (1985), Karttunen (1986a), Phillips and Thompson (1985), Ritchie et al. (1987), Russell et al. (1986), and Shieber (1985). However, the best tools in the world are of little use if the theory to be tested is not clearly formulated.

Extensibility and Modularity

Although theoretical concerns are often foremost in determining the domain of "relevant data" in linguistics (as in other disciplines), there is also a strong impetus towards completeness of descriptive coverage, especially when practical applications are involved. One difficulty which has repeatedly cropped up in computational contexts is that large grammars can be very difficult to build, maintain and extend. Take a situation in which the linguist wishes to modify an existing grammar so that it will adequately cover some new construction. The modification may involve adding a new rule, or perhaps changing an existing rule. Does the linguist have any practical method for assessing the effects that this modification will have on the existing coverage? It is a similar problem to that which arises where large unstructured computer programs need to be modified; typically, new additions propagate back into the grammar, entering into complex interactions with existing rules in ways which are extremely hard to foresee or control.

It should be emphasised that we are not doubting that large, extensive grammar fragments can be built using existing techniques. It is always possible to make *ad hoc* extensions and stipulations so as to increase descriptive coverage. What is lacking, however, is any method of building large grammars in a principled, modular fashion. Note that we are not looking for a list of the 20 most important syntactic constructions, ranked according to their statistical frequency in representative texts, which would have to be incorporated into the grammar of any "reasonably adequate" parser for English. It is rather more a question of the logical dependencies that hold within a grammar, of the kind exhibited when we speak of canonical and non-canonical constructions in a language.

An important step towards modularity would be achieved if we had adequate mechanisms for expressing high-level linguistic constraints, and Government - Binding's emphasis on cross-linguistic parametric variation has provided a useful impetus for research in this area. The level of expressive power required for this task seems to be significantly higher than that of the formalisms typically used in unification or categorial frameworks, as we wish to express global constraints which are true of the entire grammar of a language (or family of languages, or even all languages). Because the ability to state global constraints on grammars is inherently a highly modular approach to grammar development, as is the notion of parameterised grammars, research in this area should provide valuable insights on overcoming the problems which have arisen in the past for other ambitious grammar development projects.

Parsing and Parallelism

Research into natural language parsing can be pursued with the aim of developing efficient general parsing algorithms, or else of developing specialised parsers which are optimised for particular grammar formalisms. Both aims are worthy of support. Given the difficulty of constructing models of human sentence processing and the diversity of different theories of grammar, the first goal is clearly a sensible one if we want computational linguistics to have any practical application. The second area of research offers the tempting reward that we might be able to explain properties of both grammar and parser in terms of their mutual interdependence.

The rapidly increasing importance of parallel computational architectures suggests a number of useful research areas. As an initial step, it is useful to distinguish two kinds of parallelism in natural language analysis, namely "or" parallelism and "and" parallelism. The first arises where ambiguous structures are pursued simultaneously, giving rise to a disjunction of possible analyses; Crain and Steedman (1985) have argued that current psycholinguistic evidence provides support for this kind of architecture, although there are a variety of positions represented in the literature (see Briscoe, 1988, for a review). The possibility of "and" parallelism arises when the parser is computing distinct levels of description simultaneously; for example, building up a semantic analysis in tandem with a syntactic analysis. This approach seems particularly attractive for grammatical theories which adopt some version of the "rule-to-rule" hypothesis, and is closely related to theorising about the desirability of constructing an incremental semantic analysis (Haddock, 1987; Mellish, 1983, 1985; Pulman, 1985, 1987; Pareschi & Steedman, 1986).

Suppose we formulated a particular grammar as a set of axioms in a declarative logic programming language like Prolog. The semantics of the set of clauses will be provided relative to the domain of possible structural descriptions. Prolog also provides a deduction mechanism, and parsing an input string can be as viewed deducing the type of the string from the types of the lexical constituent together with the axioms (cf. Pereira & Warren, 1983). The interest of this observation is that we are not forced to use the particular (top-down, depth-first) deduction mechanism provided by Prolog, and hence the choice of a declarative language allows us to abstract away, to a certain extent, from serial computing architecture. One option, for example, would be to use a parallel deduction procedure. A rather different approach, inspired by the framework of parallel distributed programming, is proposed by Pollack and Waltz (1985). For a general review of the relation between parallelism and parsing, see Schnelle (Chapter 6).

Multi-dimensional Representations

Despite the trend of the previous sections, it should be re-emphasised that linguistic investigations do not have to be explicitly oriented towards processing or learnability considerations in order to bear on the central issues of cognitive science. As Marr (1977) has pointed out, an essential part of the solution to any information processing problem is to specify what is being computed, as well as how the computation is algorithmically implemented. Thus, even rather abstract work in grammatical theory will contribute to cognitive science to the extent that it succeeds in providing a precise account of linguistic structures and regularities. This echoes the view expressed by Gazdar et al. (1985:5) that perhaps the theoreticians' most important contribution to psycholinguistics at the present time would be "to fulfil some of the commitments made by generative grammar in respect of the provision of fully specified and precise theories of the nature of the languages that humans employ".

At a number of points throughout this chapter, we have had occasion to refer to the multi-level organisation of generative grammars, and we focussed briefly on the syntax–semantics interface. Equally interesting problems arise when one considers the syntax–phonology interface, though there has been less work of a formally precise nature in this field. At the current point in history, differing philosophies of the architecture of grammars seem to constitute a major gulf between Chomskyan and Montagovian frameworks. The contrast is ably summarised by Partee (1984: 285):

> Chomsky's skepticism towards the compositionality principle, expressed in Chomsky (1975) and elsewhere, seems to stem from two convictions: the "autonomy of syntax" thesis and the idea that the organisation of grammar is best viewed as involving a number of relatively independent subsystems, each with its own principles and constraints, which interact to jointly constrain the final output—a view of grammar very different from Montague's, which when extended to phonology as in Bach and Wheeler (1981) presents a grammar as a simultaneous recursive definition of well-formed, phonologically and semantically interpreted, expressions of the language—starting from the smallest units and building up larger ones with phonological, syntactic and semantic rules working hand in hand to construct and interpret complex expressions compositionally from their parts.

It is perhaps debatable whether a principle-based architecture is necessarily incompatible with a Montagovian framework; for example, the ID/LP rule format proposed in GPSG depends on the interaction of two distinct kinds of constraint, yet fits reasonably well within Montague's view of grammar. However, it seems useful to pose the further question as to whether a generalisation of compositionality along the lines suggested by Partee—according to which the grammatical properties (semantic, syntactic, phonological) of a complex expression are a function of the grammatical properties of its parts—can be sustained in a comprehensive way. Oehrle (1988) presents a detailed algebraic framework for accommodating this multi-level architecture, and the project of "Montague phonology" (cf. also Wheeler, 1981, 1988) also seems particularly relevant. Progress in this area may well have implications for facilitating the integration of speech research with linguistic theory.

FUTURE PROSPECTS

One of the most interesting lessons of linguistic research in the current decade is the extent to which key advances in the theoretical and computational fields have complemented and reinforced each other, giving rise to fruitful results in two related areas:

1. The grammar as logic/parsing as deduction paradigm, initiated by Pereira and Warren (1983).
2. The family of unification-based attribute-value grammar formalisms.

One area where we should expect to see a concentration of effort in the next few years is the development of more appropriate deduction techniques for the manipulation of linguistic representations, with influences coming from a variety of sources, including automatic theorem proving, logic programming (cf. Pareschi, 1988), and the sequent calculi of Gentzen and Lambek (cf. van Benthem, 1988).

As we mentioned earlier, generative grammar has achieved much of its success by ignoring functional considerations, but the price has been heavy. For example, there is very little formally precise work on the relation between intonation and pragmatics. Moreover, the prevailing model is one where syntactic well-formedness is taken as central, and other levels of representation are only related via the intermediary of syntactic structure. Yet, given the multidimensional architecture offered by recent unification frameworks, it ought to be possible to state a direct relation between, say, pitch accent and the given-new contrast, rather than mapping via syntax. In this connection, an appealing prospect is the "rehabilitation" and reconstruction of a range of insights from non-generative grammar, particularly the work of Halliday. Largely under the inspiration of Kay's (1979) work on functional unification grammar, a number of authors, including Kasper (1987), Matthiessen and Kasper (1987b), and Mellish (1988), have attempted to incorporate aspects of systemic grammar into feature-based unification frameworks. We look forward to seeing how far the interlocking array of representations which are encompassed by functional unification grammars will allow us to give a formal declarative account of a much wider range of linguistic regularities, particularly those involving aspects of discourse which are crucial to the development of adequate computational models of natural language communication.

ACKNOWLEDGEMENTS

I would like to thank the following people for their helpful comments on this chapter: Johan van Benthem, Neils Ole Bernsen, Ted Briscoe, Robin Cooper, Elisabet Engdahl, Gerald Gazdar, Antonio Sanfilippo, Helmut Schnelle, and Mary Tait. This chapter would doubtless have been much better if I had followed their advice more conscientiously. I am also grateful to Jo Calder, Fernando Pereira, Mike Reape and Henk Zeevat for a number of ideas which have influenced my views on this topic.

NOTES

1. Following Ladusaw (1985), we apply the term *strata* to multiple representations of structure which utilise the same descriptive vocabulary. Thus transformational grammar is a multistratal theory.

2. We use ∩ to indicate string concatenation.

REFERENCES

Ades, A. & Steedman, M. J. (1982). On the order of words. *Linguistics and Philosophy, 4*, 517-558.

Ajdukiewicz, K. (1935). Die syntaktische Konnexitat. *Studia Philosophica, 1*, 1-27. English translation in: *Polish Logic: 1920-1939*, ed. by Storrs McCall, pp.207-231, Oxford University Press, Oxford.

Anderson, S. R. (1982). Where's morphology? *Linguistic Inquiry, 13*, 571-612.

Anderson, S. R. (1988). Morphological theory. In F.J. Newmeyer (Ed.), *Linguistics: The Cambridge Survey*, Vol. 1: *Linguistic Theory: Foundations*, pp.146-191. Cambridge: Cambridge University Press.

Aronoff, M. (1976). *Word Formation in Generative Grammar*. Cambridge, Mass.: MIT Press.

Bach, E. (1976). An extension of classical transformational grammar. *Problems in Linguistic Metatheory*. Proceedings of the 1976 Conference at Michigan State University pp. 183-224.

Bach, E. (1979). Control in Montague grammar. *Linguistic Inquiry, 10*, 515-531.

Bach, E. (1980). In defense of passive. *Linguistics and Philosophy, 3*, 297-341.

Bach, E. (1981). Discontinuous constituents in generalised categorial grammars. In V.A. Burke and J. Pustejovsky (Eds.), *Proceedings of the 11th Annual Meeting of the North Eastern Linguistic Society*, 1981, pp.1-12.

Bach, E. (1983). On the relationship between word-grammar and phrase-grammar. *Natural Language and Linguistic Theory, 1*, 65-89.

Baker, M. (1985). The mirror principle and morphosyntactic explanation. *Linguistic Inquiry, 16*, 373-415.

Baker, M. C. (1987). *Incorporation: A Theory of Grammatical Function Changing*. Chicago, Illinois: University of Chicago Press.

Bar-Hillel, Y. (1953). A quasi-arithmetical notation for syntactic description. *Language, 29*, 47-58.

Bar-Hillel, Y. (1964). Some linguistic obstacles to machine translation. Chapter 6 in *Language and information*. Reading, Mass.: Addison-Wesley.

Bar-Hillel, Y., Gaifman, C. & Shamir, E. (1960). On categorial and phrase structure grammars. In *Language and Information*. Also appeared in The Bulletin of the Research Council of Israel, 9F.1.16.

Barton, G. E. (1985a). The computational difficulty of ID/LP parsing. In *Proceedings of the 23rd Annual Meeting of the Association for Computational Linguistics*, University of Chicago, Chicago, Illinois, July 1985, pp.76-81. @REFS. = Barton, G. E. (1985b). On the complexity of ID/LP parsing. *Computational Linguistics, 11*, 205-218.

Barton, G. E., Berwick, R. C., and Ristad, E. S. (1987) *Computational complexity and natural language*. Cambridge, Mass.: MIT Press.

Barwise, J. (1987). Noun phrases, generalized quantifiers and anaphora. In P. Gärdenfors (ed.), *Generalized Quantifiers: Linguistic and Logical Approaches*, pp.1-29. Dordrecht: D. Reidel.

van Benthem, J. (1986a). Categorial grammar. In *Essays in Logical Semantics*. Dordrecht: D. Reidel.

van Benthem, J. (1986b). Categorial grammar and lambda calculus. Research Report No. 86-03, Mathematics, University of Amsterdam, October.

van Benthem, J. (1988). The Lambek calculus. In R.T. Oehrle, E. Bach, & D. Wheeler (eds), *Categorial Grammars and Natural Language Structures*, pp.35-68. Dordrecht: D. Reidel.

Berwick, R. C. (1986). Principle-based parsing. Unpublished paper, Department of Philosophy and Linguistics, MIT, Cambridge, Mass.

Berwick, R. C. & Weinberg, A. (1984). *The Grammatical Basis of Linguistic Performance: Language Use and Acquisition.* Cambridge, Mass.: MIT Press.

Bobrow, R. J. & Webber, B. L. (1980). Knowledge representation for syntactic/semantic processing. In *Proceedings of the First Annual National Conference on Artificial Intelligence*, Stanford, Ca., 19-21, August.

Bresnan, J. (1978). A realistic transformational grammar. In M. Halle, J. Bresnan, & G.A. Miller (eds.) *Linguistic Theory and Psychological Reality*, pp.1-59. Cambridge, Mass.: MIT Press.

Bresnan, J. (1980). Polyadicity: Part 1 of The theory of lexical rules and representation. In T. Hoekstra, H. van der Hulst, & M. Moortgat (eds), *Lexical Grammar*. Dordrecht: Foris Publications.

Bresnan, J. (ed.) (1982). *The Mental Representation of Grammatical Relations.* Cambridge, Mass.: MIT Press.

Briscoe, E. (1988). *Modelling Human Speech Comprehension: A Computational Approach.* Chichester: Ellis Horwood.

Briscoe, E., Grover, C., Boguraev, B. & Carroll, J. (1987). A formalism and environment for the development of a large grammar of English. In *Proceedings of the Tenth International Joint Conference on Artificial Intelligence*, Milan, Italy, 23-28, August, pp.703-708.

Byrd, R. J., Calzolari, N., Chodorow, M. S., Klavans, J. L., Neff, M. S. & Rizk, O. A. (1987). Tools and methods for computational linguistics. *Computational Linguistics, 13,* 219-240.

Calder, J., Klein, E., & Zeevat, H. (1988). Unification categorial grammar: A concise, extendable grammar for natural language processing. In *Proceedings of the 12th International Conference on Computational Linguistics and the 24th Annual Meeting of the Association for Computational Linguistics*, Budapest, August.

Chomsky, N. (1965). *Aspects of the Theory of Syntax.* Cambridge, Mass.: MIT Press.

Chomsky, N. (1970). Remarks on nominalization. In R. Jacobs, & P. Rosenbaum (eds.), *Readings in English Transformational Grammar*, pp184-221. Waltham, Mass.: Ginn and Co..

Chomsky, N. (1981). *Lectures on Government and Binding.* Dordrecht: Foris Publications.

Chomsky, N. (1982). *Some Concepts and Consequences of the Theory of Government and Binding.* Cambridge, Mass.: MIT Press.

Chomsky, N. (1986a). *Knowledge of Language: Its Nature, Origin and Use.* New York: Praeger.

Chomsky, N. (1986b). *Barriers.* Cambridge, Mass.: MIT Press.

Cooper, R. (1983). *Quantification and Syntactic Theory.* Dordrecht: D. Reidel.

Cooper, R. (1985). Unification in situation semantics: Linguistic arguments? Unpublished paper, University of Wisconsin, Madison.

Correa, N. (1988). A binding rule for government-binding parsing. In *Proceedings of the 12th International Conference on Computational Linguistics and the 24th Annual Meeting of the Association for Computational Linguistics*, Budapest, Hungary, 22-27 August, pp.123-129.

Crain, S., & Steedman, M. J. (1985). On not being led up the garden path: the use of context by the psychological parser. In D. Dowty, L. Karttunen, & A. Zwicky (Eds), *Natural Language Parsing: Psychological, Computational, and Theoretical Perspectives*. Cambridge: Cambridge University Press.

Dalrymple, M., Kaplan, R. M., Karttunen, L., Koskenniemi, K., Shaio, S., & Wescoat, M. (1987). Tools for morphological analysis. Report No. CSLI-87-108, Center for the Study of Language and Information, September.

De Smedt, K. (1984). Using object-oriented knowledge-representation techniques in morphology and syntax programming. In T. O'Shea, (Ed.), *ECAI 84*, pp.181-184. Amsterdam: North-Holland.

Di Sciullo, A. M. & Williams, E. (1987). *On the Definition of Word.* Cambridge, Mass.: MIT Press.

Dowty, D. (1978). Governed transformations as lexical rules in a Montague grammar. *Linguistic Inquiry, 9,* 393-426.

Dowty, D. (1979). *Word Meaning and Montague Grammar.* Dordrecht: D. Reidel.

Dowty, D. (1982a). More on the categorial analysis of grammatical relations. In A. Zaenen, (Ed.),

Subjects and Other Subjects: Proceedings of the Harvard Conference on Grammatical Relations, Bloomington, Indiana. Also in *Ohio State University Working Papers in Linguistics, 26*, 102-133.

Dowty, D. (1982b). Grammatical relations and Montague Grammar. In P. Jacobson, & G.K. Pullum (Eds), *The Nature of Syntactic Representation*, pp.79-130. Dordrecht: D. Reidel.

Evans, R. (1985). ProGram — a development tool for GPSG grammars. *Linguistics, 23*, 213-243.

Evans, R. P. (1986). Direct interpretation of the GPSG formalism. Unpublished paper, Cognitive Studies Programme, University of Sussex.

Fabb, N. A. J. (1984). Syntactic affixation. Ph.D Thesis, Department of Linguistics and Philosophy, MIT.

Fenstad, J., Halvorsen, P., Langholm, T. & Benthem, J. (1987). *Situations, Language and Logic*. Dordrecht: D. Reidel.

Flickinger, D., Pollard, C., & Wasow, T. (1985). Structure-sharing in lexical representation. In *Proceedings of the 23rd Annual Meeting of the Association for Computational Linguistics*, University of Chicago, Chicago, Illinois, July, pp.262-267.

Flynn, M. (1983). A categorial theory of structure building. In G. Gazdar, E. Klein, & G.K. Pullum, (Eds), *Order, Concord and Constituency*, pp.138-174. Dordrecht: Foris Publications.

Fodor, J. D. (1985). Deterministic parsing and subjacency. *Language and Cognitive Processes, 1*, 3-42.

Freidin, R. (1975). The analysis of passives. *Language, 51*, 384-405.

Frey, W. (1985). Syntax and semantics of some noun phrases. In J. Laubsch, (Ed), *Proceedings of GWAI 1984*.

Gazdar, G. (1980). A phrase structure syntax for comparative clauses. In T. Hoekstra, H. van der Hulst, & M. Moortgat (Eds.), *Lexical Grammar*, pp.165-179. Dordrecht: Foris Publications. Also in GLOT 2, 1979, pp.379-393.

Gazdar, G. (1981a). Unbounded dependencies and coordinate structure. *Linguistic Inquiry, 12*, 155-184.

Gazdar, G. (1981b). On syntactic categories. *Philosophical Transactions (Series B) of the Royal Society, 295*, 267- 283.

Gazdar, G. (1985). Finite state morphology. Review of *Two-level morphology* by Kimmo Koskenniemi. *Linguistics, 233*, 597–607.

Gazdar, G. (1987). Grammar as a formal language: Model theory for (part of) the GPSG formalism. Paper delivered to the Spring Meeting of the Linguistics Association of Great Britain, April 1987, Westfield College, London.

Gazdar, G. & Pullum, G. K. (1981). Subcategorization, constituent order and the notion 'head'. In M. Moortgat, H. van der Hulst, & T. Hoekstra (Eds), *The Scope of Lexical Rules*, pp.107–123. Dordrecht: Foris Publications.

Gazdar, G. & Pullum, G. K. (1982). *Generalized Phrase Structure Grammar: A Theoretical Synopsis*. Bloomington, Ind.: Indiana University Linguistics Club.

Gazdar, G., Klein, E., Pullum, G., & Sag, I. (1985). *Generalized Phrase Structure Grammar*. Oxford: Basil Blackwell.

Geach, P. T. (1972). A program for syntax. In D. Davidson, & G. Harman (Eds), *Semantics of Natural Language*. Dordrecht: D. Reidel.

Groenedijk, J. & Stockhof, M. (1987). *Dynamic predicate logic: Towards a compositional and non-representational discourse theory*. Report, ITLI, University of Amsterdam: Amsterdam, March, 1987.

Haddock, N. (1987). Incremental interpretation and combinatory categorial grammar. In N.J. Haddock, E. Klein, & G. Morrill (Eds), *Edinburgh Working Papers in Cognitive Science, Vol. 1: Categorial Grammar, Unification Grammar, and Parsing*. Edinburgh: Centre for Cognitive Science.

Halliday, M. A. K. (1985). *An Introduction to Functional Grammar*. London: Edward Arnold.

Halvorsen, P. (1983). Semantics for lexical-functional grammar. *Linguistic Inquiry, 14*, 567-615.

Heim, I. (1982). The Semantics of definite and indefinite noun phrases. Ph.D. Thesis, University of Massachusetts. Distributed by Graduate Linguistic Student Association.

Heny, F. (1979). Review of Noam Chomsky, Logical structure of linguistic theory. *Synthese, 40*,

317-352.

Hoekstra, T., van der Hulst, H., & Moortgat, M. (1980). Introduction. In T. Hoekstra, H. Hulst, & M. Moortgat (Eds), *Lexical Grammar*, No. 3, pp.1-48. Dordrecht: Foris Publications.

Hoekstra, T. (1984). *Transitivity: Grammatical Relations in Government-Binding Theory*. Dordrecht: Foris Publications.

Horrocks, G. (1987). *Generative Grammar*. London: Longman.

Jackendoff, R. S. (1975). Morphological and semantic regularities in the lexicon. *Language, 51*, 639-671.

Janssen, T. M. V. (1980). Logical investigations on PTQ arising from programming requirements. *Synthese, 44*, 361-390.

Janssen, T. M. V. (1983). Foundations and applications of Montague grammar. Ph.D. Thesis, Mathematisch Centrum, Universiteit van Amsterdam.

Janssen, T. M. V. (1986). *Foundations and Applications of Montague Grammar: Part 1: Philosophy, Framework, Computer Science*. Amsterdam: Centrum voor Wiskunde en Informatica.

Jensen, J. T. & Stong-Jensen, M. (1984). Morphology is in the lexicon! *Linguistic Inquiry, 15*, 474-498.

Johnson, M. (1985). Parsing with discontinuous constituents. In *Proceedings of the 23rd Annual Meeting of the Association for Computational Linguistics*, University of Chicago, Chicago, Illinois, July, pp.127-132.

Johnson, M. E. (1987). Attribute-value logic and the theory of grammar. Ph.D. Thesis, Department of Linguistics, Stanford University.

Johnson, M. (1988). Deductive parsing with multiple levels of representation. In *Proceedings of the 26th Annual Meeting of the Association for Computational Linguistics*, State University of New York at Buffalo, Buffalo, N.Y., 7-10 June, 1988.

Johnson, M. and Klein, E. (1986). Discourse, anaphora and parsing. In *Proceedings of the 11th International Conference on Computational Linguistics and the 24th Annual Meeting of the Association for Computational Linguistics*, Institut fuer Kommunikationsforschung und Phonetik, Bonn University, Bonn, August, pp.669-675.

Kamp, H. (1981). A theory of truth and semantic representation. In J.A.G. Groenendijk, T.M. Janssen, & M.B.J. Stokhof (Eds), *Formal Methods in the Study of Language*, Vol. 136, pp.277-322. Amsterdam: Mathematical Centre Tracts.

Kaplan, R. M. (1987). Three seductions of computational psycholinguistics. In P. Whitelock, M.M.Wood, H.L. Somers, R. Johnson, & P. Bennett (Eds), *Linguistic Theory and Computer Applications*, pp.149-188. London: Academic Press.

Kaplan, R. M. & Bresnan, J. (1982). Lexical-functional grammar: a formal system for grammatical representation. In J. Bresnan (Ed.), *The Mental Representation of Grammatical Relations*, pp.173-281. Cambridge, Mass.: MIT Press.

Karttunen, L. (1986a). D-PATR: A development environment for unification-based grammars. In *Proceedings of the 11th International Conference on Computational Linguistics and the 24th Annual Meeting of the Association for Computational Linguistics*, Institut fuer Kommunikationsforschung und Phonetik, Bonn University, Bonn, 25-29 August, pp.74-80.

Karttunen, L. (1986b). Radical lexicalism. Report No. CSLI- 86-68, Center for the Study of Language and Information, December, 1986. Paper presented at the Conference on Alternative Conceptions of Phrase Structure, July 1986, New York.

Kasper, R. (1987a). A unification method for disjunctive feature descriptions. Technical Report No. RS-87-187, USC Information Sciences Institute, Marina Del Rey, Ca., April.

Kasper, R. T. (1987b). Feature structures: A logical theory with application to language analysis. Ph.D. Thesis, Electrical Engineering and Computer Science Department, University of Michigan.

Kasper, R. (1987b). *Feature structures: A logical theory with application to language analysis*. Ph.D. Thesis. Electrical Engineering and Computer Science Department, university of Michigan.

Kasper, R. T. & Rounds, W. C. (1986). A logical semantics for feature structures. In *Proceedings of the 24th Annual Meeting of the Association for Computational Linguistics*, Columbia University, New York, N.Y., 10-13 June, pp.257-266.

Kay, M. (1979). Functional grammar. In *Proceedings of the Fifth Annual Meeting of the Berkeley Linguistic Society*, pp.142-158. Berkeley: Berkeley Linguistic Society.

Kay, M. (1985). Parsing in functional unification grammar. In D.R. Dowty, L. Karttunen, & A.M. Zwicky (Eds), *Natural Language Parsing: Psychological, Computational and Theoretical Perspectives*, pp.251-278. Cambridge: Cambridge University Press.

Kiparsky, P. (1982a). From cyclic phonology to lexical phonology. In H. van der Hulst & N. Smith (Eds), *The Structure of Phonological Representations*, Vol. I, pp.131-175. Dordrecht: Foris Publications.

Kiparsky, P. (1982b). Lexical morphology and phonology. In *Linguistics in the Morning Calm: Selected Papers from SICOL-1981*, pp.3-91. Seoul: Hanshin Publishing Company.

Klein, E. & Sag, I.A. (1985). Type-driven translation. *Linguistics and Philosophy, 8*, 163-201.

Koskenniemi, K. (1983). Two-level morphology: A general computational model for word-form recognition and production. Publication 11, Department of General Linguistics, University of Helsinki, Helsinki.

Koskenniemi, K. (1984). A general computational model for word-form recognition and production. In *Proceedings of the 10th International Conference on Computational Linguistics and the 22nd Annual Meeting of the Association for Computational Linguistics*, Stanford University, Stanford, Ca., 2-6 July, pp.178-181.

Ladusaw, W. A. (1985). A proposed distinction between *levels* and *strata*. Report No. SRC-85-04, Syntax Research Centre, University of California, Santa Cruz, December, 1985. Paper read at the Winter Meeting of the Linguistic Society of America, December, Seattle.

Lambek, J. (1958). The mathematics of sentence structure. *American Mathematical Monthly, 65*, 154-170.

Lambek, J. (1961). On the calculus of syntactic types. In *Structure of Language and its Mathematical Aspects*. pp.166-178. Providence, R. I.: American Mathematical Society.

Lapointe, S. (1979). A theory of grammatical agreement. Ph.D. Dissertation, University of Massachusetts, Amherst.

Lapointe, S. (1983). A comparison of two recent theories of agreement. *CLS19P*, pp.122-134.

Lieber, R. (1980). On the organization of the lexicon. PhD Thesis, MIT. Distributed by Indiana University Linguistics Club.

Lyons, J. (1966). Towards a "notional" theory of the "parts of speech". *Journal of Linguistics, 2*, 209-236.

Lyons, J. (1968). *Introduction to Theoretical Linguistics*. Cambridge: Cambridge University Press.

Marcus, M. P. (1980). *A Theory of Syntactic Recognition for Natural Language*. Cambridge, Mass.: MIT Press.

Marr, D. (1977). Artificial intelligence — A personal view. *Artificial Intelligence, 9*, 37-48.

Marslen-Wilson, W. D. (1973). Linguistic structure and speech shadowing at very short latencies. *Nature, 244*, 522-523.

Matthiessen, C. & Kasper, R. (1987). Systemic grammar and functional unification grammar and representational issues in systemic functional grammar. Technical Report No. RS- 87-179, USC Information Sciences Institute, Marina Del Rey, Ca., April.

McCarthy, J. (1981). A prosodic theory of nonconcatenative morphology. *Linguistic Inquiry, 12*, 373-418.

McCloskey, J. (1988). Syntactic theory. In F.J. Newmeyer (Ed.), *Linguistics: The Cambridge Survey*, Vol.1: *Linguistic Theory: Foundations*, pp.18-59. Cambridge: Cambridge University Press.

Mellish, C. S. (1983). Incremental semantic interpretation. In K. Sparck-Jones and Y. Wilks (eds), *Automatic Natural Language Parsing*. Chichester: Ellis Horwood.

Mellish, C. S. (1985). *Computer Interpretation of Natural Language Descriptions*. Chichester: Ellis Horwood.

Mellish, C. S. (1988). Implementing systemic classification by unification. *Computational Linguistics, 14*, 40-51.

Montague, R. (1970). Universal grammar. *Theoria, 36*, 373- 398. Reprinted in R. H. Thomason (ed.)

(1974), *Formal Philosophy: Selected Papers of Richard Montague*, pp.222- 246. Yale University Press: New Haven, Conn.

Moortgat, M. (1987a).   Lambek categorial grammar and the autonomy thesis. INL Working Papers No. 87-03, Instituut voor Nederlandse Lexicologie, Leiden, April.

Moortgat, M. (1987b).   Lambek theorem proving. In E. Klein, & J. Benthem (Eds), *Categories, Polymorphism and Unification*, pp.169-200. Edinburgh and Amsterdam: Centre for Cognitive Science, University of Edinburgh and Institute for Language, Logic and Information, University of Amsterdam.

Moortgat, M. (1988a). *Categorial Investigations: Logical and Linguistic Aspects of the Lambek Calculus.* Dordrecht: Foris Publications.

Moortgat, M. (1988b).   Mixed composition and discontinuous dependencies. In R. Oehrle, E. Bach, & D. Wheeler, (Eds),   *Categorial Grammars and Natural Language Structures*, pp.319-390. Dordrecht: D. Reidel.

Morrill, G. (1987).   Meta-categorial grammar. In N.J. Haddock, E. Klein, & G. Morrill (Eds), *Edinburgh Working Papers in Cognitive Science*, Vol. 1: *Categorial Grammar, Unification Grammar, and Parsing.* Edinburgh: Centre for Cognitive Science.

Moshier, M. D. & Rounds, W. C. (1987).   A logic for partially specified data structures. In *ACM Symposium on the Principles of Programming Languages*, Association for Computing Machinery, Munich, West Germany.

Oehrle, R. T. (1988).   Multi-dimensional compositional functions as a basis for grammatical analysis. In R.T. Oehrle, E. Bach, & D. Wheeler (Eds), *Categorial Grammars and Natural Language Structures*, pp.349-389. Dordrecht: D. Reidel.

Pareschi, R. (1988).   A definite clause version of categorial grammar. In *Proceedings of the 26th Annual Meeting of the Association for Computational Linguistics*, State University of New York at Buffalo: Buffalo, N.Y., 7–10 June, 1988.

Pareschi, R. and Steedman, M. J. (1986).   Reduce-first parsing and the problem of non-determinism. In *Incremental Interpretation in Dialogue*. ACORD Deliverable T2.4, University of Edinburgh, Centre for Cognitive Science.

Partee, B. (1975).   Montague grammar and transformational grammar. *Linguistic Inquiry, 6*, 203-300.

Partee, B. H. (1979).   Montague grammar and the well-formedness constraint. In F. Heny, & H.S. Schnelle (Eds), *Syntax and Semantics*, Vol. 10: *Selections from the Third Groningen Round Table*, pp.275-313. London: Academic Press.

Partee, B. H. (1984).   Compositionality. In F. Landman, & F. Veltman (Eds),   *Varieties of Formal Semantics: Proceedings of The Fourth Amsterdam Colloquium*, September, Dordrecht.

Pereira, F. C. N. & Warren, D. H. D. (1983).   Parsing as deduction. In *Proceedings of the 21st Annual Meeting of the Association for Computational Linguistics*, Massachusetts Institute of Technology, Cambridge, Mass., 1983, pp.137-144.

Pereira, F. C. N. & Shieber, S. M. (1984).   The semantics of grammar formalisms seen as computer languages. In *Proceedings of the 10th International Conference on Computational Linguistics and the 22nd Annual Meeting of the Association for Computational Linguistics*, Stanford University, Stanford, Ca., 2-6 July, pp.123-129.

Perrault, C. R. (1984).   On the mathematical properties of linguistic theories.*Computational Linguistics, 10*, pp.165-176.

Pesetsky, D. (1985).   Morphology and logical form. *Linguistic Inquiry, 16*, 193-246.

Phillips, J. D. & Thompson, H. S. (1985).   GPSGP—a parser for generalised phrase structure grammars. *Linguistics, 23*, 245-261.

Pollack, J. & Waltz, D. (1985).   Massively parallel parsing: A strongly interactive model of natural language interpretation. *Cognitive Science, 9*, 51-74.

Pollard, C. J. (1984).   Generalized phrase structure grammars, head grammars, and natural languages. Ph.D. Thesis, Stanford University.

Pollard, C. J. (1985).   Lectures on HPSG. Unpublished lecture notes, CSLI, Stanford University.

Pollard, C.J. (1988).   Categorial grammar and phrase structure grammar: An excursion on the syntax–semantics frontier. In R. Oehrle, E. Bach, & D. Wheeler (Eds), *Categorial Grammar and Natural Language Structures*. Dordrecht: D. Reidel.

Pollard, C. & Sag, I. (1987). *An Information-Based App.roach to Syntax and Semantics: Volume 1 Fundamentals*. Stanford, Ca.: Center for the Study of Language and Information.

Pullum, G. K. & Gazdar, G. (1982). Natural languages and context free languages. *Linguistics and Philosophy, 4*, 471-504.

Pulman, S. G. (1985). A parser that doesn't. In *2nd European Conference, Association for Computational Linguistics*, Geneva.

Pulman, S. (1987). The syntax-semantics interface. In P. Whitelock, M.M. Wood, H.L. Somers, R. Johnson & P. Bennett (Eds), *Linguistic Theory and Computer Applications*, pp.189-224. London: Academic Press.

Reyle, U. (1988). Compositional semantics for LFG. In U. Reyle & C. Rohrer (Eds), *Natural Language Parsing and Linguistic Theories*, pp.448-474. Dordrecht: D. Reidel.

Ritchie, G. D., Pulman, S. G ., Black, A. W., & Russel, G. (1987). A computational framework for lexical description. *Computational Linguistics, 13*, pp. 290–307.

Rooth, M. (1987). Noun phrase interpretation in Montague grammar, file change semantics, and situation semantics. In P. Gärdenfors (Ed.), *Generalized Quantifiers: Linguistic and Logical Approaches*, pp.237-268. Dordrecht: D. Reidel.

Ross, J. R. (1967). Constraints on variables in syntax. Ph.D. Thesis, MIT. Indiana University Linguistics Club.

Rounds, W. C. & Kasper, R. T. (1986). A Complete logical calculus for record structures representing linguistic information. In *Proceedings of the 15th Annual Symposium on Logic in Computer Science*, Cambridge, Mass.

Russell, G., Pulman, S. G., Ritchie, G. D. & Black, A. W. (1986). A dictionary and morphological analyser for English. In *Proceedings of the 11th International Conference on Computational Linguistics and the 24th Annual Meeting of the Association for Computational Linguistics*, Institut fuer Kommunikationsforschung und Phonetik, Bonn University, Bonn, August.

Scalise, S. (1984). *Generative morphology*. Dordrecht: Foris Publications.

Selkirk, E. O. (1982). *The Syntax of Words*. Cambridge, Mass.: MIT Press.

Selkirk, E. O. (1984). *Phonology and Syntax: The Relation between Sound and Structure*. Cambridge, Mass.: MIT Press.

Sells, P. (1986). *Lectures on Contemporary Syntactic Theories*. Chicago, Ill.: University of Chicago Press.

Shieber, S. M. (1985). Criteria for designing computer facilities for linguistic analysis. *Linguistics, 23*, 189-211.

Shieber, S. M. (1986). A simple reconstruction of GPSG. In *Proceedings of the 11th International Conference on Computational Linguistics and the 24th Annual Meeting of the Association for Computational Linguistics*, Institut fuer Kommunikationsforschung und Phonetik, Bonn University, Bonn, August.

Shieber, S. M. (1986). *An Introduction to Unification-based Approaches to Grammar*. Chicago, Ill.: University of Chicago Press.

Shieber, S. M. (1988). Separating linguistic analyses from linguistic theories. In U. Reyle, & C. Rohrer (Eds), *Natural Language Parsing and Linguistic Theories*, pp.33- 68. Dordrecht: D. Reidel.

Shieber, S., Uszkoreit, H., Pereira, F. C. N., Robinson, J. J. & Tyson, M. (1983). The formalism and implementation of PATR-II. In B. Grosz, & M. E. Stickel (Eds), *Research on Interactive Acquisition and Use of Knowledge*, pp.39-79, Menlo Park, Ca.: SRI International.

Shieber, S. M., Karttunen, L. & Pereira, F. C. N. (1984). Notes from the unification underground. Technical Note 327, SRI International, Menlo Park, Ca., June.

Smolka, G. (1988). A feature logic with subsorts. LILOG- Report No. 33, IBM Deutschland GmbH, Stuttgart, May.

Sproat, R. (1984). On bracketing paradoxes. In M. Speas & R. Sproat (Eds), *MIT Working Papers in Linguistics*, Vol.7: *Papers from the January 1984 MIT Workshop in Morphology*, pp.110-130.

Stabler, E. P. Jr.(1987). Restricting logic grammars with government-binding theory. *Computational Linguistics, 13*, 1-10.

Steedman, M. (1985). Dependency and coordination in the grammar of Dutch and English. *Language, 61*, 523-568.

Steedman, M. (1987). Combinatory grammars and parasitic gaps. *Natural Language and Linguistic Theory, 5*, 403-439.

Stowell, T. (1981). Origins of phrase structure. Ph.D. Thesis, Department of Linguistics and Philosophy, MIT.

Thomason, R. H. (1976a). Some extensions of Montague grammar. In B. Partee, (Ed.), *Montague Grammar*, pp.75-117. London: Academic Press.

Thomason, R. H. (1976b). *On the Semantic Interpretation of the Thomason 1972 Fragment.* Bloomington, Ind.: Indiana University Linguistics Club.

Thompson, H. (1982). Handling metarules in a parser for GPSG. In M. Barlow, D. Flickinger, & I.A. Sag (Eds), *Developments in Generalized Phrase Structure Grammar: Stanford Working Papers in Grammatical Theory*, Vol. 2, pp.26-37. Bloomington, Ind.: Indiana University Linguistics Club.

Wasow, T. (1977). Transformations and the lexicon. In P.W. Culicover, T. Wasow, & A. Akmajian (Eds), *Formal Syntax*, pp.327-360. London: Academic Press.

Wasow, T. (1980). Major and minor rules in lexical grammar. In T. Hoekstra, (Ed.), *Lexical Grammar*. Dordrecht: Foris Publications.

Wheeler, D. (1981). Aspects of a categorial theory of phonology. Ph.D. Thesis, Linguistics, University of Massachusetts at Amherst. Distributed by Graduate Linguistics Student Association, University of Massachusetts.

Wheeler, D. 91988). Consequences of some categorially motivated phonological assumptions. In Oehrle, R. T., Wheeler, D., & Bach, E. (Eds.), *Categorial grammar and natural language structures*. Dordrecht: D. Reidel.

Williams, E. (1981). On the notions "lexically related" and "head of a word". *Linguistic Inquiry, 12*, 245-274.

Zeevat, H. (1988). Combining categorial grammar and unification. In U. Reyle, & C. Rohrer (Eds). *Natural Language Parsing and Linguistic Theories*, pp.202-229. Dordrecht: D. Reidel.

Zeevat, H., Klein, E. & Calder, J. (1987). An introduction to unification categorial grammar. In N. J.Haddock, E. Klein, & G. Morrill (Eds), *Edinburgh Working Papers in Cognitive Science*, Vol.1: *Categorial Grammar, Unification Grammar, and Parsing.* Edinburgh: Centre for Cognitive Science.

CHAPTER 4

Logical Semantics

Johan van Benthem

Institute for Language, Logic and Information,
Faculty of Mathematics and Computer Science,
University of Amsterdam, Roetersstraat 15, 1018
WB Amsterdam, The Netherlands

1. LOGIC AND LANGUAGE

Semantics is the study of meaning of language, viewed as a medium of communication. Philosophers have debated for a long time what meaning *is*: whether it is some kind of object associated with linguistic structures, or some kind of phenomenon emerging in every successful use of language. We do not have to decide (and perhaps, should not even decide) this issue to see that there is a broad field of enquiry here. Understanding a language is having a grasp of its meaning: A competent speaker is one who does not merely broadcast grammatically correct sentences, but one who is able to paraphrase the same meaning in different words, translate it into another language, or infer other meanings from it. A thorough study of meaning, then, carries the promise of making us understand the various functions of language use, and thereby the process of cognitive communication.

Thus described, semantics lies at the borderline of various disciplines, notably, linguistics and logic. And in fact, throughout Western history, there have been lively contacts between these two fields—witness the joint development of "logic and grammar" in such philosophical schools as the Stoics in Antiquity, the Scholastics in the Middle Ages, or the Port-Royal at the beginning of the modern era. There has always been a (healthy) tension between the semantics of specific natural languages and the "universal grammar" underlying all of them, with the logicians concentrating on the latter. The resulting development, up until this century, might be described as an alternation of mutual attraction and repulsion—with the former phase gaining predominance again these days.

Being interested in universal aspects of meaning, logicians have tended to keep their distance from the syntactic peculiarities of any given language (whether traditional Latin or modern European). Instead, they produced so-called *formal languages*, bringing out semantic structure more clearly, so as to facilitate the study of meaning and inference. For instance, the following sentences all express the same meaning:

She wants John to love his sister,
Elle veut que Jean aime sa soeur,
Sie will dass Johann seine Schwester liebt.

In representing this meaning, a logician would wish to employ a formalism abstracting away from such syntactic peculiarities as different word order, or the presence/absence of a particle preceding what is wanted. This is not to say that the above differences in syntactic structure reflect no difference in meaning whatsoever; but, it is of primary importance to bring out the similarity.

A number of widely applicable formal languages has been constructed in modern logic, starting with the work of George Boole (1854) and especially Gottlob Frege (1879)—the inventor of so-called *Predicate Logic*. The basic idea of the latter formalism is as follows. Atomic statements of a language assert that some predicate holds of certain individuals, e.g.

LOVES (John, Mary) or GREATER THAN (7,5).

Out of these, complex statements are then built up by logical operations, involving such key notions as:

Boolean operators: negation / conjunction / disjunction, and
quantifiers: "some", "all", "no", "one", ...

On the pattern of this predicate logic, various richer formal languages have been developed in this century, incorporating other important kinds of operators (e.g. temporal indicators such as Future, Past, or epistemic modes, such as "know (that)"). As these formal languages were used, they became more than just a symbolic notation. Due to their simple perspicuous structure, logical formalisms started serving as a central vehicle for thinking about linguistic meaning, and how it comes about.

The general semantic scheme to arise out of this reflection may be summarised as follows:

Language	*Interpretation*	*World*
syntactic structure,		semantic structure,
or "logical form"		or "model"

On the one hand, there is an as yet uninterpreted language, with a certain grammatical structure and, on the other, a situation ("world") which this language is used to talk about. Grammatical structures now become meaningful assertions about this situation by a process of interpretation, linking various linguistic elements with actual objects in the semantic structure. This process starts from interpretations of basic lexical predicates and names (which may have been learned, or inferred, beforehand), and then creates more complex interpretations for logical compounds following the above "logical construction" of the sentence.

The key point here is this. Although there is a potential infinity of linguistic forms to be interpreted, the number of construction rules producing these is *finite*—and it suffices to give an interpretation of the latter: all possible meanings will arise through suitable combinations and repetitions of these. It is this observation, called Frege's Principle of *Compositionality*, which is generally held to account for the *learnability* of languages; in particular, our ability to understand and produce new meanings which we had not encountered before. On the other hand, there is also a Fregean Principle of *Contextuality*, stating that in practice meanings are often to be determined in context, rather than in isolation. That is, determining which meanings apply in a particular context may not be a smooth bottom-up procedure, but rather a trial-and-error process with local decisions being postponed, or even reversed, in the light of further (con-)textual evidence. Again, this would fit in well with known general features of human learning procedures.

There is a lot of fine-structure to the above schema. For instance, linguistic expressions may vary in their mode of interpretation. Some expressions denote concrete objects, others apply rather abstract "logical glue", or merely convey some instruction in a language game. Some words have stable meanings across a wide range of situations ("table", "prime number"), whereas others have highly context-dependent behaviour: To know who is meant by pronouns such as "I" or "she", one needs to appeal to the specific *context of utterance* of a statement. Thus, interpretation is a more delicate process than may have appeared at first.

Another complicating factor is the nature of the "models" in the above. Sometimes, these are to be thought of realistically, as parts of the actual world—then again, they rather serve as (mathematical) *representations* of aspects of that world. In fact, for many purposes, the proper semantic perspective is as in the following *triangle*:

language   reality

representation
structure

Here any kind of system can, in principle, model any other; and semantics in the broader sense is the study of all these possible relations, and their interplay. (In all, there are nine possibilities in the schema. For instance, languages *describe* reality or representations of it, while representation structures *model* reality or *realise* text; but also, languages can interpret or *translate* one another, etc.)

As an illustration of the unifying power of the semantic perspective, it may be noted that the above considerations apply equally well to *programming languages*, as well as other formalisms being used in computer science. Programs have a pure syntax; but, the important task is to understand what they mean. And, for this purpose, it is often advantageous to interpolate a well-chosen representation of the computing process, in between the text and the physical whirlpool inside the computer.

The semantic triangle reflects an important historical development. Language is a highly successful evolutionary instrument for interacting with the real world. Surely, exploring its underlying meaning structures, whether through linguistic syntax, or its associated representations, will point at the cognitive patterns which are serving us so well, and hence at efficient ways of representing knowledge. Or at least, such is the hypothesis inspiring much contemporary work.

2. SEMANTIC FRAMEWORKS

Nothing in the preceding section cannot be found, presumably, in one or other general philosophy of meaning propounded in this century. After all, modern philosophy has undergone what has been called a *linguistic turn*: with a deep interest in language and meaning resulting in various philosophical traditions, both Anglo-Saxon and continental. The important point for present purposes, however, is that these ideas have turned out to be implementable in exact mathematical frameworks. This move guarantees precise statement, and hence theoretical progress, but also the possibility of application.

The first such precise scheme was proposed by the Polish logician Alfred Tarski. Its central notion is as follows:

M,I,b *verifies* φ:

sentence φ is true in model M under interpretation I for its vocabulary and assignment b to its contextual parameters.

Note that "truth" is actually a *relation* here, involving several degrees of freedom: choice of a sentence, a model, and a mode of interpretation (divided up into a more global and a more context-dependent component). This view at once suggests various directions for semantic research, such as:

Describing the world:
given a model M and interpretation /assignment I,b:
which sentences will be true in M?

Learning how a (foreign) language applies to the world:
given a model M and sentence φ:
which interpretations I will make φ true in M?

Or, perhaps more abstractly,

Exploring a range of application:
given a sentence φ :
which combinations M,I,b will serve as models for φ?

All these directions have been pursued in the logical literature —and new ones are still becoming relevant. For instance, in the semantics of programs, the program text φ is given, as well as the model M plus an assignment I, but the interesting parameter is the assignment b, which stores current values of the program variables. As consecutive commands are executed, the assignment changes, recording changes in values stored. But again, this process can be formulated and studied smoothly within the Tarskian framework.

The above semantics was developed for formal logical languages. A linguistic breakthrough occurred with the work of Richard Montague, who showed how the above view of semantic interpretation could be extended to natural languages, in roughly the following way. One starts with a linguistically oriented grammar for analysing sentences of natural language, and then provides a systematic rule-by-rule *translation* from its grammatical forms to formulae in some suitably rich logical language. Thus, the already available Tarskian semantics for the latter can be transported to the former. Once this procedure became fully understood, however, it also turned out to be possible to formulate the interpretation procedure directly on grammatical forms, without any (overt) formal language intermediary.

Although the specific proposals made by Montague have often been considerably modified, his general format of interpretation has been extremely influential—both in more theoretical linguistics and in more practical projects of natural language processing. (An example is the Philips PHLIQUA project at Eindhoven, for querying databases in natural language, as well as its current successor ROSETTA aiming at automatic translation.)

In recent years, various semantic paradigms have attracted attention, which can all be viewed as enriching the Montague format in essential ways. First, it has been proposed to add a component of *discourse representation*, mediating between grammatical structures and actual models. Arguments for introducing such an additional level in semantics are found in the nature of discourse, where various processes occur which are neither purely syntactic nor really part of the outside world. Such processes concern the way in which we arrange and present our information. A prominent example is *anaphoric connection*, as in the following piece of text:

A sailor$_1$ was teaching *his*$_1$ parrot$_2$ a song$_3$.
It$_2$ needed a lot of rum from *him*$_1$ to learn *it*$_3$ really well.

Evidently, our picture of this situation is entirely dependent on the anaphoric identifications made when hearing this story. Hans Kamp and Irene Heim have proposed a formal theory of discourse representation for describing the anaphoric process (as well as many other discourse phenomena). A related, more informal approach due to Pieter Seuren and Gilles Fauconnier has also concentrated on broad principles governing discourse representation, such as "least mental effort" in selecting anaphoric connections, or "maximal coherence" in understanding texts.

Another prominent new paradigm is that of *Situation Semantics*, developed by Jon Barwise and John Perry. This theory stresses the *context-dependence* of meaning; so much so, that meaning itself is taken to consist in a relation between a situation of utterance and a described situation, allowing for flow of information between the two.

Situations are always thought of as small, partial pieces of the world and, hence, situation semantics focusses especially on the dynamics of what happens when we move from one situation to another in our use of language. Which pieces of information remain valid, which ones are lost? For instance, if I know that

Johnny B. Goode kissed a teacher

in one small situation, this fact will remain true in larger situations containing this one; but the same need not hold for the perhaps only limited generalisation:

Johnny B. Goode kissed every teacher.

So, one additional task for semantics is to chart "persistence" of information across situations, something which turns out to be important also in computer science, when using changing databases containing facts about varying situations.

Finally, the dynamics of discourse has also been made a central feature in the *Game-theoretical Semantics* of Jaakko Hintikka, which views language use as a game about truth, played between ourselves and "Nature", a somewhat malevolent opponent testing our wits. This approach is also congenial to modelling *dialogue* (witness the earlier work of Paul Lorenzen on the dialogical foundations of logic). In such a perspective, the mathematical notions of Game Theory can be enlisted to make precise sense of the earlier-mentioned principles of discourse, as winning strategies in language games.

Summing up, this century has seen an outburst of linguistic and philosophical studies concerning natural language. What logic has offered here is a set of notions and results for formulating such insights in precise, testable frameworks. Thus, there is no essential opposition between what are sometimes called the "natural language" and "formal language" approaches to the linguistic and philosophical study of language. For instance, more informal work in analytic philosophy on speech acts (Austin, Searle) or conversational postulates (Grice) is still guiding contemporary technical approaches. In fact, the subject to be understood is so vast that no one, on whatever side of whatever academic fence, can afford the luxury of not learning from insights, and failures, encountered elsewhere.

3. SPECIFIC SEMANTIC THEMES

In the scientific climate encouraged by the above, more systematic semantic frameworks, a wealth of specific case studies has been undertaken. Some of the main areas will be mentioned here, to give a more concrete idea of important current topics in the literature.

For a start, a distinction may be made between *lexical semantics*, being concerned with the semantic behaviour of words or unit phrases, and *structural semantics*, being the study of the interpretative effects of further grammatical constructions. Lexical semantics looks at such things as the search for enlightening classifications of word meanings, resulting in natural clusters or "semantic networks" of, for example, expressions for spatio-temporal positioning, or main types of activity verbs. Structural semantics is mainly interested in the process of how more complex meanings arise out of given ones. Different research traditions may have a different emphasis here. For instance, the Montagovian approach is stronger on the structural side, whereas classical British semantic research has a more lexical orientation. However, with many linguistic phenomena, both aspects can be discerned. For instance, Boolean operators (NOT, AND, OR) can be studied as a lexical word class, but also as a means of creating compound logical structure in many other grammatical categories.

The following list of topics, by no means a complete survey, will not only give an idea of the research into specific grammatical categories of expression, but also into more general semantic mechanisms across whole languages.

3.1 Determiners and Quantifiers

To introduce our first example, we take a brief look at basic syntax. A fundamental sentence pattern in natural languages is given in the rule:

S ⇒ NP VP

Any sentence can be decomposed into a subject nounphrase and a verbphrase predicated of it. Decomposing the NP gives either a proper name ("John") or a complex expression:

NP ⇒ Det N

For example, the *determiner* "every" combines with the noun "sailor" to form the complex nounphrase "every sailor". Thus, a crucial sentence pattern arises:

S ⇒ Det N VP

which may be viewed as follows. The determiner establishes a relation between two predicates, one given by the noun, the other by the verbphrase. So-called logical quantifiers from Predicate Logic are an example:

Every sailor swears:
SAILOR is *contained* in SWEARING.

Some sailor swears:
SAILOR *overlaps* with SWEARING.

But also other, less standard determiners are possible, as in "*Most* sailors swear", "*Many* sailors swear". This relational pattern plays a basic role in conveying information and drawing inferences, and hence it has been studied extensively —resulting in the so-called *Theory of Generalised Quantifiers*, describing both logical quantifiers and linguistic determiners in general.

3.2 Boolean Operators

Another basic logical operation is that of Boolean compounding, as in classical propositional calculus. Boolean particles also play a pervasive linguistic role, however,

LL—I

as they can modify most major types of expression, e.g. "not" negates such diverse categories as verbs ("does not walk"), adverbs ("not nicely"), nounphrases ("not every sailor"), or prepositional phrases ("not with a knife"). And conjunction ("and") and disjunction ("or") have a similar freedom of movement ("stand or fall", "nicely and easily").

The effect of this ubiquity is to make all such categories "inferentially sensitive", in the sense of allowing inferences to be drawn. Thus, not only can sentences imply one another, but also the above types of expression:

"nicely and easily" implies "easily",
"not with a knife" implies "not with a bowie knife".

These observations have been systematised into a coherent theory. One key notion here, and in contemporary semantics generally, is *monotonicity*. An occurrence of an expression X in another expression Y= ... X ... is positive monotone if, whenever X is replaced by some X* implied by X, then Y*= ... X* ... is also implied by Y. Monotonicity effects have been observed for many types of expression, notably the earlier determiners and quantifiers. For instance, the position X_2 in the sentence pattern "*all* X_1 X_2" is monotone:

Since "ruined" implies "poor",
"all nobles are ruined" implies "all nobles are poor".

(Incidentally, the other argument X_1 is *downward* monotone here:

if "all nobles are ruined",
then "all British nobles are ruined",
since "British noble" implies "noble".)

These observations suggest that natural language has a strongly inferential "design".

3.3 Plurals and Collectivity

One striking aspect of linguistic description is our ability to gather individuals into collections (sets, groups), thus creating a new level of entities with their own emergent patterns of behaviour. Quite recently, there has been an upsurge of interest in these phenomena, with various proposals to model them, whether inside or outside standard set theory. In particular, the process of how collective meanings arise out of more individual ones is still to be understood. Given the ubiquity of "collectivisation", this process must certainly play a central role in our representation of the world—the advantages of which are already amply demonstrated in ordinary Set Theory. Natural languages seem to form various kinds of collectives, however, beyond bare sets; and these may yield valuable clues as to our actual cognitive operations.

These issues show various analogies with the so-called "mass-count" distinction, which reflects another basic duality in our ways of thinking about the world. On the one hand, reality is divided up into countable sets of objects; on the other, it comes in non-countable "substances", such as water, time, or happiness. There are striking linguistic dualities between countable pluralities and mass items; witness parallel pairs such as:

all sailors cheered—all the water disappeared
many sailors were flogged—much water was drunk.

Given the tenacity of this dual world view, formal semantic theories will eventually have to come to terms with it. There are some promising proposals for integrated pictures in the recent literature, which show why mass and count perspectives can co-exist peacefully.

3.4 Properties and Types

The earlier presentation of basic sentence patterns, when introducing determiners, presupposes a common distinction between *individual objects* (referred to by proper names, and quantified over by determiners-cum-common nouns) and *properties* predicated of these (expressed by verbphrases). This picture suggests a natural division into *types* of semantic objects associated with these linguistic categories: properties are higher predicates "operating on" individual objects. And repeating this process, a whole semantic hierarchy arises. This is the viewpoint of *Categorial Grammar* in linguistic description, and also that of a whole family of related grammar formalisms sharing the Montagovian heritage: (See Klein, Chapter 3). Moreover, this hierarchy is also the habitat of Bertrand Russell's famous *Theory of Types* in the foundations of mathematics—and, in fact, technical research into logical type theories is becoming increasingly relevant to linguistic (as well as computational) practice.

Nevertheless, recent research is questioning this convenient distinction to a certain extent, for there are constructions which seem to reverse the picture, turning predicates into objects, viz. such *nominalisations* as:

work-*ing*: working can be pleasant
to lie: to lie is sinful.

Thus, the picture becomes a more Protean one, where entities in one type can undergo a metamorphosis, ending up in a quite different level of the semantic hierarchy. Much current research on flexible or *polymorphic typing* is directed towards accounting for this freedom of movement.

Polymorphism is a subject with many ramifications. Flexible typing is actually needed for quite a few more domestic linguistic purposes, such as the proper description of co-ordination, dislocated constituents, or various scope ambiguities. Accordingly, there is a large body of work on calculi of so-called "type shifting", trying to provide a principled logical account of which metamorphoses are possible and which ones are not. (For instance, the Boolean particle "not" has a great freedom of occurrence, as was observed earlier; but there are limits. Unlike the earlier example, *it* cannot be nominalised to denote an individual object.)

There are also several analogous developments in other areas. Polymorphism is a central issue in the semantics of programming languages these days, with examples reminiscent of the above. For instance, *procedures* in programs are naturally seen as (higher) operations on data, but can also be regarded themselves as being stored data on which computation can be performed. Again, this calls for free typing, as in current systems of *Denotational Semantics*, due to Scott. And, finally, in contemporary philosophy, there is a lively interest in so-called *Property Theories*, treating individual objects and properties on a par. There is a growing trade in ideas to be observed across these various fields.

3.5 Temporal Perspective

Most of our discourse takes place in a temporal setting, referring to changing situations. In natural language, this is reflected in the syntactic fact that all sentences are tensed, while often containing a variety of other temporal expressions as well. To account for this semantically is not just a simple matter of adding an occasional temporal parameter in earlier static modellings, as has often been thought. Instead, a thoroughly temporalised view of meaning is needed, together with an account of the interactions between temporal and other expressions.

There is an extensive literature on this topic, with early logical contributions by Hans Reichenbach and Arthur Prior, the founder of so-called "Tense Logic". A sizeable body of linguistic temporal description has been accumulated within the Montagovian paradigm. Recently, there have been attempts to develop a more sensitive theory of temporal *representation*, in line with an earlier-mentioned general trend. For instance, although many tenses can be modelled relatively simply, as indications of temporal position on the time line (with respect to the moment of utterance), there are subtleties coming to light. A pair of tenses like French *imparfait* and *passé simple* may describe the same real event (*"Maurice mangeait"*, *"Maurice mangea"*), while conveying duration in the one case, and instantaneity in the other. An account of this difference will have to be found at a representational level: the same event is being *presented* in different ways.

In order to achieve descriptive success here, it seems necessary to set one's aims higher than traditional Tense Logic, and demand a description of the temporal system in its entirety, including tenses, aspects, Aktionsarte, temporal abverbials, quantifiers, and connectives.

This is an area where many disciplines have related concerns (see van Benthem, Chapter 8). Temporal representation has become a focal topic, not just in linguistics and logic, but also in computer science and psychology. Many of the leading questions here are again tied up with possible *inference*. We usually have partial information about what goes on during certain periods. In order to plan and think ahead, we need to extrapolate: If an assertion holds for a certain period, will it also hold during its subperiods or during later periods? Expressions fall into different classes of "temporal persistence" here, which are presently being charted and analysed logically.

Finally, temporal expressions are just one way of "taking our bearings" in the world, of course. A similar task lies ahead as regards *spatial* indicators.

3.6 Intensionality

Perhaps the most characteristic feature of human language is its intensionality. We do not only communicate brute facts, but also meaningful relations between them, as well as our intentions, attitudes, and expectations towards them. This is abundantly reflected in the structure of natural language, which has a plethora of expressions for modality, causality, wishing, believing, knowing, etc. Various major classes of such expressions have been studied, both in logic and linguistics, often within the broad setting of so-called "Possible Worlds Semantics". (There are even such subdisciplines of this paradigm as Modal Logic, Deontic Logic, and Epistemic Logic.) The latter approach may be described roughly as modelling by *multiple reference*: Our uncertainty as to the actual state of the world is represented by a logical space of alternative worlds, which gives a range of possibilities to be entertained. For instance, we "know" only those statements which hold in our entire epistemic range. This idea has proved very powerful beyond its original uses. For instance, it has also become the core of the so-called Dynamic Logic semantics for programming languages (see Section 5).

Recently, however, various alternative approaches to intensional modelling have been proposed, both within Situation Semantics and within Discourse Representation Theory (see Section 2). For instance, on the latter view, discourse representations are themselves a kind of knowledge structure, providing a speaker's or hearer's model of the world, which is, moreover, computationally tractable—so that one can connect up the semantic *description* of cognitive notions with an account of cognitive *processing* (see Guenthner, Chapter 5). In fact, it can be said quite generally that contemporary semantics is moving from a view of language as a medium for the recording of truths about the world to one in which language is a cognitive instrument to interact with the world.

As is so often the case, these general ideas assume a practical shape in artificial intelligence. For instance, we live in a world not just consisting of facts, but also structured by regularities as perceived by us. Thus, we organise facts intensionally through *causal connections*. This process needs to be understood, both as regards semantic structures and processing strategies, in order to arrive at workable models emulating our competence in organising data, and planning actions on this basis.

4. GENERAL ISSUES

The above list may have given an idea of at least some of the main themes in contemporary semantics, and their diversity. Nevertheless, there are also general issues permeating many of these separate directions of research. A few of these will be brought out for their potential cognitive significance.

One general theme is the question of whether, in all these various semantic proposals, the earlier hypothesis of *compositional* stepwise interpretation can be maintained. As was mentioned in Section 2, this hypothesis is tied up with explaining the indubitable learnability of human languages. But, on the other hand, the latter achievement could tolerate a certain amount of *contextuality*, i.e. the phenomenon of certain expressions only being fully interpretable in a wider context. At present, these boundaries are being probed. For instance, recent research into generalised quantifiers is bringing out "emergent" semantic phenomena, when putting together sentence meanings, which show that the whole is sometimes (a bit) more than its parts. Another relevant development here is the current research into the "dynamics of interpretation" (See van Benthem, Chapter 8).

Then, in many of the above special areas, there is a distinction to be made between language-specific facts and *semantic universals*, stable across human languages. For instance, the major laws of generalised quantifiers, or free Boolean operators, hold in all human languages—modulo some syntactic idiosyncracies. One notable example is the monotonicity (in the earlier sense) of the basic determiners everywhere. It is here where semanticists are looking for the cognitive grounding of their discipline: Such regularities contain valuable clues for a theory of cognition and communication.

Another instance of this attempt at finding a suitable level of abstraction for semantic theorising can be found in Section 3. After a long period of concentration on specific lexical items, there is now a tendency towards describing what might be called *semantic mechanisms* and their dynamic behaviour, e.g. Boolean compounding, or the creation of a temporal perspective. This fits in well with recent attempts at constructing semantically well-motivated grammars stressing type-analogies across the whole of a language. (A prominent example is the earlier-mentioned "categorial grammar", relating grammatical categories to logical types.) Evidently, more global semantic mechanisms form precisely the level of abstraction where one expects to find significant semantic universals.

A final pervasive issue throughout semantics is the role of *inference*. An important test for proposed theories is that they should account for our pre-theoretical logical judgements of validity. Of course, eventually, theoretical developments can also influence and reshape such judgements. (Here is where semantic theory interacts with cognitive practice.) One important feature of modern research in this area is a certain *multiplicity*. It has been found that there need not be one single notion of validity for all logical purposes, but different ones for different functions of reasoning. For instance, classical logic is *monotone* (in a sense connected with the earlier-mentioned one):

> if B follows from A,
> then B also follows from A plus C.

Thus, additional information does not affect conclusions already reached. This stability is bought at a price, however. Classically, we can only draw those conclusions at any instant of which we are absolutely sure—and there may be few of those. In many practical situations, where decisions have to be made, this will not do; and there are rules for drawing additional inferences. For instance, one might temporarily assume to hold what has not been disproved yet. Naturally, such less absolute conclusions are less robust, and may have to be withdrawn in the light of further evidence. Thus, many important varieties of practical reasoning are *non-monotone*. There is a very lively research going on, both in general semantics and in the field of artificial intelligence, into finding the most useful types of non-monotone inference, striking the right balance between boldness and prudence (see van Benthem, Chapter 8).

Another basic feature of reasoning is the interaction of *inference* and advantageous *representation* of the data to perform inference upon. One way of looking at the earlier list of topics in the semantics of natural language is as being an attempt to find logical theories that optimise both.

5. THE COMPUTATIONAL CONNECTION

One of the notable developments in recent years has been the confluence of concerns in linguistic semantics and logic on the one hand, and those in computer science and artificial intelligence on the other. It turns out that many of the above themes are common ground—and researchers on both sides of the fence are beginning to appreciate, and apply each other's work. In a sense, these parallels are not surprising, given the fact that computer languages are a subspecies of the genus "language", both in their grammatical structure and their communicative functions. But even so, the extent of the above commonality is striking. Some examples may exemplify this trend, reinforcing the similar point made by van Benthem (Chapter 8).

In the semantics of programming languages, many of the earlier topics return. For instance, so-called Operational or Dynamic Semantics employs a form of the possible worlds framework, where "worlds" are possible memory states of the computer, and "correctness statements" about a running program express that a certain desired outcome holds in all (relevant or "reachable") states. Thus, proof techniques from intensional logic have become applicable for the purpose of proving program correctness.

Standard logical modelling is even more natural for those programming languages which have themselves been developed on the analogy of certain formal logical languages. A prime example is the declarative language PROLOG, whose semantics is of the ordinary Tarskian variety (see Section 2). There is a twist, however. PROLOG programs are interpreted by reference not to *all* their Tarski models, but just the smallest, or *minimal* ones (in a suitable sense of "closest fit"). This restriction to minimal models increases the number of inferences that may be drawn about a PROLOG program (typically, one obtains certain principles of "Induction" and "Completion"). On the other hand, such inferences may have to be withdrawn or modified as the program increases: reasoning in the semantics of PROLOG is non-monotone. This minimal model semantics can be extended to include all of Fregean predicate logic, as has been done, for example, in the theory of *circumscription* in artificial intelligence.

Another point of contact between the above semantic investigations and computational concerns is the use of so-called "common sense" or "naive physics" representations in artificial intelligence. For example, it has been found that providing planning systems with a fully-fledged "scientific" world picture is unworkable. What is needed instead is a relatively simple heuristic representation—for which clues are being sought in natural language. A major example is again the temporal or spatial perspective.

In this same setting, more general intensional aspects have also turned out to be increasingly important. Planning systems often need to reflect on their knowledge, or lack of it, in order to guide their course of action. Thus, epistemic logics, and epistemic trends in modern semantics generally, are becoming of practical importance. Another illustration of this same phenomenon may be observed in automated dialogue systems: successful discourse techniques depend heavily on the mutual knowledge which participants have about each other's knowledge and expectations. For instance, a correct answer to a question is one which will direct the listener to the true state of affairs given *his* or *her* particular state of knowledge. But, of course, the same holds for man–machine dialogues in natural language processing.

In addition, at a much more specific level of detail, analogies with natural language semantics emerge throughout. For instance, like natural languages, programming languages have a Boolean structure, though be it with a more dynamic flavour (IF THEN means conditional choice, AND means sequential conjunction). Similar correspondences arise with anaphoric relations (see Section 2) binding terms to each other across pieces of text. Also, the notion of general linguistic category structure, with its attendant logical type theory, has proved a striking unifying theme across natural languages and programming languages.

Actually, there is two-way traffic in many of these cases. Logical formalisms provide a general inspiration for various computing formalisms. But, conversely, the more dynamic twist to which these have been put there, also turns out quite useful for a better understanding of natural languages— witness recent "dynamic logics" for describing anaphora and Boolean control in natural language. Thus, ordinary semantics is becoming more dynamically and computationally oriented in the process of application.

6. DIRECTIONS TO BE PURSUED

From the preceding overview, various promising directions of research are discernible which can be expected to come to fruition within the next few years. We list a few desiderata which seem reasonably realistic:

- To create a semantically well-motivated, generally acceptable grammatical theory which can serve as a common framework for theoretical investigation and practical purposes, such as natural language processing.

Given the present converging tendencies in linguistic semantics, this seems a reasonable expectation. Such a uniform theory would encourage the exchange of linguistic results, while preventing unnecessary duplications in writing parsers and other paraphernalia in current European projects in this area.

- To arrive at a general framework for discourse representation which is precise enough to admit of a stable theory and a useful computational implementation.

Some variant of the theories described in Guenthner (Chapter 5) can presumably do this job. An additional test of adequacy here will be if the framework can bridge the still existing gap between more detailed formal studies at the sentence level, and more informal, but often descriptively richer studies in text linguistics and analytic philosophy of language (Speech Act Theory), and more computationally oriented studies of discourse.

- To find a new logical paradigm of an epistemic slant, to replace (or at least, reform) possible worlds semantics as a covering framework for foundational investigations into semantic theories.

There is a multitude of proposals on the market these days, carrying banners such as "partiality" and "verification", and already a certain theoretical unification can be seen in progress.

- To introduce a dynamic perspective into semantics, linking up more closely with computational concerns.

Again, there are already quite a few proposals to this effect in the literature, but the list of desiderata to be fulfilled is large. The proper theory should give a good account of the various functions of language, of the dynamic phenomenon of "linguistic control" in communication, and also of the logical dynamics described in the earlier passage on varieties of inference.

This list may seem over-ambitious at first sight. But, it is grounded in already existing tendencies in semantic research. Moreover, in pursuing both theoretical and practical aims in cognitive science, we may have to set our sights higher than is usually done in the "piece-meal strategies" of normal science. Perhaps, this is illustrated most easily on the practical side. If we are to have any hope of intelligent natural language processing systems, which are able to carry on a meaningful dialogue with their users, virtually all of the above desiderata become urgent concerns, within the realm of one single application. Thus, practical requirements may actually serve to remind the theorists of their wider obligations.

BIBLIOGRAPHY

Historical

Boole, G. (1854). *An investigation of the laws of thought, on which are founded the mathematical theory of logic and probabilities.* London: Walton and Maberley.

Frege, G. (1879). *Begriffsschrift, eine der arithmetischen nach gebildete Formelsprache des reinen Denkens.* Halle: Nebert Verlag.

Kneale, W. & Kneale, M. (1962). *The development of logic.* Oxford: Clarendon Press.

Parret, H. (Ed.) (1976). *History of Linguistic Thought and Contemporary Linguistics.* Berlin: De Gruyter.

Logic and Language

Davidson, D. & Harman, G. (Eds) (1972). *Semantics of Natural Language*. Dordrecht: Reidel.
Dummett, M. (1973). *Frege. The philosophy of language*. London: Duckworth.
Flew, A. (Ed.) (1952/1953). *Logic and language*. Oxford: Blackwell.

Semantic Frameworks

Austin, J. (1962). *How to do Things with Words*. Oxford: Oxford University Press.
Barwise, J. & Perry, J. (1983). *Situations and attitudes*. Cambridge, Mass.: Bradford Books/MIT Press.
van Benthem, J. (1988). Games in logic: A survey. In J. Hoepelman (Ed.), *Representation and reasoning*. Tübingen: Niemeyer Verlag.
Creswell, M. J. (1973). *Logics and languages*. London: Methuen.
Fauconnier, G. (1985). *Mental spaces*. Cambridge, Mass.: MIT Press.
Fenstad, J.E., Halvorsen, P.K., Langholm, T., & van Benthem, J. (1987). *Situations, language and logic*. Dordrecht: Reidel.
Grice, P. (1975). Logic and conversation. In P. Cole & J. Morgan (Eds), *Syntax and semantics. Vol. III: Speech acts*. London and San Diego: Academic Press.
Gries, D. (1981). *The science of programming*. Heidelberg: Springer.
Heim, I. (1982). *The semantics of definite and indefinite noun phrases*. Dissertation. Department of Linguistics, Massachusetts Institute of Technology.
Hintikka, J. & Kulas, J. (1983). *The game of language*. Dordrecht: Reidel.
Kamp, H. (1984). A theory of truth and semantic representation. In J. Groenendijk, T. Janssen, & M. Stokhof, (Eds), *Truth, interpretation and information*, pp. 1-41. Dordrecht: Foris.
Lorenzen, P. & Lorenz, K. (1978). *Dialogische Logik*. Darmstadt: Wissenschaftliche Buchgesellschaft.
Montague, R. (1974). *Formal philosophy*, (edited by R.H. Thomason). New Haven: Yale University Press.
Searle, J. (1969). *Speech acts*. Cambridge: Cambridge University Press.
Seuren, P. (1985). *Discourse semantics*. Oxford: Blackwell.
Tarski, A. (1956). *Logic, semantics, metamathematics*. Oxford: Oxford University Press.

Semantic Themes

Leach, G. (1977). *Semantics*. Harmondsworth: Penguin.
Lyons, J. (1968). *Introduction to theoretical linguistics*. Cambridge: Cambridge University Press.

Determiners and Generalised Quantifiers

van Benthem, J. (1986). *Essays in logical semantics*. Dordrecht: Reidel.
Cooper, R. (1983). *Quantification and syntactic theory*. Dordrecht: Reidel.
van Eyck, J. (1985). *Aspects of quantification in natural language*. Dissertation. Rijksuniversiteit Groningen. (To appear with Reidel, Dordrecht.)
Westerstahl, D. (1986). *Quantifiers in formal and natural languages*. Report 86-55, Center for the Study of Language and Information, Stanford. (To appear in D. Wunderlich & A. von Stechow (Eds), *Handbook of semantics*. Berlin: De Gruyter.)

Boolean Operators

Keenan, E. & Faltz, L. (1985). *Boolean semantics for natural language*. Dordrecht: Reidel.

Collectives, Plurals, Mass Terms

Carlson, G. (1977). *Reference to kinds in English*. Dissertation. University of Massachusetts. Department of Linguistics.
Link, G. (1983). The logical analysis of plurality and mass terms: A lattice-theoretical approach. In R. Bauerle et al. (Eds), *Meaning, use and interpretation of language*, pp.302-323. Berlin: De Gruyter.

Pelletier, J. (Ed.) (1979). *Mass terms*. Dordrecht: Reidel.

Properties and Types

de Bakker, J. (1980). *A mathematical theory of program correctness*. London: Prentice Hall.

Bealer, G. (1982). *Quality and concept*. Oxford: Clarendon Press.

Buszkowski,W., Marciszewski, W., & van Benthem, J. (Eds) (1988).*Categorial grammar*. Amsterdam and Philadelphia: John Benjamin.

Chierchia, G. (1985). Formal semantics and the grammar of predication. *Linguistic inquiry, 16*(3), 417-443.

Chierchia, G., Partee, B., & Turner, R. (Eds) (1988). *Properties, types and meanings*. Dordrecht: Reidel.

Scott, D. (1982). Domains for denotational semantics. In H. Nielsen & E. M. Schmidt (Eds), *Automata, languages and programming*, pp.577-613.

Turner, R. (1983). Montague semantics, nominalization and Scott's domains. *Linguistics and Philosophy, 6*, 259-288.

Temporal Perspective

Allen, J. (1983). Maintaining knowledge about temporal intervals. *Communications of the Association for Computing Machinery 26*, 832-843.

van Benthem, J. (1983). *The logic of time*. Dordrecht: Reidel.

Dowty, D. (1979). *Word meaning and Montague Grammar*. Dordrecht: Reidel.

van Eynde, F. (1987). *Time. A unified treatment of tense, aspect and aktionsart*. Leuven: Catholic University, EUROTRA Research Report.

Galton, A. (1984). *The logic of aspect*. Oxford: Oxford University Press.

Kamp, H. (1979). Instants, events and temporal discourse. In R. Bauerle et al. (Eds), *Semantics from different points of view*, pp.376-417. Berlin: Springer.

Michon, J. & Jackson, J. (Eds) (1985). *Time, mind and behavior*. Berlin: Springer.

Prior, A. (1967). *Past, present and future*. Oxford: Clarendon Press.

Reichenbach, H. (1947). *Elements of symbolic logic*. Berkeley: University of California Press.

Verkuyl, H. (1972). *On the compositional nature of the aspects*. Dordrecht: Reidel.

Intensionality

Asher,N. (1986). Belief in discourse representation theory. *Journal of Philosophical Logic, 15*, 127-189.

Cresswell, M. (1985). *Structured meanings*. Cambridge, Mass.: Bradford Books / MIT Press.

Gabbay, D. & Guenther, F. (Eds) (1984/1985). *Handbook of Philosophical Logic. Vols II and III*. Dordrecht: Reidel.

Stalnaker, R. (1984). *Inquiry*. Cambridge, Mass.: Bradford Books/MIT Press.

General Issues

Barwise, J. & Cooper, R. (1981). Generalized quantifiers and natural language. *Linguistics and Philosophy, 4*, 159-219.

Janssen, T. (1983). *Foundations and applications of Montague Grammar*. Dissertation. Amsterdam: Mathematical Centre.

Oehrle, R. et al. (Eds) (1988). *Categorial grammars and natural language structures*. Dordrecht: Reidel.

Partee, B. (1984). Compositionality. In F. Landman & F. Veltman (Eds), *Varieties of formal semantics*, pp.281-311.Dordrecht: Foris.

Zaefferer, D. (Ed.) (forthcoming). *Semantic universals and universal semantics*. Dordrecht: Foris.

Computational Aspects

Barwise, J. (1987). Noun phrases, generalized quantifiers and anaphora. In P. Gärdenfors (Ed), *Generalized quantifiers. Linguistic and logical approaches*, pp.1-29. Dordrecht: Reidel.

van Benthem, J. (1987a). Semantic automata. In J. Groenendijk, D. de Jongh, & M. Stokhof (Eds), *Studies in the theory of generalized quantifiers and discourse representation*, pp. 1-25. Dordrecht: Foris.

van Benthem, J. (1987b). Towards a computational semantics. In P. Gärdenfors (Ed), *Generalized quantifiers. Linguistic and logical approaches*, pp.31-71. Dordrecht: Reidel.

Goldblatt, R. I. (1982). *Axiomatizing the logic of computer programming*. Heidelberg: Springer.

Hobbs, J. (Ed.) (1985). *Common sense summer: Final report*. Report 85-35, Center for the Study of Language and Information, Stanford.

Lloyd, J. W. (1984). *Foundations of logic programming*. Heidelberg; Springer.

Newer Directions

van Benthem, J. (forthcoming). Semantic parallels in natural languages and computation. To appear in M. Garrido (Ed.), *Logic colloquium. Granada 1987*. Amsterdam: North-Holland.

Blamey, S. (1986). Partial logic. In D. Gabbay & F. Guenther (Eds), *Handbook of Philosophical Logic. Vol. III*, pp.1-70. Dordrecht: Reidel.

Gärdenfors, P. (1988). *Knowledge in flux: Modelling the dynamics of epistemic states*. Cambridge, Mass.: MIT Press / Bradford Books.

Groenendijk, J. & Stokhof, M. (1985). *On the semantics of questions and the pragmatics of answers*. Dissertation. Filosofisch Instituut, University of Amsterdam. (To appear with Oxford University Press.)

van der Sandt, R. (1988). *Context and presupposition*. London: Croom Helm.

Veltman, F. (1986). *Logics for conditionals*. Dissertation. Filosofisch Instituut, University of Amsterdam. (To appear with Cambridge University Press.)

CHAPTER 5

Discourse: Understanding in Context

Franz Guenthner

*Seminar für natürlich-sprachliche Systeme (SNS),
University of Tübingen, Tübingen, Federal Republic
of Germany*

If semantics is, as we maintain, the empirical study of how humans understand or interpret uttered sentences the way they do, there is no escape from the fact that semantics is part of cognitive science. (Seuren, 1985:284).

The general moral of all this is a lesson that some of us have taken too long too learn. Neither semantics nor cognition can be studied fruitfully on its own. Only by looking at them together can we hope to arrive, eventually, at a viable theory of either. (Kamp, 1984/1985:261).

1. INTRODUCTION: "MEANING" BEYOND THE SENTENCE

1.1 Three Levels of "Meaning"

Recent theories of discourse semantics share a number of common features that set them apart from most previous systematic attempts to come to grips with the meaning of natural language utterances within the confines of isolated sentences. Although it has always seemed obvious that an adequate account of the semantics and pragmatics of linguistic communication cannot limit itself to the examination of single speech acts, few theories of meaning and communicative intention have been able to bridge the gap between sentence meanings and the more complex meaning relations which govern communication in the form of discourses.

Sentence meanings have been described in detail in various accounts using techniques and concepts from formal logic (cf. the accompanying chapter on "Logic and Linguistics" and Section 1.2, below). These theories have made it clear that the relation between utterances and "world" (in the form of model-theoretic constructs) must play a central role in any semantic theory; but in taking this relation as their starting point, these theories produced concepts of meaning which are in many ways not adequate for a more comprehensive account of the complexities of either meaning or communicative interaction. Even though it was realised very early that in addition to descriptions of meaning expressed in purely *extensional* (or truth-conditional) terms, another level of description involving *intensional* entities was necessary, many kinds of semantic phenomena still remained beyond the reach of the theories developed in formal semantics.

One reason for the inadequacy of describing the meaning of natural language utterances in terms of their extensional and intensional properties alone can be found in the fact that neither of these levels are sufficient to capture all the meaning relations into which utterances may enter. Clearly extensional (or denotational) equivalence in a model says little about meaning equivalence; but even intensional equivalence (in the sense that intension may be said to determine extension) does not suffice. Many utterances may determine the same set of models (i.e. be true in exactly the same situations) without being semantically equivalent in all respects. A still finer grained notion of meaning is required. Various recent developments in discourse semantics (e.g. Kamp's "Discourse Representation Theory" and the related "file card semantics" due to Heim, Barwise, and Perry's "situation semantics", or Seuren's "discourse semantics") have introduced a concept of meaning—which we shall call "linguistic meaning" in the strict sense here—that is based on considerations concerning context-dependence somewhat different from earlier approaches. Already in work by Stalnaker (1978) and Kaplan (1977) contextual features (in particular indexical parameters) played a role in determining the interpretation of utterances (e.g. the proposition expressed in a context), with the result that the linguistic meaning of a sentence was identified with a function from contexts to propositions (where propositions are taken to be sets of so-called "possible worlds").

In the theories of discourse semantics mentioned above we can take the idea of the generalised context-dependence of meaning one step further. Here we can take the concept of "linguistic meaning" to be a function from representations to representations. Representations are in general available from the background as well as from previous discourse; the linguistic meaning of an utterance is thus taken to extend (or modify in some other way) representations into other representations. Below we shall give some examples of the kind of phenomena that can be accommodated within such accounts. Among the advantages of being able to describe semantic properties of utterances at the level of their extension (in a model), their interpretation (in terms of representations having definite truth conditions), and in terms of a function from representations to representations (their "linguistic meaning"), is that we can also set priorities right in terms of which levels of meaning description determine which other levels. It is the level of linguistic meaning which determines the level of interpretation and the latter determines extension.

1.2 The Limits of Formal Semantics

The methods of formal semantics have been very successful in relating the levels of interpretation and denotation via model-theoretically formulated truth conditions. These methods have found their way into computational accounts of meaning as well. Most varieties of natural language interfaces to databases (e.g. USL, Chat-80, TEAM, INTELLECT, and many others; cf. Wahlster, Chapter 7, below) have been based on either a direct or indirect use of translations into predicate logic (or predicate logic like query languages, e.g. SQL or even Prolog) to account for the retrieval of information from collections of facts in the form usually of relationally formatted databases. Such databases are in most essential respects quite similar to the model structures used in formal semantics to represent the "world".

The reason why these techniques (both in the setting of formal semantics and database querying) have been so successful resides in the fact that the models and their structures are known in advance. From a semantic point of view the meaning of queries is thus nothing more than the evaluation procedure (the truth conditions) which determine the truth values (or the satisfaction sets) of queries in the database. In such structures the meaning of the logical connectives can be given in a uniform manner as they can in the semantics of predicate logic; similarly, the extension of the lexical constants can be regarded as determining appropriate sets and relations in the database. In fact, it is even possible to determine in an exact way what the class of all "computable answers" with respect to such a database is.

As a model of communication, however, the presupposition that the structures underlying the exchange of information are always completely determined in advance is not realistic; on the contrary, quite a few characteristic features of ordinary discourse must necessarily remain neglected in such approaches. As a result, the methods and techniques developed for model-theoretic evaluation in "closed-world" type databases do not carry over very easily into theories whose goal it is to describe what is going on in communicative interactions where discourse functions play a fundamental role. What is needed is an account of discourse understanding which fares equally well with the restricted situation described above and with discourse phenomena which transcend the bounds of isolated sentences and their relations to models.

The following are just a couple of examples of the kinds of problems which arise once we leave the single sentence as the domain of linguistic description:

1. *Anaphoric links in a discourse*: almost every sentence in a discourse is implicitly or explicitly "connected" to elements of the part of the discourse that precedes it; the most obvious links are anaphoric constructions (in the personal, temporal or spatial domains).

2. *Discourse domains for quantifiers*: the range of most quantificational expressions (e.g. *every, no, sometimes, everywhere*, and many others) is rarely the domain of all objects, times or locations that exist but is always restricted by other conditions introduced in the discourse; these domains usually vary from sentence to sentence and have to be reconstructed in the comprehension process.

These and other examples make it clear that a proper treatment of the information conveyed in discourse cannot be reduced to purely model-theoretic properties of the constructions involved, for in many if not most cases the parameters of evaluation are not available independently of the discourses in question.

1.3 Towards a Theory of Communication and Understanding

In characterising the linguistic meaning of utterances as functions from representations to representations, we can also invoke representations in a general description of communication. For in the larger setting of information exchange, the participants (typically the "speaker" and the "recipient" of a discourse) will encode and decode the pieces of discourse that make up a "conversation" in function of the representations available to them. At least three such representations have to be distinguished: the representational set-ups of the speaker and of the recipient and the representation structure which is the point of the communicative interaction. In the context of the present discussion we may assume that all of these can be described in some format appropriate for characterising representational structures. A communicative act then involves the identification on the part of the speaker of the representation to be verbalised; how the speaker chooses (among the many possibilities) the appropriate verbalisation for this representation is one of the central problems in the theory of communication. Among other things, the speaker will use the fact that the representation the hearer can decode from his discourse has to result in the addition of a representation in the hearer's set-up which is interpretationally equivalent with the one he intends to communicate. There are quite a few requirements to be formulated with respect to this criterion, the minimal one being that the representations have identical truth conditions (cf. Appelt, 1986, for an extensive discussion of these matters).

A linguistically adequate theory of semantic representation must tell us how given a context the rules of linguistic meaning are instrumental in associating a representation with (i.e. in determining an interpretation for) a given discourse as well as of course a perhaps partial explanation of how this can fail to come about. Processing a discourse does not stop however when an interpretation is obtained; understanding what and why something is said certainly presupposes the presence of an interpretation. But the interpretation thus obtained will interact in many ways with the representations already present. Many new inferences will be drawn; some of these will depend on the idiosyncratic properties of particular representational set-ups, others will be of a more general nature. Indeed it seems that many of these inferential processes that go beyond interpretation can be controlled with linguistic means. The function of certain particles (e.g. *but, nevertheless, however*, etc.) has little if no effect on interpretation, but rather on how the interpretation of an utterance is to be related to other information (cf. Saeboe, 1987, for an account of discourse particles in the setting dialogues in natural language man–machine communication).

2. DISCOURSE AND REPRESENTATION

2.1 The Nature of Representations

In the rest of this survey of aspects and problems of discourse semantics we will have recourse to some of the central features of the framework of "discourse representation theory" (originally due to Kamp, 1981), as it allows a concise formulation of some of the current issues of research in this area; many of the features discussed here are of course present in other theories as well, just as many concepts developed in other approaches to discourse semantics can and should be carried over to this framework.

Most if not all approaches to discourse semantics agree in dividing up the general structure of a theory of discourse into the following components:

1. A *syntactic* account of the language under consideration.
2. A *mapping* from syntactic structures to representations.
3. A *specification* of the form of possible representations.
4. An *interpretation* of representations in models.

In terms of the concept of linguistic meaning mentioned above the construction of representations (i.e. component 2) takes on the central role both from an empirical as well as from a theoretical point of view. This component has to be sensitive both to the input coming from the syntax (in the form of syntactic analyses) as well as to the representations built up from prior portions of discourse.

The form of representations derived from natural language discourses is a matter of much discussion in all theories of discourse semantics. Even though it seems unquestionable that the expressive power of representations should include at least some version of standard predicate logic, semantic theories vary in the way such a version is to be encoded and how much additional expressive power is required in order to treat, for instance, various modal and temporal phenomena. As recent work—especially in the theory of anaphora—has shown, even the standard version of predicate logic is not an adequate tool for the accommodation of even very simple cases of pronominalisation.

Let us look at the form of semantic representations in Kamp's theory more closely. In its original formulation (Kamp, 1979; 1981) the theory was intended to cope with certain problems of anaphora on the one hand and with problems arising in the treatment of the distinction between certain tense forms in French (in particular, the distinction between the *passé simple* and the *imparfait*) on the other. For different reasons both of these issues are difficult to treat within a predicate logic framework as employed, for instance, in Montague Grammar.

Kamp calls the representations associated with a discourse "discourse representation structures" (DRSs). A DRS is defined to be a pair, <U,Con> consisting of a domain of "discourse referents" and a set of "conditions" on them. In the general case the referents in U will belong to different sorts (e.g. individuals, times, events, propositions, etc.) of first- and higher-order entities. We will consider only the one-sorted first-order case here. Given a discourse D the DRS K(D) constructed via the construction algorithm will thus contain the individuals explicitly introduced in D (the members of DR) as well as the set of conditions in which they are involved. The conditions are either atomic or complex; the latter include the traditional Boolean types (e.g. negation, disjunction, implication). Complex conditions are themselves constructed out of discourse representation structures. One of the most interesting applications of having complex conditions is that the discourse referents embedded in them are not available for pronominalisation in the same way as discourse referents introduced in the main DRS for the discourse. In this way many typical "binding" phenomena can be explained in terms of the structure of the conditions occurring in the representation. For instance, discourse referents introduced via universally quantified nounphrases can only be linked to pronouns in sub-DRSs at least as deeply embedded as the DRS in which the nounphrases occur. As a result, bindings of the following type are ruled out on configurational grounds:

Every man attended a party. *He enjoyed himself.

(For details concerning the "accessibility relation", which is responsible for ruling out the above anaphoric chain, cf. Kamp (1984).

On the other hand, there are binding phenomena where the force of a quantifier seems to be quite different from the natural translation into predicate logic:

If a student fails the exam, he has to take it again.

The indefinite article cannot simply be translated into an existential quantifier here, for such a translation would not allow for the "cross-reference" with the pronoun "he". The force of the quantifier is rendered more appropriately by a "universal" quantifier of the form:

$$\forall x \forall y (\text{student}(x) \ \& \ \text{exam}(y) \ \& \ \text{fail}(x,y) \rightarrow \text{has to take again}(x,y))$$

In discourse representation theory the "universal" effect of such nounphrases is dealt with in terms of interpretation of the conditional. The antecedent gives rise to exactly the same DRS as if it occurred alone, i.e. into a sub-DRS of the form:

x   y
student (x)
fail (x,y)
exam (y)

When such a DRS occurs as the antecedent of a conditional, pronouns in the consequent may be linked to discourse referents occurring in the antecedent:

The truth conditions of implicational conditions give rise to the universal

interpretation of the indefinite nounphrase: very informally, an implicational condition is true (with respect to a model) if every way of making the antecedent true constitutes a way of making the consequent true. (For a more formal definition of the syntax and semantics of the language of discourse representation theory, cf. Asher, 1986 and Guenthner, 1986.)

Equally interesting is the general notion of truth for discourse representation structures. A DRS K is said to be true (with respect to a model) if the domain U of K can be embedded into the domain of the model in such a way that all the conditions of K are true in M. What this means is roughly that the representation structure we derive from a discourse must be compatible with the way the world is. When K contains only atomic conditions, this actually boils down to saying that the representation can itself be taken for a submodel (or rather as a structure isomorphic to a submodel) of the world, (see van Benthem & van Eijck, 1982).

One of the attractive features of the use of DRSs is their manifold application. From a syntactic (and inferential) point of view, we may regard them as simply a set of formulas with certain semantic and deductive properties. This interpretation makes them very attractive for computational uses. Once we have derived such representations from natural language discourses we need to have access—depending on the particular type of interactive purposes—to the information they express. Given that the various types of conditions in representations have certain logical properties, it becomes possible to define deductive inference procedures on them. In addition to deductive manipulation, DRSs may be regarded as model-theoretic constructs in their own right, in the sense that each of them is in fact quite similar to a partial model corresponding to particular information states.

The representations constructed from discourses can also fruitfully be regarded from a psychological point of view as a kind of "mental model" that recipients of the discourse build up in response to utterances. From this point of view representations are to be studied in terms of their short- and long-term semantic memory properties. It is here that semantic and psychological theories of memory and comprehension will have to be co-ordinated most. Much attention will also have to paid to the way the information provided by the formal properties of the discourse interacts with various aspects of world knowledge and inferences made in terms of general background assumptions.

2.2 Aspects of Constructing Representations

The main goal of an integrated theory of discourse understanding is to associate representation structures with discourses as a function of their linguistic form and their context of occurrence. As already pointed out, the algorithm that accounts for the construction of the representation must be sensitive to both the representation derived for preceding parts of the discourse as well as to some representation of the non-linguistic context including background knowledge.

Some of the areas where systematic progress has been made are the following.

2.2.1 Nounphrases and Anaphora

The discourse function of indefinite and definite nounphrases as well as various constraints on anaphoric relations has received ample attention from linguistic, psychological, and computational points of view. Several important concepts for discourse analysis have been introduced specifically in connection with the problem of identifying the local domains with respect to which the resolution of cross-reference links is to be constrained; for instance, the notion of *focus* (Grosz, 1981; Sidner, 1983), *salience orderings* in the sense of Smaby, (1979; 1981) and Lewis (1981), and *mental spaces* (Fauconnier, 1985) constitute different attempts to structure the representations with respect to the availability of possible discourse antecedents for pronominal elements.

2.2.2 Tense and Events

Discourse structure is not only organised around individuals and their relations but also around temporal structures involving various temporal entities (states, processes, events, time periods, etc.). In many respects the linguistic means for temporal reference and temporal anaphora are quite similar to those in the domain of individuals, and it is therefore not surprising that much recent research has concerned the temporal organisation of discourse. For instance, Kamp's discourse representation framework originated from a concern with the treatment of certain tense forms in French (the *passé simple* and the *imparfait*) whose main functions cannot be described in purely truth-conditional terms but rather in the way they impose constraints on the overlap and separability of the events they introduce (cf. Kamp, 1979; 1981; Partee, 1984; Dowty, 1986). Recent work on event structures and event and proposition anaphora by Bäuerle (1987) provides a unified account of various kinds of anaphoric relations based on a Davidson approach to events within discourse representation theory, where events are taken to be basic entities and where the relational structure of propositions reduces to the specification of thematic roles of the various "arguments" of the event.

2.2.3 Propositional Attitude Reports

The semantics of indirect discourse remains a major research area in several disciplines and any comprehensive account of discourse understanding will have to tackle this problem, not only because ordinary discourses abound with "psychological verbs" like believe, know, etc. but also because the relations expressed by these verbs play a central role in any theory of understanding. Recent studies of propositional attitudes have shown that the central issue in this area should be regarded as the interaction of a number of cognitive states (of the person uttering the sentence containing the report, of the person to whom the attitude is attributed, as well as the person receiving the report) and their connections to the world. Some promising work on belief and related attitudes has been advanced in the context of discourse representation theory (cf. Asher, 1986; 1987). These studies rely on the characterisation of attitudes in terms of representation structures in an essential way.

2.2.4 Macrostructures of Discourse

One can approach the question of discourse structures from below in terms of the effect of linguistic constructions (like the ones mentioned up to now), but this approach alone cannot suffice for a general characterisation of what makes a sequence of sentences into a text or into a dialogue. Much of the early work in discourse analysis has been concerned with the so-called "macrostructures" of discourse in one way or another. This work seems to fall into several traditions depending on the source discipline. For instance, several concepts of "story grammars" have been employed by psychologists interested in comprehension; more prominently, such concepts as Minsky's "frames" or Schank's "scripts" have been used widely in AI research in text understanding. A survey of linguistic approaches to the global architecture of discourse can be found in van Dijk (1977; 1981); a computational approach to higher-level discourse structures is outlined in Polanyi (1986).

One of the major desiderata in discourse theory is relating the "macro-" and "microstructure" approaches into a single framework for neither of these can reach an adequate account of discourse alone. This gap is felt most severely in the setting of computational treatments of discourse where both approaches must be carried out simultaneously if workable models of discourse understanding are to be realised.

2.3 Manipulating Representations

One of the most pressing goals in discourse processing is a proper theory of how representations can be "manipulated". Inferential processes concern representations in at least two ways: First, it has become widely acknowledged that the construction of representations will involve inferential steps at every corner, because a lot of the information needed to make the appropriate links between various bits of representations is in general not given explicitly in the discourse itself. Well-known examples are to be found in the area of anaphora resolution for pronouns and definite nounphrases or in the construction of implicit temporal links between the events introduced in a discourse. Even though inferences of this type are clearly rather restricted, little is known about their formal properties. Secondly, if one is interested in deriving information that is only implicitly given in a representation, more general inference mechanisms have to be applied.

One approach consists in using techniques from automatic theorem proving where representations play the role of a "deductive" database much in the style of logic programming. This method can be used—within the general limits of theorem proving for predicate logic—as long as the representations have an interpretation in terms of standard logic.

Another approach might be keyed more towards the particular form of the representation language itself. For instance, the representation language underlying Kamp's discourse representation theory is in many respects a "quantifier-free" version of predicate logic; the quantificational force of the discourse referents is provided by their particular occurrence in conditions. An inference system for this language seems in many respects to be much closer to actual steps of reasoning than what goes on in say resolution (or other) types of automated theorem proving. For instance, the rules for manipulating the standard Boolean connectives must take the quantifiers into account as well. As a result, many of the inferences that humans seem to make spontaneously turn out to be one-step inference rules here as opposed to applications of several inference rules in predicate logic. An interesting example is the generality of the rule of modus ponens in such a system: It combines the standard rule of modus ponens together with the rules for universal instantiation and existential generalisation into one. With it we can derive quite a few inferences in one step as in the following example:

> every student likes a professor that he knows
> John is a student
> _____
>
> John likes a professor
> John knows a professor

An extremely interesting inference system for such quantifier-free presentations of predicate logic was in fact already invented by Peirce towards the end of the last century with the motivation of capturing "immediate" inferences in a systematic way. Peirce's system contains five rules of inference all of which affect Boolean connectives and quantifiers at the same time (see Roberts, 1973, for a presentation of Peirce's inference system).

A major area for research stands in wait of new discoveries here: How can the complexity of what we might call "natural reasoning" be characterised. Clearly a substantial part of ordinary reasoning with classical inference schemata can be performed in real time by humans, e.g. all forms of the generalised modus ponens discussed above. But the inference schemata that are performed automatically so to speak are in general of a quite shallow nature. Determining the "depth" of spontaneous inferences in terms of the syntactic and semantic structure of the discourses and the representations on which they are based will be of great importance both for the psychology of reasoning as well as for the construction of more feasible systems of discourse comprehension. Work in this direction can be found in various approaches to reasoning (cf. Johnson-Laird, 1983; Evans, 1982; and the collection of papers in Myers et al., 1986).

Besides inferences of the classical, i.e. monotonic, sort—which in the long run is appropriate only when the domains of discourse are held constant—it is more than imperative to address attention to reasoning processes which govern the dynamic development of discourse domains. Recent attempts to capture the many varieties of so-called default and non-monotonic reasoning are central to a theory of inference geared towards discourse. At present it is still unclear to what extent there are common underlying principles at work here; many examples from the area of default assumptions in the theory of frames seem to be of a different nature from the problems that arise in connection with the incremental nature of knowledge due to incoming new information. Separating out the various issues and the principles that govern them is one of the most urgent desiderata for all theories of discourse understanding.

3. TYPES OF MEANING RELATIONS

The processing of a discourse should result in a representation structure which we may regard as the "information content" of the discourse; this representation may then enter into a variety of relations with the "world" (models, situations, etc.). Semantic theories have in general concentrated on such relations in one way or another. In particular, the concept of truth has played the fundamental role here.

Given the concept of a representation there are, however, other semantic relations which do not necessarily involve reference to the world in any essential way. These are relations that govern the way representations may be extended or modified in the course of a discourse.

We shall call relations of the first kind T-relations (for "truth"-relations) and relations of the second kind D-relations (for "discourse"-relations). In diagrammatic form:

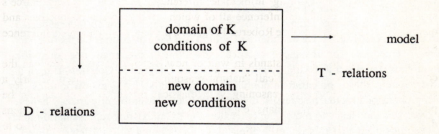

Besides truth a number of related concepts can be defined in terms of how a representation may be related to the world. Among these are such notions as (logical) consequence or entailment between representations, or the consistency of a representation. Other T-relations are such concepts as "fictional" or various notions of "probability", as well as the notion of vagueness which concerns the criteria (or absence of such) of the way predicates in the representation are related to extensions.

More central to discourse processing are relations that describe the conditions under which sentences may be incorporated into existing representations by extending or modifying them. Foremost among these relations are such notions as presupposition and ambiguity. Both of these have most often been studied from the point of view of truth relations, but it seems more appropriate to consider them as relations internal to the structure of representation.

The discourse approach to presupposition has been pursued in the work of Heim (1983), van der Sandt (1982), and others. These theories have demonstrated that many instances of the so-called "projection" problem of presuppositions can be dealt with if one starts from the idea that the presuppositions of a sentence have to be entailed by the context into which the sentences (or rather their assertional content) is to be incorporated. Take for instance a conditional sentence like

if Fred is ill, his children will take care of him

whose consequent (and thus the sentence as a whole) presupposes that Fred has children. On the other hand, a conditional with the same consequent like

if Fred has children then his children will take care of him

does not carry the presupposition. The reason why the second conditional behaves in the way it does is due to the fact that the appropriate condition on the context will already have been added to the context (i.e. to the representation) when the consequent is processed.

Many cases of presupposition are such that it is the finer structure of the representation (e.g. in terms of the discourse referents introduced) and not some semantic correlate of the context (e.g. like Stalnaker's set of possible worlds) which must be invoked in determining the presuppositional properties of expressions. This remains particularly problematic in constructions involving complement constructions in non-extensional contexts (cf. for instance, Asher, 1987).

Ambiguity is another semantic problem which has been a major obstacle especially to computationally effective treatments of natural language discourse. On the one hand, many sentences (for instance sentences involving more than one quantified nounphrase) turn out to be highly ambiguous when analysed in isolation. But on the other hand, these potential ambiguities very rarely lead to difficulties for comprehension in actual discourses. If we take the view that ambiguity arises whenever a given sentence leads to more than one extension of an existing representation, then it becomes clear that this representation plays an essential role in determining the proper analysis of incoming sentences. This is easy to see in the case of purely lexical ambiguities, but less obvious at the level of "structural" ones. A major research topic in this area is thus the "co-routining" of syntactic analysis with the construction of representations. Consider a typical case: The ambiguities in a sentence like

He saw a girl with the telescope

are most often resolved once the representation built up prior to this sentence is known, as for instance in:

> John received a telescope for his birthday. He saw a girl with the telescope

Only a systematic account of the interplay of syntactic, representational as well as default assumptions will lead to an adequate account of how ambiguities are resolved in discourse processing. The important consequence to draw from a discourse account of phenomena like presupposition and ambiguity is that they have little if anything to do with T-relations; they concern the internal well-formedness of representations whose relations to the world are entirely another matter.

Besides presupposition and ambiguity we want to include accounts of "coherence", "redundancy", and "informativeness" as further properties of utterances to be studied as conditions on the way representations may be extended. For instance, a representation might be qualified as incoherent if there are no links (e.g. between discourse referents) in the representation. Of course, an extensive study of such phenomena is still outstanding; it will have to include not just the local properties of representations in terms of discourse referents and their conditions but also structures of a higher level which are usually not given in an explicit manner. It is here that the study of such notions as frames and scripts will have to interact with the linguistic features we have been discussing so far.

4. STRUCTURING DISCOURSE

4.1 Varieties of Discourse Structure

An alternative approach to the more content-oriented macrostructure theories of the global structure of discourse has recently been put forth in Grosz and Sidner (1986). These authors propose a computational model that supplements the actual linguistic structure of a discourse (as given by the sequence of sentences making up the discourse) with a level consisting of discourse "intentions" and a level consisting of "attentional states". This theory aims at an integration of work in speech act theory and intentional theories of meaning in the Gricean tradition with previous work on focussing in discourse. Both the intentional and attentional levels are regarded as hierarchically organised; it is the intentional structure of a discourse which determines to a large extent the attentional one and it is the latter which is taken to be responsible for the control of the contextual information relevant for the processing of utterances at a particular point in the discourse.

4.2 Approaches to "Focus"

The concept of "focus of attention" is used in several AI-based theories of discourse comprehension, in particular those connected with issues concerning the resolution of anaphora. Grosz (1981) and examines task-oriented dialogues and develop several levels of focussing ("immediate focus", "global focus", etc.) as well as diverse internal structures of focus representation.

Sidner (1983) extends the above work in attempting to provide an algorithmic characterisation of the establishment and change of focus domains. Further ramifications of these approaches can be found in Reichman (1985), whose notion of "context spaces" is a propositionally richer structure than the focus concepts.

The above work is an interesting and necessary complement to approaches like Kamp's discourse representation theory or Smaby's pronoun resolution algorithm and related theories; what has been missing, however, is an integration of the more structurally and algorithm-oriented theories like the latter with the more psychological ones in the style of Grosz and Sidner. Perhaps the recent work on "centering" described for instance in Grosz, Joshi, and Weinstein (1983) might form a starting point for a synthesis of the two approaches.

4.3 Approaches to "Relevance"

Sperber and Wilson (1986) present a theory of discourse and communication in which they pursue earlier work by Grice on conversational maxims. Their account is oriented towards the calculation of "contextual effects" of new information on background assumptions and involves detailed use of deductive operations in the process of determining which context sets are involved in communicative intentions. Like the concept of focus, the notion of relevance will certainly be central to any future theory of discourse processing; precise operational accounts of these notions have up to now not been available.

4.4 Combining Speech Act Theory and Discourse Semantics

That the encoding and decoding of discourse is a pragmatic activity which is governed by general principles of cooperative action is something that has long been realised; the various approaches to speech act theory are thus eminently relevant here. Already in the work of Grosz and others on task-oriented dialogues (cf. Grosz, 1981; Litman & Allen, 1987) the emphasis on the plan structure and on other intentional aspects forms the basis of a general approach to discourse structure. More recently, the relation between illocutionary acts and the intended perlocutionary effects has been studied in the context of default rules; here again we find a convergence between different strands of analysis of speech act theory, planning, non-monotonic reasoning, and discourse understanding (cf. Perrault, 1987, for a first synthesis).

5. PROSPECTS AND APPLICATIONS

The question of what makes a sequence of sentences into a coherent and meaningful whole is a research issue which is being pursued from many different angles and within all the disciplines interested in explaining the cognitive aspects of language and communication. Each discipline sheds a different light on the many factors that must be considered if we want to grasp what underlies the human capacity to communicate in ever changing contexts.

A more adequate account of discourse understanding can only be achieved via an integration of the insights that linguistics, psychology, artificial intelligence, and logic bring to bear on the processes and constraints involved in relating utterances to the effects of understanding these bring about.

In spite of the seemingly great divergence in this field, there is a common consensus that progress can only be achieved by trying to provide descriptions of discourse production and comprehension that make sense from a computational perspective. All of the approaches mentioned in this brief survey are to be considered as small steps towards isolating and then integrating the many mental operations that characterise the ability of humans to manipulate the information available to them in a linguistically and cognitively manageable way. The role of computational modelling of such processes has turned out to be methodologically and theoretically extremely illuminating; not only do these constitute the only way of presenting analyses of communicative acts in such a way that their assumptions and predictions can be appropriately characterised and falsified, but they also help pave the way for applications which would otherwise not stand a chance of being realised. Sophisticated man–machine communication in all areas will only be possible once mechanisms governing ordinary communication are integrated in precise theories of discourse.

REFERENCES

Appelt, D.(1986). *Planning English sentences*. Cambridge: Cambridge University Press.

Artificial Intelligence (1980). Special Issue on "Non-monotonic logic", *13*, 1–2.

Asher, N. (1986). Belief in discourse representation theory. *Journal of Philosophical Logic, 15*, 127-189

Asher, N. (1987). A typology of attitude verbs and their anaphoric properties. *Linguistics and Philosophy, 16*, 125-197.

Barwise, J. & Perry, J. (1983). *Situations and attitudes*. Cambridge, Mass.: Bradford.

Bäuerle, R. (1987). *Ereignisse und Repräsentationen*. FNS-Script, University of Tübingen.

Bosch, P. (1983). *Agreement and anaphora*. London and San Diego: Academic Press.

Brady, M. & Berwick, R. (Eds) (1983). *Computational models of discourse*. Cambridge, Mass.: MIT Press.

Clark, H. (1981). Definite reference and mutual knowledge. In A. Joshi, I. Sag, & B. Webber (Eds) *Elements of discourse understanding*. Cambridge: Cambridge University Press.

Dowty, D. (Ed.) (1986). Special Issue of *Linguistics and Philosophy* on "Temporal reference".

Evans, J.(1982). *The psychology of deductive reasoning*. London: Routledge and Kegan Paul.

Fauconnier, G.(1985). *Mental spaces*. London: Bradford.

Gazdar, G. (1979). *Pragmatics: Implicature, presupposition and logical form*. London and San Diego: Academic Press.

Gazdar, G. (1982). On a notion of relevance. In N. Smith (Ed.), *Mutual knowledge*. London and San Diego: Academic Press.

Grice, P. (1975). Logic and conversation. In P. Cole & J. Morgan, (Eds), *Speech Acts*. Syntax and Semantics, Vol. 3, pp.41-58. London and San Diego: Academic Press.

Grosz, B. (1981). Focusing and description in natural language dialogues. In A. Joshi, I. Sag, & B. Webber (Eds), *Elements of discourse understanding*. Cambridge: Cambridge University Press.

Grosz, B. & Sidner, C. (1986). Attention, intentions, and the structure of discourse. *Computational Linguistics, 12*, (3), 175-204.

Grosz, B., Joshi, A., & Weinstein, S. (1983). Providing a unified account of definite noun phrase anaphora. *Proceedings of the 21st Annual Meeting, ACL.*

Guenthner, F. (1986). Linguistic meaning in discourse representation theory. *FNS-Bericht-86-4*, 569-598. University of Tübingen.

Heim, I. (1982). Definite and indefinite noun phrases. Ph.D. Dissertation, University of Massachusetts.

Heim, I. (1983). On the projection problem for presuppositions. In *Proceedings from the Second Annual West Coast Conference on Formal Linguistics.*

Johnson-Laird, P. (1983). *Mental models.* Cambridge: Cambridge University Press.

Joshi, A., Webber, B., & Sag, I. (Eds) (1981). *Elements of discourse understanding.* Cambridge: Cambridge University Press.

Kamp, H. (1979). Instants, events and temporal reference. In R. Bäuerle et al. (Eds), *Semantics from different points of view*, pp.376-417. Heidelberg: Springer.

Kamp, H. (1981). Belief attribution and context. *FNS-Bericht-86-13.* University of Tübingen.

Kamp, H. (1984). A theory of truth and semantic interpretation. In J. Groenendijk, M. Stokhof, & T. Janssen, (Eds), *Truth, interpretation and information.* (First published in Groenendijk et al. (Eds) *Formal methods in the study of language*, Mathematical Centre Tracts 136, Mathematisch Centrum, Amsterdam, 1981.) Dordrecht: Foris Publications.

Kamp, H. (1984/85). Context, thought and communication. *Proc. Aristotelian Society*, N.S., *XXXV*, 239-261.

Kaplan, D. (1977). *Demonstratives.* Unpublished ms.

Lewis, D. (1981). Score-keeping in a language game. In R. Bäuerle et al. (Eds), *Semantics from different points of view*, pp.172-187. Heidelberg: Springer.

Litman, D. & Allen, J. (1987). A plan recognition model for subdialogues in conversation. *Cognitive Science, 11*, 162-200.

Myers, T. et al. (Eds) (1986). *Reasoning and discourse processes.* London and San Diego: Academic Press.

Partee, B. (1984). Nominal and temporal anaphora. *Linguistics and Philosophy, 7*, 243-286.

Perrault, R. (1987). *An application of default logic to speech act theory.* CSLI-Report.

Polanyi, L. (1986). *The linguistic discourse model: Towards a formal theory of discourse.* BBN Report No. 6409.

Reichman, R. (1985). *How to make computers talk like you and me.* Cambridge, Mass.: Bradford.

Reinhart, T. (1980). Pragmatics and linguistics: An analysis of sentence topics. *Philosophica.*

Roberts, D. (1973). *The existential graphs of Charles S. Pierce.* The Hague: Mouton.

Saeboe, K. (1987). Semantics of discourse particles. *SNS-Bericht*, University of Tübingen.

Seuren, P. (1985). *Discourse Semantics.* Oxford: Basil Blackwell.

Sidner, C. (1983). Focusing in the comprehension of definite anaphora. In M. Brady & R. Berwick (Eds) *Computational models of discourse*, pp.264-330. Cambridge, Mass.: MIT Press.

Smaby, R.(1979). Ambiguous coreference with quantifiers. In F. Guenthner & S. Schmidt (Eds), *Formal semantics and pragmatics for natural languages.* Dordrecht: Reidel.

Smaby, R. (1981). Pronouns and ambiguity: A simple case. In U. Mönnich (Ed.), *Aspects of philosophical logic.* Dordrecht: Reidel.

Smith, N. (Ed.) (1982). *Mutual Knowledge.* London and San Diego: Academic Press.

Sowa, J. (1983). *Conceptual Structures.* London and San Diego: Academic Press.

Sperber, D. & Wilson, D. (1985). *Relevance.* Oxford: Basil Blackwell.

Stalnaker, R. (1978). Assertion. In P. Cole (Ed.), *Pragmatics.* Syntax and Semantics, Vol.9. London and Dan Diego: Academic Press.

van Benthem, J. & van Eijck, J. (1982). The dynamics of interpretation. *Journal of Semantics.*

van Dijk, T. (1977). *Text and context: Explorations in the semantics and pragmatics of discourse.* London: Longman.

van Dijk, T. (1981). *Studies in the pragmatics of discourse.* The Hague: Mouton.

van der Sandt, R. (1982). Kontekst en Presuppositie. Ph.D. Dissertation, Nijmegen.

Webber, B. (1978). A formal approach to discourse anaphora. *Tech. Report 3761*, BBN.

CHAPTER 6

The Challenge of Concrete Linguistic Description: Connectionism, Massively Parallel Distributed Processing, Net- linguistics.

Helmut Schnelle

Ruhr-Universität Bochum
Sprachwissenschaftliches Institut
Postfach 102148
D-4630 Bochum
Federal Republic of Germany

1. THE HISTORICAL CONTEXT

At least since Herder (1772), *language* has been conceived as the culminating *characteristic* of human *nature*. It has developed structurally on the basis of, and in relation to audition, the central sensory endowment of human beings. This central part of human nature is called "internal language" by Herder. In contrast to the internal language, uttered words and sentences are considered merely as manifestations and are called "outer language" (cf. Herder, 1772: 57). Herder summarises:

> Since all our senses cooperate, we are in the school of nature—through our hearing—learn to abstract and, at the same time, to speak . ... Could I only take together all pieces and visualize the tissue called human nature: really a tissue for language.

Language is thus primarily a natural faculty and only secondarily a collection of products of this faculty.

In contrast to this conception, the tradition since Greek and Roman times has been to think of *language* as *a collection of sequences of signs* (words), a tool used by human nature, which is essentially determined by the language-independent, rational, deliberating mind. Thinking is done by means of ideas which are only secondarily expressed by signs. Condillac, who is attacked in Herder's treatise, still confines his studies to the "operations by which we assign signs to our ideas" (Condillac, 1746), though he concedes "that the use of signs is the real cause for the progress of imagination, reflexion and memory" (ibid.). In the second part of his book, Condillac studies language starting from the question, "how human beings could have invented a language, i.e. an appropriate means for communication". This question seems natural if language is conceived merely as a system of signs or as a tool with certain structural properties. It is problematic, though, if language is in fact primarily part of the central tissue of the human organism, made up of complicated internal processes which are only partially represented by the sounds generated as outward manifestations.

Ever since the eighteenth century, there has been a basic conflict among linguists about the primary object of their discipline. There are those, who take it to be language, taken as sets of structured words and sentences, and there are the others who consider this "outer language" only as a partial (external) property of a more embracing complex of mental phenomena, which includes at least the faculty of speaking and understanding. Linguists working in the latter half of the last century were mostly interested in explaining language as a mental phenomenon whose essential feature was a capacity for development as determined by mental and physiological regularities (i.e. the internal properties). In contrast to this, the modern linguist of our century insisted on a restriction of the problem area, arguing that linguistics should confine its studies to the explanation of the forms and meanings of words and sentences (i.e. the manifestations) and should avoid any reference to mental phenomena. Modern linguistics added, however, an additional feature: The forms and meanings were no longer to be understood as a mere collection of facts but they were to form a system.

In the attempt to understand language as determined by a system, *linguistics was helped by formal logic.* The concentrated effort of formal logic had provided a powerful descriptive apparatus for specifying systems of expressions: the rules of formal symbol systems (calculi). The modification and adaptation of formal logical methods led to the precise concept of formal grammar on the one hand and to the notions of algorithm- and program-controlled universal automata on the other. The successes of these powerful descriptive means resulted in the quasi-unanimous view that linguistic knowledge is knowledge about symbolic expressions and must therefore be expressed in terms of symbolic rules or principles.

Only recently have alternative views again started to be voiced, views according to which it must eventually be possible to represent directly the "tissue of the internal language". I shall now try to give an introduction to the state of the art of this new development in theoretical linguistics and to the challenges posed by the problems it raises.

Let me first state again the problem of concrete linguistic description in its modern setting, which is to study the processes in the human organism (or in a similar machine) which organise and control speech acts in production and understanding. These studies should be concerned with evidence from neuroanatomy, neurophysiology and from the microbiology of the brain on the one side and with empirical linguistic observations and the linguistic models derived from these observations on the other. It should aim to *build a bridge between observations and structural generalisations about the linguistic behaviour of the human organism as a speaker/hearer, and observations and structural generalisations of the microbiological behaviour and form assigned to neurons, neuron modules (several hundred neurons), brain areas, etc.*

Many scientists still believe that attempts to build this bridge are premature because of the paucity of detailed results in the brain sciences. It is certainly true that the results obtained from the correlations of brain lesions and behaviour usually concern millions of neurons and that the impossibility of specific experiments on the human brain prevents a more detailed probing of the local processing in the speech areas of the cortex. Even so, there is a considerable amount of information available, such as neuroanatomic evidence about the structure and functioning of cortical units and modules in primates (e.g. in the visual area), global indications that the speech areas in the cortex area have a similar organisation, etc.

Admittedly, the empirical basis is certainly relatively sparse. This, however, does not at all prevent the development of theoretical linguistic modelling with the aim of building a bridge toward neurobiological modelling. We could and should try to develop methods of description which represent those features already known to exist in brain tissue. One of these features is, for example, that the system is made up of operational units which have numerical states of activities, and whose interaction in the changing of their states depends on the immediately preceding activities of their neighbours. The connectivities and the interactivities (regularities of interaction) of the units in the network, i.e. the network structure, which could also be called the connectivity state of the network, determine processes which are triggered by the (input-) events at sensory neurons and produce the (output-) events at motor neurons activating muscles. There is a sense in which the connectivity state of a linguistic network *embodies* the rules specifying the behaviour the network is to exhibit.

There has been much research activity in this direction during the last 10 years, an activity having its roots in a particular "prehistory". Basic ideas, such as those of McCulloch and Pitts (1943), Hebb (1949), and von Neumann (1949) had been transformed into technological design principles for the logical design of circuits by Burks and Wright (1953) and Burks and Wang (1957), and into theoretical nerve system analyses such as those of Rosenblatt (1962).

Some early attempts had even been made to apply the concepts to linguistics by Schnelle (1964), Lamb (1973), Reich (1967, 1973), and Hays (1973), but these descriptions were still too schematic. More important were the proposals of linguistic feature detection by Anderson et al. (1977) and Kohonen (1977).

An important event was the 1979 conference in La Jolla on *Parallel models of associative memory* (Hinton & Anderson, 1981). The study of language processing was much more specifically developed some years later by Cottrell and Small (1983, 1984), Dell (1986), Shastri and Feldman (1984), Waltz and Pollack (1985), Gigley (1985), McClelland and Rummelhart (1981), Schnelle (1981;1984), Schnelle and Job (1983), and Schnelle and Rothacker (1984). A decisive event was, undoubtedly, the appearance of the two PDP volumes edited by Rumelhart and McClelland (1986) and the handbook McClelland and Rumelhart (1988). The articles published in these volumes will be important references for future research in linguistics (e.g. Chs 15, 18, and 19). But the volumes also provide detailed discussions of theory and basic methodological questions.

It seems to me that the main challenge for concrete linguistic description at the moment is the definition of *a theoretical language for the specification of interactive networks, which is complete in that every process which can be defined by symbol manipulation rules can in principle also be definied in this language.* Such a theoretical language should be developed and applied to linguistic description as an alternative to the current theoretical languages which only directly specify regularities of language behaviour and leave it open as to how brain style specifications could be derived from rule specifications.

The main obstacle to the development and application of such a formal language to the description of dynamic tissue, instead of systems of sets of structured symbolic objects, is the previous success of symbolic formalisation and the ensuing habitual ways of conceptualising problems. According to Pinker and Prince (1988) it is the

'central dogma' of modern cognitive science, ... that intelligence is the result of manipulation of symbolic expressions... one of the reasons that the strategy has remained compelling is that it has given us precise, revealing, predictive models of cognitive competences that have required few assumptions about the underlying neural hardware other than that it makes available some very general elementary processes of comparing and transforming symbolic expressions (Pinker & Prince, 1988: 74).

It seems clear, however, that the "elementary processes" appear only elementary for us, because we are animals trained to read. Considered from the point of view of their realisation in the brain they are much less elementary. In any case, a reactive unit, such as a neuron or one of its idealisations is much more elementary. Our reading ability makes us believe that strings (or configurations) of symbols are elementary entities. In a mechanism, they are of course not elementary; a corresponding ability to distinguish and identify symbols and strings must be constructed. But the primary contrasting feature is actually something else: symbols are passive, keep their shape and change only under the control of a surveying agent! This is what makes them ideal entities for controlled activity, such as calculating and precisely controlled reasoning. However, our brain does not seem to have available such passive entities for "conceptual manipulation" (except perhaps in its long-term episodic memory).

We seem to be confronted with a deep split in our approach over a range of theoretical mathematical methods:

1. *Symbolic methods*, in formal logic, formal linguistics, theoretical computer science, basic research in mathematics; and
2. *Signal-theoretic (numerical) methods* in electronics, neurobiology, thermodynamics, concrete linguistics.

The former try to solve their problems by specifying rules operating on representations or, correspondingly, by programming instructions operating on stored non-numerical data (symbol configurations), the latter by designing the circuitry (i.e. the connections or, in the case of a continuum, the topology of a dynamic medium) of a system which channels (transmits and transforms) a data flow from input ports to output ports.

There are various possible levels of abstraction for signal-theoretic methods, according to how many empirical or technological details are represented. We may thus contrast a formal level of network analysis which merely specifies models in terms of units and their degrees of activities and interactivities with a level describing the empirical or technological details of neural wetware or electronic hardware (cf. Sejnowski & Rosenberg, 1987: 146; Smolensky, 1988). The formal level of network analysis has a similar role as have field-theoretic models to empirically observable fields (hydrodynamic, electromagnetic, etc.); in the latter case we have a system of partial differential equations describing the behaviour of spatio-temporal continua of interactive points with quantitative magnitudes.

But signal-theoretic methods (discrete or continuous) are almost totally unknown in academic circles used to thinking in terms of rules and representations of instructions. This makes it all the more particularly difficult to advocate alternative methods in the field of logic and linguistics, methods which, moreover, are often derived from the methods of associationism, the arch enemy of linguistic structuralism. By advocating their application we seem to be entering the lion's den in sheep's clothing.

Hence, the argument for a new descriptive method must be carefully prepared. The discussion of basic questions cannot be avoided, for many current conceptualisations about parallel processing are still rather confused. There are in point of fact two different approaches which will be discussed on pp. 156–157. Section 3 deals with those systems in which the structure of processing is still determined by stored control symbols (programs), which control concurrent activities in a set or collection of computers. These systems implement the current ordinary instruction/data (rule/representation) concepts directly into parallel processing systems—the collectionist approach to parallelism, as I shall call it. In Sections 4 and 5 this collectionist approach will be sharply contrasted with the connectionist approach, in which the system's knowledge is embodied in the connections among interactive units and not in the complexities of their states or state configurations and the co-ordinations of the latter. In spite of the technical differences of the collectionist and the connectionist approaches, the challenge with which they are confronted is common to both; its specification is the task of the next section.

2. SPECIFYING THE CHALLENGE

It is a basic assumption in cognitive linguistics, that the competence of *language is embodied in biological tissue* and that this embodiment differs from tissues embodying other competencies, such as conceptualising or inferencing on the one hand, or articulation and auditory discrimination on the other. Moreover, the different tissues involved cooperate in producing speech and understanding. In this sense, the classical assumption, that we have just one system of general intelligence, specifiable either by unconstrained formal symbol manipulation or by arbitrary "associative" connections between operational units, has been abandoned.

If formal linguistics is understood as a cognitive science, the statements it makes would have to be taken as *specifications of linguistic competence on a level which is still very abstract*. The theoretical language it uses does not make reference to parts of the tissues implementing the modules nor to idealisations of cells, etc.; it is satisfied with a reference to phonemes, words, sentences, and meanings corresponding to phonological, syntactic and semantic categories, and particular relations among such metalinguistic concepts. The fact that symbolic referents to metalinguistic concepts are used and combined into representations of strings, trees, etc., has not been considered to be in conflict with the ultimate task of linguistics of rendering the structure of language as it is embodied in a biological module, though it is obvious that there are no strings, trees, etc., in biological tissue. For the time being, linguistic specification is unwilling to leave the abstract level because the notational systems provided for defining complicated symbolic structures are so powerful and so well understood—mainly through the development of formal logic—that it seems foolish to change the representational system unless it were clear how the complexities which must be expressed in linguistics could—at least in principle—be rendered in other (perhaps more concrete) representational systems.

Formal cognitive linguistics does not exclude complementary *studies of algorithmic implementation*, including those using parallel processes. Indeed, some of these studies can be made on the basis of inessential and unproblematic changes in the formal approach. Studies of parallel implementation could be based on the following argument: Linguistics itself assumes a partitioning of its definition of language competence into components, such as phonology, syntax, semantics, etc. Conceiving these *components* as *working in parallel* seems to be empirically justified and can be linguistically as well as physiologically motivated. It is obvious that this move alone does not require a change of the notational and representational scheme. Even going further and thinking of *applying* particular *rules concurrently*, whenever the conditions for application are mutually independent, or even combining words and concepts with rules and developing *"word experts"* which apply their rules concurrently, merely results in particular systems of implementation—albeit parallel implementations, though—which refer to the symbolic forms of the same type as the formal definitions of grammatical structure. Abstract linguistics and such implementations are both compatible domains for symbol manipulation. Thus Fodor and Pylyshin (1988) suggest that "Classical models" of symbol manipulation may be implemented in "Classical machines" having:

> a 'message passing' architecture, like that of Hewitt's Actors . ... Classical architecture is. .. neutral on the question whether the operations on the symbols are constrained to occur one at a time or whether many operations can occur at the same time (ibid.: 14–15).

The essential character of these implementations is that the messages passed, stored, and retrieved "have a combinatorial structure which is causally implicated in the processing"(ibid.). This contrasts with *connectionism*. Connectionism is an essentially different approach as it does not use symbols, symbol configurations or symbol structures, whether stored, retrieved, or transmitted but merely specifies causal changes in the activities of units, activities which can be rendered numerically.

There are *two varieties of connectionism, localist and distributed*. In localist connectionist representations of a linguistic system, the individual units correspond to linguistic entities and concepts. In distributed connectionism, each linguistic entity or concept is "distributed" over many units such that the sets of units "embodying" different linguistic entities and concepts do not have to be completely distinct but may share some of their units. By this means, similarities between concepts appear to be easily implementable by the overlapping of sets of units.

The distinction between localist and distributed connectionism is not completely clear-cut, however. It is well-known from linguistic feature systems for sounds that similarities between two sound-concepts can be expressed through the features which are shared by the two sound-concepts. Because both levels are conceptual (the level of sound-concepts and the level of features), their connectionist counterpart would be localist as the units correspond to concepts, and at the same time distributed with respect to the level of sound concepts. Would this be an instance of localist or of distributed connectionism?

Net-linguistics is a variety of localist connectionism (which certainly would not exclude the last type of "distribution"). The concepts are occurrences of phonemes, words, phonological, syntactic, and semantic concepts and features, each of them represented by an interactive unit. The system is localist in that there is a one-to-one mapping between the occurrences of meta-linguistic concepts and units—it is distributed in the same way that, for example, bundles of phonological feature concepts provide a distributed representation of phoneme concepts. The basic activity values assumed are binary (active, non-active). Linguistic structures are represented by the set of those units which are, or have been, active since the beginning of a process of speech production or understanding of speech. In this sense, there is a homomorphism between rule systems and connectivities on the one hand and symbolic configurations and activity processes on the other.

There is one essential *difference between common connectionism and net-linguistics*: Common connectionism tries to model features of processing which are determined indiscriminately by linguistic, psychological, and physiological observations, whereas net-linguistics tries to isolate the purely linguistic aspects in the hope that the psychological and physiological aspects of typical performance processes will turn out to depend on merely gradual variations and a fine-grained subsymbolic distribution of large-grained net-linguistically defined structures. Even if this assumption is proved wrong it may be interesting to compare purely linguistically motivated networks—those of net-linguistics—with networks which superimpose empirical data and theoretical assumptions from different disciplines in a way that makes it impossible to indicate which structural features of the networks correlate with which discipline.

Whether connectionist or collectionist, all implementations of classical systems share a number of *basic features*. Mathematically, these systems may be presented as a set (of units, cells, places, or sites) with a topology (the connectivity among the units which defines the neighbourhood of each unit). There are, in addition, other sets to be considered (the possible activity and interactivity values) and also the class of possible mappings which assign activity and interactivity values to the units and neighbourhoods. The activity values represent the unit and local environment activities which may change from moment to moment, and the interactivity values represent the current interactivity "rules" or "laws" (i.e. regular interdependencies of activities and of interactivity changes).

We may render the mathematical "rules" by the following equations:

$$u' = F \left[\{ \ u \ \} \right]$$
$$F' = G \left[\{ \ u \ \}, \{ \ F \ \} \right]$$

The formulae indicate that u',the next state of unit u, depends on the current states of its neighbours ({ u }) in a way indicated by the interactivity function F. We assume that there is one such pair of equations for each unit, such that, in general, these formulae are different for different units. The first formula is sometimes called the *activation equation* and the second the *learning equation*. The system thus consists of an inhomogeneous, non-stationary dynamic field of interactivities. Note that u may itself be a member of its neighbourhood. Moreover, the interactivity F may change at the unit u as indicated by the learning equation, i.e. the next interactivity F' depends on the current activity of u and its neighbours and on the current interactivities of u and the neighbours that the learning function G indicates.

These specifications are still very general; nothing has been said as yet about the possible activity values of the units and their possible interactivity functions. We may, for instance, allow that the different activity states be rendered by strings of symbols and that the possible interactivities F be recursive functions on strings of symbols. In this case, the system would be equivalent to a network of Turing machines or universal computers whose communication would be defined by the interactivity functions. We could even introduce a distinction between proper units and the channel units placed between them. In this case, the structures representing the activity states of the channels would be messages transmitted from one "proper" unit to the other.

At the other extreme, we could just allow ourselves a binary set of activity values with Boolean interactivity functions. The corresponding networks would be logical nets such as those found in logical designs of hardware (Burks & Wright, 1953; Burks & Wang, 1957). Instead of Boolean functions we might take simple threshold functions; the corresponding nets would then be so-called formal nerve nets, first studied by McCulloch and Pitts (1943) or, alternatively, threshold logic nets (cf. Winder, 1968). There are well-known nets whose activity value sets and functions lie between these extremes, e.g. the cellular automata (see, e.g. Wolfram, 1986) and the systolic arrays. In the latter case the units are finite state automata. We shall not go into detail here, rather we shall turn to the currently most interesting systems—connectionist nets.

Typical connectionist nets satisfy our general specification, and the structures of their activity sets and interactivity functions are of a complexity lying between the extremes mentioned above. A brief characterisation of the *properties of typical connectionist nets* is given by Smolensky:

> The kind of connectionist model I will consider can be described as a net of very simple processors, units, each possessing a numerical activation value that is dynamically determined by the values of the other processors in the net. The activation equation governing this interaction has numerical parameters, which determine the direction and magnitude of the influence of one activation value on another; these parameters are called the connection strengths or weights. The activation equation is a differential equation (usually approximated by the finite difference equation that arises from discrete time slices).... The weights modulate the behaviour of the net: they constitute the "program" for this architecture. ... The learning rule is the differential equation governing the weight changes. The knowledge in a connectionist system lies in its connection strengths (Smolensky, 1988, §1.3, following hypothesis 6).

There is an important new feature concerning the activation equation given above. It now takes the form:

$$u' = H \, [\{ \, u,w \, \}]$$

where $\{ \, u,w \, \}$ is the set of pairs of neighbours' activities and connection strengths w to the neighbours, one connection strength for each neighbour of u. Usually, connectionist models assume a specific structure for F, namely:

$$u_i' = F_i \, [u_i, \, \Sigma \, w_{ij} * f_j(u_j)].$$

where f_j is a non-linear function, determining the output of the unit u_j on the basis of its activity. Each output of a neighbour u_j of unit u_i is multiplied by the connection strength or weight w_{ij}, characterising the connection from unit u_j to unit u_i. Then the weighted outputs from the neighbours are summed up and combined with the current activity of the unit u_i itself. The essential characteristic is that the activity of a unit is now linearly dependent on the outputs of its neighbours. This makes such a connectionist net very similar to the dynamical systems governed by linear differential equations known from physics.

The challenge can now be put as follows: Linguistic competences have up until now been defined in terms of rule systems able to *identify and manipulate symbolic structures*; able, for example, to form and store more complicated and still identifiable structures from simpler ones. Moreover, the semantics of a linguistic expression is also usually represented by symbolic structures such that it can be shown how the meanings of complicated expressions can be composed from the meanings of simple ones.

In contrast to this approach there is a "space" or *tissue of units* with neighbours with *regularly changing numerical activity values*, such that the regularities may change in a learning process. These units will not represent all the details of the biological properties of neural cells or neural nets. Nevertheless, they may be considered as idealised cells, such that each cell is a numerically specified unit that interacts with its neighbours to produce the behaviour of the net as an overall effect. The behaviour corresponds to a "surface" property of the net's activity.

There is a sense in which we may *correlate* the structure or *connectivity* state of a net *with knowledge representation*. We may say that the net has knowledge and that the knowledge of the whole system lies in the regularities with which its units become activated or change their activities determined by the activities of their neighbours. Applying the language of knowledge representation, we would say that single units in a local net or sets of units in a distributed net correspond to concepts and may be taken to be hypotheses about whether the corresponding concept currently applies to the situation. The activity value then expresses the current degree of confidence in the applicability of the concept. The connection strengths correspond, in this interpretation, to the constraints existing between the hypotheses (cf. Smolensky, 1986: 392).

If this is the case, there immediately arises *the question whether linguistic knowledge that is representable in classical architectures by symbol manipulation can also be represented in connectionist architectures by numerical interdependencies between conceptual or subconceptual units*. There are two ways we could try to meet the challenge: Either we map linguistic concepts (linguistic unit concepts—of phonemes, words, phrases—as well as concepts of linguistic categories and features on the various levels) on to the units of connectionist, i.e. net-linguistic, nets, and render the interdependencies determining the processes of production and understanding of speech by the "rules" of interactivity, or we try a more complicated approach, in which the concepts are mapped directly on to distributed configurations which also render psychological aspects, and may be generating the speech errors or speech reductions that occur in fast speech, etc. Given that connectionism is still in its infancy, I would suggest we start with studies of the simpler solution in order to find out whether we can map classically known linguistic solutions into nets.

The relation between classical and connectionist approaches also provides *a converse challenge*: Given that some psycholinguistically (or neurobiologically) motivated properties of language use can be explained by connectionist nets, but that it is presently unknown how they can be expressed by classical rule systems, can we devise classical systems that do?

One may question the net-linguistic approach. At best it merely seems to provide alternatives to already existing empirical descriptions. Should we not rather try to directly develop a broader perspective on connectionism by showing that connectionism can provide explanations, where classical rule systems cannot, just as classical rule systems can provide explanations where connectionism fails, as is commonly believed? If both views were correct, we would simply have to form hybrid systems to define the full complexity of language performance. I believe, however, that there is a sense in which both approaches are, in principle, equivalent. In my view, von Neumann's growing automata are essentially equivalent to growing connectionist nets. If so, then both approaches have in principle the same expressive, and perhaps, the same structural power. The essential challenge is then how to translate between equivalent explanations of the two approaches.

The word "translate" here is crucial to the issue. Fodor and Pylyshin (1988:67) concede that it might be possible to "treat connectionism as an implementation theory" i.e. to conceive "nets as potential implementation models". Let us assume that it can be shown—as I believe it can—that a connectionist implementation exactly renders a rule system in generating the sentences generated by the rule system and represent the structure of each sentence temporally by the structure (e.g. the "branchings") of the processing flow. Let us further assume that the representation of the rule system can be obtained by retranslation. Now, which representation would be the implementation of which? Would not both representations merely be notational and operational variants whose equivalence defined the really abstract linguistic structure? After all, a set of symbol configurations is merely an instantiation of a semi-group, albeit one particularly appropriate for visualising and communicating the really abstract mathematical structure.

Thus the question is not about a relation between form and implementation but about a *relation between alternatives of representation*. Is it necessarily so, that recursive definitions of configurations and their structures must be specified by symbol manipulation, or is this an historical accident reflecting certain ideas about the formalism of Hilbert, Post, etc.? Are not von Neumann's growing automata examples of structure specifications which are not symbol manipulations, and did not von Neumann plausibly conjecture that there are cases for which the specification of a net would provide a better description than a description in terms of structured expressions? (cf. Schnelle, 1988b). It is still unclear how connectionist structures could be designed in order to fully implement computational structure as well as rules do for symbol manipulation. This is no proof, however, that the former cannot do what the latter can.

The challenge is then to work through the details and to study the ranges of applicability of connectionist systems. I shall now discuss some of these details, starting with the theoretically simpler cases of implementation on a collection of ordinary computers working in parallel.

3. PARALLEL PROCESSING AMONG PROGRAMMABLE PROCESSORS: THE COLLECTIONIST APPROACH

As Fodor and Pylyshin (1988) indicate, *implementation on parallel machines* seems to be straightforward. The symbol structures occurring in manipulations defined by rule systems in an abstract way are stored, retrieved, and manipulated in a machine as indicated in the rule system. The implementations merely add specifications of sequentiality or parallelity of manipulation, and technical details of implementation are left unspecified in the rule system because their specification is not structure-relevant. Nevertheless, some technical details and terminology may be worth specifying.

The basic conception of a computational system derives from Turing and consists of marks (written on paper or stored in a tape) and a reading/writing head moving over the tape and changing here and there some of the marks or adding new ones. According to an ingenious idea the movement of the head and the reading and writing operations at certain positions can be made dependent on the marks which the head reads at other positions. What it reads at these other positions can be conceived as instructions for the subsequent operation of the head at other positions of the store containing the data to be operated upon.

Turing was able to show that there is a machine of this type which can solve every mathematical problem that can be solved at all by effective mathematical methods, provided that the storage space and the time allowed for solving the problem is unlimited. Such a machine is a universal Turing machine.

Von Neumann and others developed this concept into a practical machine by specifying the structure of an instruction to be composed of an operation specifier and an address. In this way it was easy to separate the act of *finding the data* to be operated upon from the actual *transformation of the data*. Moreover, instead of moving the reading/writing head over the tape, the addressed data were moved to a central processing unit (CPU), where they were transformed, and then returned to the store, perhaps to another position. All of this was done under the control of an instruction fetched from the store and momentarily stored in the central processor unit before the data to be addressed were called up. The instruction itself can also be changed systematically when it passes the central processing unit (either in the address part or in the operation specifier part) in order to be appropriately applicable later on. The set of instructions stored is called a *program*.

The basic idea of the functioning of such a machine is that the processes executed occur on two streams of information flowing from the store through the central processor unit and back to the store: *the stream of instructions* (or of control information) and the *stream of data*. In general, each stream is transformed during its passage through the central processor unit—the changes in the instructions are usually systematic, whereas the changes in the data depend wholly on the instruction stream flowing parallel to the data.

Let us exemplify this by looking at the process of traditional linguistic parsing. Here, linguistic facts are thought to be represented in a storage space as symbol configurations, and linguistic processes—such as grammatical analyses or semantic interpretations—as sequences of operations leading from initially stored information (e.g. a sentence) to the information representing the result (e.g. the interpretation of the sentence).

To be more specific we might refer to parsing. Here, the initial fact is represented by a string of symbols and the solution consists in representations of form added to the stored string: an annotated tree representing the syntactic form, a sequence of phonetic symbols representing the phonological form, and a bracketed sequence of symbol configurations designating the concepts representing the semantic form (cf. Klein, Chapter 3). The process of computation is conceived as a gradual build up of these representations.

Ordinarily, the processing is sequential in that at each moment just one rule or instruction is applied to a section of the initial representation or some part of the intermediate representations. Of course, high-level programming languages partly obscure what is actually going on in the machine. The automatic processes for the translation of the high-level languages into machine instruction code (compilation or interpretation) are added to the execution of the intended change of data structures. But what is going on is always an interconnected bi-directional flowing of instructions and data. In the case of parsing this double stream generates a gradual addition of stored representations of linguistic information to the initially stored string. Neglecting interpretation or compilation processes, each moment is characterised by the application of a specific instruction or rule to a specific section of data representation, changing it and/or moving it to another place.

Let us now turn to the implementation of *parallel* processing. The idea is simple: Whenever two rules or procedures apply to totally different sections of the stored representations, they should be applied simultaneously or concurrently. Various programming languages have been developed recently in which concurrent application of rules can be specified, and at the same time hardware has become available which provides arrays of central processor units—not just one —all working simultaneously in applying different parts of the program concurrently, possibly on different parts of the data. In this case we are faced with a system with a multiple instruction stream and a multiple data stream "pumped" through a corresponding configuration of processor units. Such *parallel processors* are of the MIMD (multiple instruction stream–multiple data stream) type, whereas the ordinary computers are of SISD (single instruction stream–single data stream) type. There are also intermediate types (SIMD or MISD) which will not be discussed here.

One can also analyse the situation from the point of view of concurrent programs—viewed rather more as agents than as streams of control data—and their accessibility to the stored data. In this case several programs (and their instructions) may have access to the same data. This is the so-called *blackboard model* according to which different programs—for example, programs for syntactic, semantic, and phonological processing—have access to the same data (a syntactic processor can "see" phonological and semantic data, a phonological processor syntactic and semantic data, etc.

This example gives a hint of the additional programming problems which arise in parallel processing. Obviously, one must make sure, among other things, that two programs do not try to operate on the same piece of information simultaneously. The output may then be unpredictable.

The additional problems hinted at stem from the general feature that the processor units form a "society" solving a problem in cooperation, i.e. by distribution of labour. In contrast to the activity of a simple unit, the actions of the different units must now be co-ordinated. The units must "know", to some degree, what they are doing presently, what they are about to do next, or what they plan to do and what has already been done. This requires communication between the units, involving the *sending and receiving of messages* and facilities for *interpreting the meaning of the messages* controlling the activities.

I will now briefly touch on some linguistic applications of parallel processing, e.g. parsing. One assumption usually made is that the rules or instructions of *different linguistic levels are assigned to different processors*. It is sometimes even assumed that the tasks of individual levels be further subdivided and assigned to different processors. We might then have a *processor for the syntactic analysis of nounphrases*, another one for *relative clauses*, another one for the analysis of the synthetic *forms of verbs* (the auxiliaries + modals + main verb constructions), and so on.

Another way of distributing the tasks is to keep available several processors for syntactic analysis. If during a parsing process several paths seem possible, each path is assigned its own processor. In this way the various *alternatives of syntactic interpretation are followed in parallel*.

Both of these aspects—processing of levels in parallel and parallel syntactic parse route processing—seem to be present in Crain and Steedman's work (1985: 325, 328f.) From the parse routes first created in parallel the selection of the appropriate parse is dependent on the information concurrently computed on another level (semantics, pragmatics). In this way the activity of the semantic and pragmatic processors form the context for the selective evaluation of the syntactic alternatives concurrently computed in the array of syntactic processors.

Yet another approach consists of applying the techniques of concurrent programming to specific linguistic tasks. A relatively perspicuous system is PARALLEL PROLOG. In using it we may transform a solution programmed in PROLOG into a concurrent system. As already indicated by Klein (Chapter 3) a grammar can first be formulated as a set of axioms in PROLOG. We can then use a parallel deduction procedure for deducing the statements which are true of a given string relative to the axioms of grammar. The set of true statements corresponds to the structural description assigned to the given string. Particular specifications of this general idea are currently under investigation in the U.S. and similar implementations are being developed in Germany (cf.Hahn, 1987a; 1987b).

The guiding principles at the root of these implementations are similar to those of *constraint satisfaction systems*, i.e. both are approaches seeking to satisfy the constraints between a given system (grammar) and a given datum (e.g. input string).

All the systems discussed so far are systems whose processing is determined by instructions and stored data. Instructions and data can be assigned to a single processing unit plus store, or they may be distributed by assigning different parts of the programs to different processors and different sections of the data to storage spaces accessible to only one processor or a small number of processors. Access to data can be controlled by addressing and operation by operator specifications contained in an instruction.

This contrasts strongly with the systems which will be discussed subsequently. In their case no distinction is made between storage space and central processor units and, correspondingly, they do not distinguish streams of instructions from data. As a consequence, there is no concept of addressing, no concept of a data variable, no denotation of the data used in instructions or rules.

This is so because—in the simplest case—each "processing unit" has only one instruction and, accordingly, it always operates in the same way. It becomes meaningless to call such a unit a processing unit. What is more, each unit has a fixed assignment of data upon which its instruction is to be applied: this is just the data of its "immediate neighbourhood"—where "immediate neigbourhood" is determined through the connections ("wires") the unit has with other units. Each unit is connected to only a very small subset of the set of all the units in the system. (The neurons of the brain are of this kind: They have up to several hundred or thousand neighbours, a small number compaired with the 10 billion neurons of the brain.) Cooperative processing is possible because neighbouring units influence each other (with a certain time delay).

As a consequence of these properties *problems can be solved*, not by substitution of stored symbols, but *by data flows* which are in fact changing the activities over a field of units, as has already been emphasised in Schnelle (1964: Fig. 3b). The specific character of a system which determines its behaviour is not a stored program but the specific connectivities which determine which data flows are possible and which are not. This leads us to the discussion of a style of "programming" in terms of nets and connections.

4. PARALLEL PROCESSING BY CONNECTIONIST NETS OF INTERACTIVE UNITS

We shall first show, that *a syntactic tree* can be conceived *as a connectivity net* of interdependencies between the activities of the nodes representing syntactic categories. Let us consider a slight modification of the syntactic representation in Klein (Chapter 3), reproduced here as Fig.1.

Suppose that each box assigned to a word is not a configuration but a mechanism which, when confronted with ink spots on a piece of paper, will either be active at its output or inactive. It will be active exactly when the ink spots on the paper have the

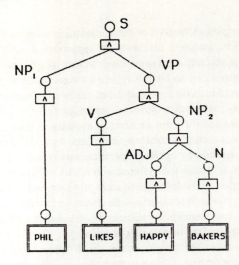

FIG. 6.1

form of a standard print for that word. If then the input has indeed the written configurations of standard print corresponding to the realisation of the words **Phil, likes, happy, bakers** in that sequence, all four word mechanisms will indeed be active. The tree is then to be understood as a logical design of a circuit. Each circle represents a binary storage element (e.g. a flip-flop) and each box a circuit realising the logical AND-function. An element, together with the box whose output it is, will be called a node. A node **S** will become active if the nodes **NP1** and **VP** have been active. In turn the node **VP** will become active when the nodes **V** and **NP2** have been active and, simultaneously, the node **NP1** becomes active when the node **N1** has been active.

What then does the activity of node **S** represent? It does not yet represent the concept **S** but merely the fact that the system considers the utterance **Phil likes happy bakers** to be present. This presence has been "computed" by logical switching on the basis of the presence of the detections of the words **Phil, likes, happy,** and **bakers**. So far the example is extremely simple but it already illustrates a straightforward kind of parallelism in that the bottom-up information flow is concurrent wherever possible. We have exploited the fact that the units of a circuit always operate in parallel (perhaps synchronously if dependent on a clock), and they operate whenever the conditions for their operation are satisfied in their neighbourhood.

There is another interesting feature of the system—the constituent structure rendered by the tree is like a wired circuit which in turn implies a tree, i.e. the information-flow tree. The structure contained in an input configuration is rendered by the connectivity of the interactive units (nodes) detecting the presence of a complex unit in the presence of elementary units.

We can also analyse each of the word-boxes detecting words from configurations of ink spots as a net of the same kind as that already presented, i.e where horizontal or vertical line components are detected as conjunctions of single ink spots, letters are detected as conjunctions of line components and words as conjunctions of letters. Each configuration is registered by a particular node on the basis of its connectivities to the nodes recording the presence of the constituent components. Each initial node records the presence (or absence) of an ink spot at the particular position to which it is assigned. The complete system is like a collection of measuring instruments, each measuring a configurational property of ink-spot configurations. The more embracing properties are implemented as combinations of simpler properties.

What has been said so far can be rephrased in a way more in line with logical analyses. Each node may be taken to represent a hypothesis about what is present at the periphery of the system. The nodes assigned to the boxes may be read, when active, as hypotheses like " The word **Phil** is momentarily present" and "The word **bakers** is momentarily present", and the other nodes represent hypotheses like "The verb-phrase constituent **happy bakers** is momentarily present" or "The sentence **Phil likes happy bakers** is momentarily present." The activities representing the degrees of confidence of these hypotheses are obviously interdependent, as can be seen from the tree, and may emerge in a temporal process from bottom to top. If the system is further developed to include alternatives—as will be discussed in the next paragraph—then the alternatives should be incompatible hypotheses to be related in such a way that their "confidence-activities" inhibit each other.

As Smolensky has very clearly formulated:

> This way of thinking about cognition can be summarized by saying that behaviour rests on a set of internal entities called hypotheses that are positively and negatively related in a knowledge base that is used for inference, the propagation of confidence. The hypotheses relate directly to our way of thinking about a given cognitive process; e.g. for language processing the hypotheses relate to words, syntactic categories, phonemes, meanings (Smolensky, 1986: 392).

If the nodes are understood as representations of hypotheses which may change their momentary truth values or binary degrees of confidence, it is clear that the system can also be formulated in propositional logic. The process of derivation is technically, however, quite different if this derivation is a manipulation of symbolic expressions of sentences, as is usual in ordinary propositional logic, or if it is directly given in terms of the flowing of activities over the connectivities of storage elements. It should be quite obvious that the latter requires much less space (in terms of storage units, e.g. flip-flops,) in the machine than the corresponding symbolic inferential device.

At the start of Section 4 we presented a tree as a logical net with nodes reacting to the conjunction of activities. It is obvious how this approach can be extended to integrate alternatives of partial trees: we simply introduce the Boolean function OR as well.

Let us assume that instead of Fig.1 we have Fig.2 in which each of the nodes **N1**, **V**, **ADJ**, and **N2** is connected to several word detectors. Then the corresponding nodes

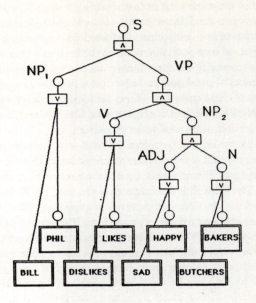

FIG. 6.2

are active whenever one of the nodes recording the presence of a word of its category is connected to it. These nodes thus no longer record words but the presence of members of word-classes (parts of speech). The same holds for the rules. Let us assume that we have the rules:

$$NP \rightarrow DEF + N$$
$$NP \rightarrow INDEF + N.$$

We would have to connect the NP node through an OR to one AND-detector connecting **DEF** and **N**, and another connecting **INDEF** and **N**.

We also need NOT. For the rules:

$$VP \rightarrow V$$
$$VP \rightarrow V + NP.$$

we would need to connect the VP node via OR to one node connected through an AND to **V** and **NP** and to another node connected through an AND to **V** and NOT-NP (following **V**).

Let us summarise these very simple illustrations. The recording of the presence of units and syntactic categories of an expression in a configuration of ink spots is *caused by a net of causal connectivities*. The structure of the net represents the constituent structure. The *structure of expressions is contained in the specific wirings connecting inner (or higher) nodes to the periphery* (perhaps also to other inner nodes representing the context). This is the basic idea contained in our extremely primitive example. We would have to add a large number of details and modifications before the reader would be able to acknowledge the proposal as useful, which is not possible in the present context. The interested reader should study the research literature on parallel processing (see Kohonen, 1984; Rumelhart et al., 1986 and the references given there), connectionist nets (see Feldman & Ballard, 1982), and net-linguistic approaches (see Schnelle, 1988a; 1989 and references given there). But let us emphasise once more the fact that simple as our examples are, they already show the property of parallel processing and of the specific representation of structure by connectionist wiring.

We shall now turn to an example which goes beyond the limits of mere structural processing. It is related to the problems of context dependency of analyses addressed by Crain and Steedman (1985) and referred to on p.156. The German word **Wachtraum** is structurally and semantically ambiguous. It is a composed word which can be split as **Wach-traum** or **Wacht-raum**. The former means **daydream**, the latter **guardroom**. In syntax both of the following sentences are well-formed:

1. **Der Patient hatte einen Wachtraum**
   (The patient had a daydream/guardroom)
2. **Die Kaserne hatte einen Wachtraum**
   (The barracks had a guardroom/daydream)

Semantically, of course, the interpretation with **daydream** is dominant in the first case and with guardroom in the second.

The inner-sentential semantic context of the subject of the sentence thus selects the dominant interpretation. This selection could only be rejected by strong counter evidence from the wider, nonsentential context, e.g. in the following:

The patient had a daydream/guardroom in which he was supposed to stay during heavy rain. Due to his claustrophobia he preferred to stay outside.

As indicated by Crain and Steedman (1985; and see p.151), the selection among the possible word-structure parses (**Wach-traum/Wacht-raum**) is made under the influence of some other level of linguistic processing, the semantic level, which takes into account that the affinities of:

PATIENT-HAVING (-PSYCHOLOGICALLY)-DAYDREAM

versus

BARRACKS-HAVING (-AS-A-PART)-GUARDROOM

are—in the absence of additional contextual information—much more intensive than the affinity:

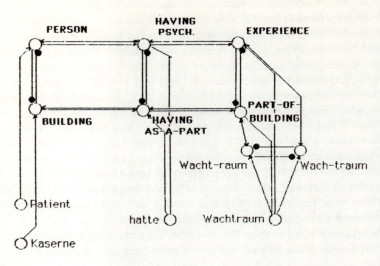

FIG. 6.3

PATIENT-HAVING-AVAILABLE-GUARDROOM

This situation requires processing by means of a gradation of activity values and gradations of the interdependencies between activities. A rough solution is given in Fig.3.

Let us first indicate the process with **Kaserne (barracks)** as a subject. The word **Wachtraum** activates both of the morphological parses, whose incompatibility is expressed by the mutually inhibitory connection (indicated in Fig.3 by a line ending in a black dot) which causes a decrease in the activity of a neighbour of an active node. Because both alternatives have the same strength they inhibit each other initially to the same degree. However, the word **Kaserne** activates the notion **BUILDING** and through this notion the sentential concept **BUILDING HAVING-AS-A-PART PART-OF-A-BUILDING**, which is simultaneously activated by the corresponding **HAVING** notion and the notion **PART-OF-A-BUILDING**. These latter notions are, however, incompatible with their alternatives which had also become active due to the ambiguity of the words. But now, the higher levels spread activation downward as well, that is, the activity of **BUILDING HAVING (-AS-A-PART) PART OF A BUILDING** adds to the activity of its constituent, whereas its alternatives—lacking the constituent (**PERSON**)—have not become active and thus cannot support their constituents. This then leads to the strengthening of the activities **HAVING (AS-A-PART)** and **PART-OF-A-BUILDING**, whose inhibitory activity against their alternative becomes stronger and succeeds in overpowering the neighbour activity. This in turn acts back on the activities of the alternative morphological parses and leads **Wacht-raum** to win over **Wach-traum**.

The situation becomes slightly different in the context of the sentences in which the word claustrophobia is mentioned. There the incoming words of the first sentence favour the interpretation of a patient having a daydream due to the stronger support of the connection to **DAYDREAM** compared to the connection of **GUARDROOM**. This alternative seems to win at first. But then its opponent gets support from the pragmatics of the wider context (the claustrophobia information and the information about staying in a daydream/guard room) which finally allows it to win, to overpower the activity of its opponent, and to cause its constituents [**GUARDROOM** and **HAVING (AVAILABLE)**] to defeat their respective opponents and to select once again the morphological parse **Wacht-raum** (for further details, see Schnelle, 1984).

The example shows up two points. First, it is very useful in many cases to have available particular degrees of activities during a relaxation time in order to be able to take into account contextual effects stepwise during the course of processing. Secondly, the situation tends to become quickly complicated and may require more systematic insight into the principles of this type of processing.

But a complicated system can only be understood when not only the thousands and millions of connectivities are given, but also when they can be grouped into subnets whose functions can be named and systematically specified. In other words, we must understand the *design principles for the functional architectures* of nets.

It is to be expected that the grouping into functional subunits also plays a decisive role in the *learning process*. A system may not be able to learn successfully if all possible connectivities must be tried. Quick adaptation requires adaptational selection at decisive positions in an architecture. A deep insight into the design principles for functional architecture is thus a prerequisite for trying to define sufficiently strong principles of learning.

The literature provides a wealth of indications of possible learning functions. It is impossible to summarise them here (see References). A relatively interesting though linguistically rather *ad-hoc* example of learning phonemic differences on the basis of contextual configurations is presented by Sejnowski and Rosenberg (1988).

Let us illustrate another processing feature which has been especially developed in net-linguistics and which has been lacking so far in other approaches to parallel processing as well as in connectionist approaches, in spite of the fact that it must be considered as basic for linguistic processing: How do we represent *temporal order in connectionist nets*?

The careful reader may already have remarked that our analyses of sentences presupposed that the words were represented in a sequence. But in fact they did not have anything which constituted a real representation of temporal order. The different registerings of the words of a sentence as well of its constituents were rather considered to be simultaneously present. But how do the words of a sentence become simultaneously available, when they enter the ear one after the other? How are they read in through hearing, or how is a written text scanned by eye movements?

In typical connectionist approaches to lexical access, such as in the TRACE model (see McClelland 1985: 115; McClelland et al., 1986: 123), we have three levels of analysis, the level on which the sequence of phonetic features are read in, a level for the detection of phonemes, and a level for the words. The feature level is mapped onto the phoneme level by phoneme detector units and, correspondingly, the phoneme configurations are mapped onto the word representations. Initially, the features are entered into a register in a stepwise manner from left to right and, simultaneously, the detectors react to the feature configurations read in at each moment.

In order to be able to detect the order of phonemes (or words) an array of $n*l$ detectors is assumed when a sequence of l letters of n different letter types is to be detected. Thus the TRACE model which operates on a register of length 15 has to have 15 identical detector connectivities from the possible occurrences of each phoneme type to the feature submatrix, which has the corresponding position in the complete matrix at the lowest level.

The authors concede that their model has deficiencies. They write:

> One fundamental deficiency is the fact that the model requires reduplication of units and connections, copying over and over again the connection patterns that determine which features activate which phonemes and which phonemes activate which words (McClelland & Elman 1986: 119).

Now, let us assume that initially the feature bundles are not simultaneously present but read in at each time-step into the right most edge of the matrix and then shifted to the left. At each time step, all feature bundles already entered so far are shifted one step to the left and a new feature bundle is read in at the right border. Technically speaking, we assume the matrix scheme to be a shift register instead of a fixed store.

Next let us assume that only the right-most phonemes are connected to the detectors of the features. As soon as a phoneme has indeed been detected, it is also shifted to the left simultaneously to the shifting of its corresponding feature bundles. In this way each detected phoneme keeps its position relative to the feature submatrix on the basis of which it was detected. Subsequent feature bundles flowing in from the right lead to the detection of other phonemes which start to get shifted the very moment they have been detected. As soon as the matrix has been completely entered into the feature shift register, the sequence of phonemes detected correspondingly fills the phoneme shift register.

The same holds for syllables or words. They are similarly detected on the basis of a right-most phoneme sequence as soon as the latter has been shifted into the phoneme level shift register. Because the detected words are also shifted to the left on their level they keep their relative positions with regard to the phonemes and feature bundles which are their constituents.

We now see that instead of 15 connectivities for each phoneme and word occurrence we have only one per shift register. But we see moreover, that there is no limitation whatsoever to the length of phoneme or word sequences to be detected, as there is no principled limitation to the length of the shift register. I have discussed application of this concept in various publications. Though it constitutes a powerful approach and deserves thorough study, I shall not enter into further detail. Let me only remark that the NETtalk system assumes the input level to be a shift register with a "seven letter window" through which the higher level units depend on those of the lowest level, such that the text is "stepped through the window letter-by-letter" (Sejnowski & Rosenberg, 1988: 150).

Let me add a fundamental remark: Theoretical linguistics tries to capture the idea of an unlimited sequence by the notion of a string. As it is usually presented, this notion is strictly neutral with respect to the question as to whether sequentiality is expressed in time or space. *The notion of a shift register with (temporally) sequential input is the correlate of the notion of a symbol string*, as it incorporates (in principle) unlimited extension, and—by providing sequential to parallel conversion—is equally neutral with respect to space and time, as everything which occurs at one position in the temporal sequence is also represented in the spatial sequence simultaneously. I assume here a shift register can be implemented by a connectionist network. An unbounded net of this type thus corresponds to the class of concatenated symbols in the classical approach.

Let us now turn to the *crucial issue of unlimited combinatorial structure and recursivity*. Critics of connectionism have insisted on challenging connectionists to show how combinatorially unlimited structure-sensitive processes could be realised in connectionist networks. The article by Fodor and Pylyshin contains a first answer to this challenge from a point of view which takes a biological network to be an implementation of a rule system. Fodor and Pylyshin make the following proposal:

> Because, in general, Classical models assume that the expressions that get physically instantiated in brains [or, we may add, in some idealised connectionist nets] have a generative syntax, the definition of an appropriate physical instantiation mapping has to be built up in terms of (a) the definition of a primitive mapping from atomic symbols to relatively elementary physical states and (b) a specification of how the structure of complex expressions maps onto the structure of relatively complex or composite physical states. Such a structure preserving mapping is typically given recursively, making use of the combinatorial syntax, by which complex expressions are built up out of simpler ones (Fodor & Pylyshin, 1988: 14).

Since **S**, **NP** and **VP** are atomic symbols in a generative syntax, they will get mapped onto elementary physical entities. In fact, all terminal and non-terminal symbols of a given generative grammar will also. Activity of these entities may indicate that the current input is analysed as being of the category which the active unit encodes. Fodor and Pylyshin suggest that there are physical relations between the physical states which encode the formally defined relations between the symbols representing the categories. The examples we have discussed illustrate this proposal.

However, present research at my institute follows a different line for the derivation a connectionist representation equivalent to a given grammar in its weak and strong generative capacity. Instead of implementing a grammar directly, we *implement the Earley-parser* for that grammar. An Earley-parser can be viewed as extending the class of symbols which get manipulated. In fact, each grammatical rule is transformed into a so-called dotted rule, and is then taken as a symbol (and no longer as a rule) to be manipulated. The rules of Earley's algorithm specify how pairs of dotted grammatical rule symbols and numbers indicating their scope in the string of terminal symbols get added to stacks during the process of building up the structure tree. What is important to bear in mind is that grammatical structure can also be represented in this way. In our proposal, Earley's algorithm is implemented by assigning to each dotted rule symbol a single primary unit of a connectionist network and an infinite sequence of auxiliary units. The auxiliary units of each dotted rule form a shift register, i.e. a completely regular infinite structure which could also be conceived as a regularly growing structure. The connectivities of the primary units are specific and implement the grammatical interdependencies of the symbols, i.e. the structure of the grammar.

Earley's algorithm is implemented as the combination of a parser network and a top-down, left-to-right generator network. The activity pattern on the set of shift registers represents a correct parse shifted onto the shift-register net by the parser net in the course of its parsing activity. This same activity pattern causes the generator network to reconstitute the causal pattern of category dependencies representing the structure if necessary. But the activity pattern can also be transformed by activity changing rules, such that the transformed pattern generates another structure, e.g. the structure of a transformed or logically implied sequential input/output process (temporal string) (for details, see Schnelle & Doust, 1989.)

The essential idea is this: In *implementing a rule system*, we are not confined to implement it directly in the way indicated by Fodor and Pylyshin (1988). We may first *derive another rule system with an enriched symbol set* and then *translate this enriched system into a net*. Enriching the system is necessary in order to secure that recursive processing does not interfere in a conflicting way with a maximal parallel implementation. In our system possible alternative paths in the computation of parse lists are really parallel. All who study Earley's algorithm will see that a number of rule applications are independent of each other and can thus be straightforwardly parallelised.

Another point here is worth being stressed: Because our implementation allows us to specify regular processes of activity patterns which control different generation processes, we can implement transformations, paraphrases, and implications. It seems to us that this meets the challenge raised by critics of the connectionist approach. Though our approach might be characterised as implementational by Fodor and Pylyshin, we would consider this to be due to a historical accident, which has given symbol manipulation implementations of abstract mathematical structures a more established position with respect to network representations. Had formal methods of the definition of networks first been developed in history, symbol manipulation would appear as "mere" implementations of networks.

5. HOW TO MEET THE CHALLENGE

The discipline of connectionist and massively parallel modelling is still very young. This holds, in particular, with regard to its applications to linguistic processing. We need then at the moment mainly to take both *foundational and paradigmatic steps*, to provide typical solutions on the one hand and clarifications and a greater perspicuity of methods on the other. Let me discuss these points in turn.

The ranges of application to linguistic problems should certainly be extended. It seems that the phonetic, phonological, and morphological data connected with the problem of *lexical access* (such as in the TRACE model or in the various models of feature detection mentioned above) and the *phenomena of speech production* (as exemplified by Dell, 1986; Mackay, 1987) provide the best problem areas with which to start.

Another problem area is provided by the field of *massively parallel parsing*. This will probably be the field in which comparative studies of concurrent programs defined on arrays of communicating processors with purely connectionist data flow solutions will be of interest. It seems that functions which must be realised again and again are best learned in such a way that no communicatively controlled interaction is necessary and pure data flow is sufficient. This will certainly have to be clarified in future work.

Another area of research is *inferencing in knowledge bases* in cases where the "knowledge" simply consists of the presence of connectivities. Which actions "follow" in such systems from which others? Which constraints are expressed in physical connectivities and not in the symbolic conditions of a symbol manipulating device?

In all of these cases the conjecture is that the processes could be speeded up to a very high degree if, only given the regularities of behaviour, one knew how to specify the connectivities. It may well be that simple aspects of lexical access could be successfully modelled very soon in such a way that automatic word recognisers could be implemented in the hardware of input/output equipment for future computers or intelligent machines.

Given that common visual problems have been treated much more extensively than linguistic ones, it seems advisable that linguistic solutions are not sought in isolation from the former. Much can be learned from comparing different methods and studying their possible applications as well as from considerations in which respect linguistic processing must have its own specific properties.

Building stronger links with research on vision may offer another chance of reactivating concepts and approaches in linguistics which were once fruitful, but which have since disappeared into oblivion during the decades in which linguistics emphasised those of its concerns which were definitely not in the domain of any neighbouring discipline. A general attempt was made to deemphasise situation-determined language, i.e. language use which is highly dependent on the concurrent perception of a situation and the accompanying action. The fact that, among children, language is mainly used in the context of action and is also learned in this context has been neglected, as well as the possibility that even the understanding of syntactic structure may, in deictic and anaphoric units, still depend on inner visual orientations. The analysis of deictic language in real-world situations should be considered a very important research topic. It also promises important practical results because language understanding is often important in situations where a rapid linguistic influence on machines or a quick interaction is required. The neglect of linguistic research of this area should be rectified and concrete contacts with research on vision and action may give important inspirations for this approach.

The clarification and perspicuity of method should be sought in connection with the best *design principles of structured programming or the structured design of hardware*. Methods of classification and characterisation will need to be developed, starting, for example, from the characterisation of configurations (sequences) of sets of units, cascades of such sequences, and so on. Further, possible topological constraints should be studied, e.g. the topology-preserving mapping of Kohonen (1984: 135) should be related to findings in the neurosciences.

Whether the introduction of concrete modelling (e.g. electrical circuit modelling—Koch & Poggio, 1985) is equally relevant for linguistic modelling is rather doubtful. This kind of modelling seems to be more important for the periphery of the nervous system which is determined by a high density of information processing. In central processing at the level of phonemes, words, or sentences, the specific units become more rarely activated—even if expressed in a distributed way by microfeatures. In this case, digital and localistic analyses seem to be more fruitful.

In summary, we see that we are confronted with a wealth of research directions with much promise for solutions in the processing of speech and language. The field should become the primary one in the most important centres of research in cognitive science.

REFERENCES

Anderson, J.A., Silverstein, J.H., Ritz, S.A., & Jones, R.S. (1977). Distinctive features, categorial perception and probability learning. *Psychological Review, 84*, 413-451.

Burks, A.W. & Wang, H. (1957). The logic of automata. *Journal of the Association for Computing Machinery, 4*, 193-218, 279-297.

Burks, A.W. & Wright, J.B. (1953). Theory of logical nets. *Proceedings of the Institute of Radio Engineers, 41*, 1357-1365.

Condillac, E.B. de Mably de (1746). *Essai sur l'origine des connoissances humaines*. Amsterdam: Pierre Mortier (Repr. Paris: Galiläe, 1973.)

Cottrell, G.W. & Small, S.L. (1983). A connectionist scheme for modelling word sense disambiguation. *Cognition and Brain Theory, 6*, 89-120.

Cottrell, W.G. & Small, S.L. (1984). Viewing parsing as word sense discrimination: A connectionist approach. In B.G. Bora, & G. Guida (Eds), *Computational models of natural language processing* pp.91-119. Amsterdam: Elsevier.

Crain, S. & Steedman, M. (1985). On not being led up the garden path: The use of context by the psychological syntax processor. In D.R. Dowty, L. Karttunen, & A.M. Zwicky (Eds), *Natural language parsing,) pp.320-358. Cambridge: Cambridge University Press.*

Dell, G.S. (1986). A spreading-activation theory of retrieval in sentence production. *Psychological Review, 93*, 283-321.

Feldman, J.A. & Ballard, D.M. (1982). Connectionist models and their properties. *Cognitive Science, 6*, 205-254.

Fodor, J.A. & Pylyshin, Z.W. (1988). Connectionism and cognitive architecture: A critical analysis. *Cognition, 28*, 3-71.

Gigley, H. (1985). HOPE—AI and the dynamics of language behavior. *Cognition and Brain Theory, 6*, 39-88.

Hahn, U.(1987a). *Lexikalisch verteiltes Text-Parsing. Eine objekt-orientierte Spezifikation eines Wortexpertensystems auf der Grundlage des Aktorenmodells*. Konstanz:University of Konstanz.

Hahn, U.(1987b). Modeling text understanding. *Proc. 1st. Intl. Symp. Artificial. Intelligence and Expert Systems*. Berlin.

Hays, D.G. (1973). *Cognitive structures: A prospectus*. Mimeo. Buffalo: SUNY.

Hebb, D.O. (1949). *The organization of behavior*. New York: John Wiley.

Herder, J.G. (1772). *Abhandlung über den Ursprung der Sprache*. Berlin (Repr. Stuttgart: Reclam, 1966).

Hinton, G.E. & Anderson, J.A. (Eds) (1981). *Parallel models of associative memory*. Hillsdale, N.J.: Lawrence Erlbaum Associates Inc.

Koch, C. & Poggio T. (1985). Biophysics of computation: Neurons, synapses and membranes. A.I. Memo 795. Cambridge, Mass.: Massachusetts Institute of Technology, A.I. Lab Center for Biological Information Processing.

Kohonen, T. (1977). *Associative memory*. Berlin: Springer.

Kohonen, T. (1984). *Self-organization and associative memory*. Berlin: Springer.

Lamb, S. (1973). The crooked path of progress in cognitive linguistics. In A. Makkai & D.G. Lockwood (Eds), *Readings in stratificational linguistics*, pp.12-33. Alabama: University of Alabama Press.

MacKay, D.G. (1987). *The organization of perception and action—A theory of language and other cognitive skills*. Berlin: Springer.

McClelland, J.L. (1985). Putting knowledge in its place: A scheme for programming parallel processing structures on the fly. *Cognitive Science, 9*, 113-146. (Also in McClelland, J.L., Rumelhart, D.E., & PDP Research Group (Eds), 1986, *Parallel distributed processing Vol.2: Psychological and biological models*. Cambridge, Mass.: MIT Press.)

McClelland, J.L. & Elman, J.L. (1986). The TRACE model of speech perception. *Cognitive Psychology, 18*, 1-86.

McClelland, J.L. & Rumelhart, D.E. (1981). An interactive activation model of context effects in letter perception. *Psychological Review, 88*, 375-407.

McClelland, J.L., Rumelhart, D.E. & PDP Research Group (Eds) (1986). *Parallel distributed processing: Vol. 2: Psychological and biological models*. Cambridge, Mass.: MIT Press.

McClelland, J.L. & Rumelhart, D.E. (1988). *Explorations in parallel distributed processing*. Cambridge, Mass.: MIT Press.

McCulloch, W.S. & Pitts, W.A. (1943). A logical calculus of ideas immunent in nervous activity. *Bulletin of Mathematical Biophysics, 5*, 115-133.

Neumann, J. von (1949). The general and logical theory of automata. In A.H. Taub (Ed.), *J.v. Neumann—Collected Works V*. Oxford: Pergamon Press.

Pinker, S. & Prince, A. (1988). On language and connectionism: Analysis of a parallel distributed processing model of language acquisition. *Cognition, 28*, 73- 193.

Reich, P.A. (1967). Competence, performance, and relational networks. Reprinted in A. Makkai & D.G. Lockwood (Eds), *Readings in stratificational linguistics*, pp.84-91. Alabama: University of Alabama Press, 1973.

Reich, P.A. (1973). Symbols, relations and structural complexity. Reprinted in A. Makkai & D.G. Lockwood (Eds), *Readings in stratificational linguistics*, pp.92-115. Alabama: University of Alabama Press.

Rosenblatt, F. (1962). *Principles of Neurodynamics*. New York: Spartan.

Rumelhart, D.E., McClelland, J.L., & PDP Research Group (Eds) (1986). *Parallel distributed processing Vol. 1: Foundations*. Cambridge, Mass: MIT Press.

Schnelle, H. (1964). Programmieren linguistischer Automaten. In K. Steinbuch & S.W. Wagner (Eds), *Neuere Ergebnisse der Kybernetik*, pp.109-136. München: Oldenbourg.

Schnelle, H. (1980). Introductory remarks on theoretical neurolinguistics. *Language Research (Seoul)*, *16*, 225-236.

Schnelle, H. (1981). Elements of theoretical net-linguistics, Pt. 1: Syntactical and morphological nets. *Theoretical Linguistics, 8*, 67-100.

Schnelle, H. (1984). Programmierung netzlinguistischer Prozess-Systeme. Mimeo. *GENET, 17*, Bochum: Sprachwissenschaftliches Institut).

Schnelle, H. (1986). Array logic for syntactic production processors. In J.L. Mey (Ed.), *Language and discourse*, pp.477-511. Amsterdam: Benjamins.

Schnelle, H. (1988a). Ansätze zur prozessualen Linguistik. In H. Schnelle & G. Rickheit (Eds.) *Sprache in Mensch und Computer*. Wiesbaden: Westdeutscher Verlag.

Schnelle, H. (1988b). Turing naturalized: Von Neumann's unfinished project. In R. Herken (Ed.) *The universal Turing-machine — A half-century survey*, pp.501-520. Oxford: Oxford University Press.

Schnelle, H. (1989). *Die natur der sprache*. Berlin: de Gruyter.

Schnelle, H. & Job, D.M. (1983). Elements of theoretical net-linguistics, Pt. 2: Phonological nets. *Theoretical Linguistics, 10*, 179-203.

Schnelle, H. & Rothacker, E. (1984). Elements of theoretical net-linguistics, Pt. 3: Principles and fundamentals of dynamic nets for language processing. *Theoretical Linguistics, 11*, 87-116.

Schnelle, H. & Doust, R. (1989). An implementation of the Earley algorithm using connectionist network. In R. Reilly (Ed.), *Connectionist approaches to language processing*. Amsterdam: North-Holland.

Sejnowski, T.J. & Rosenberg, C.R. (1988). Parallel networks that learn to pronounce English text. *Complex Systems, 1*, 145- 168.

Shastri, L. & Feldman, J.A. (1984). Semantic networks and neural nets. *Techn. Rep. No. 131*. Rochester, N.Y.: University of Rochester, Computer Science Deptartment.

Smolensky, P. (1986). Neural and conceptual interpretation of PDP models. In McClelland, J.L., Rumelhart, D.E, & PDP Research Group (Eds), *Parallel distributed processing Vol.2: Psychological and biological models*. Cambridge, Mass.: MIT Press.

Smolensky, P. (1988). On the proper treatment of connectionism. *Behavioral and Brain Sciences, 11*, 1-74.

Waltz, D.L. & Pollack, J.B. (1985). Massively parallel parsing. *Cognitive Science, 9*, 51-74.

Winder, R.O.(1968). Fundamentals of threshold logic. In J.T. Tou (Ed.), *Applied automata theory*, pp.235-318. London and San Diego: Academic Press.

Wolfram, S.(1986). *Theory and applications of cellular automata*. Singapore: World Scientific Publications.

CHAPTER 7

Natural Language Systems: Some Research Trends

Wolfgang Wahlster

*Computer Science Department,
University of Saarbrücken, 6600 Saarbrücken 11,
Federal Republic of Germany*

1. THE IMPORTANCE OF NATURAL LANGUAGE SYSTEMS

In an economy based on the generation and dissemination of information and knowledge, basic research in natural language (NL) understanding and generation can have important positive impacts (cf. Waltz, 1983):

1. It can make computer applications available to segments of the population that are unable or unwilling to learn a formal language.
2. It can increase knowledge productivity in providing automatic means for manipulating knowledge expressed in natural language.

Natural language processing (cf. Allen, 1987) is a prerequisite for advanced knowledge-based systems because the ability to acquire, retrieve, exploit, and present knowledge critically depends on natural language comprehension and production. Natural language concepts guide the interpretation of what we see, hear, read, or experience with other senses.

The knowledge base of a natural language system includes both *linguistic* (e.g. lexicon, grammar, dialogue rules) and *nonlinguistic* (e.g. a description of the objects in the domain of discourse) subparts. Whereas, ideally, the construction of the nonlinguistic part of the knowledge base is based on joint research of computer scientists and application specialists, the design and implementation of the linguistic parts rely on cooperation among computer scientists and linguists. For centuries linguists have gathered knowledge about various natural languages. In most cases, unfortunately, this knowledge cannot be used directly in natural language systems because it is represented in computationally untractable formats or because it is not detailed enough for transformation into algorithmic systems. Thus, it is often a collaborative effort among linguists as "experts for language" and computer scientists as "experts for the formal representation of knowledge" to construct linguistic knowledge sources for natural language systems.

A piece of software is called a *natural language system*, if

1. A subset of the input and/or output of the system is coded in a natural language.
2. The processing of the input and/or the generation of the output is based on knowledge about syntactic, semantic, and/or pragmatic aspects of a natural language.

2. KNOWLEDGE SOURCES FOR NATURAL LANGUAGE SYSTEMS

Let us use a simple example to demonstrate the role of natural language in advanced information systems.

Usually, a clerk at an information desk in a train station uses a time-table and a price list to respond to questions of an information-seeking customer. As formatted mass data, these tables and lists are contained in manuals or in a database system. As external data, they are not a part of his internalised knowledge. Because for the clerk, the access to these tables and lists is of critical importance, it is clear that he must be familiar with the organisation of the manuals or the database.

For adequate consultation however, the clerk must, aside from such *access knowledge*, activate other areas of knowledge as well:

1. If the customer says "My son must be on the train to Saarbrücken on Monday. Does it have intercity connections?", he shortens his second sentence by using the pronoun "it" instead of "the train". The clerk's *linguistic knowledge* helps him to select the correct referent for the pronoun. He is able to rule out "My son", "Saarbrücken", and "Monday" as possible antecedents for "it". Furthermore, the clerk can use his linguistic knowledge about speech acts to recognise that the client does not just expect a yes/no answer, but also the departure times of suitable intercity trains to Saarbrücken.

2. If the customer asks "What is the difference between a sleeping-car and a couchette car" the clerk cannot find the answer in his timetable or his price list. But the clerk *can* use his *conceptual knowledge* to compare both concepts and to identify the distinguishing features of both alternatives for spending the night on a train.

3. If the customer says "I am going to Greece on an excursion together with my professor and our archaeological seminar. Can I use a Eurorail ticket?", the clerk exploits his *inferential knowledge* referring to a rule like "If the client is a student and is under 27 years old, then he can buy a Eurorail ticket". He can apply this rule in a backward chaining mode, which means, that he has to test the if-part of the rule. Using

an inference rule like "If someone is attending a university course, then he is a student", the clerk can infer that the customer is a student. Then the clerk can respond with "Yes" if the customer gives an affirmative answer to the clerk's question "Are you under 27?"

4. If the customer says "A return ticket to the Hanover Fair, please" the clerk will most probably offer him a first-class ticket. This response is based on a *user model* which the clerk derives from the assumption that a visitor to a professional fair is on a business trip. With the user class "businessman" the clerk associates certain stereotypical knowledge, e.g. that travel costs are usually reimbursed for business trips. Thus the clerk assumes that a first-class ticket will be preferred by the customer.

In the 1970s, there were many computer science projects which tried to replace the clerk by an information system. In such a scenario, the customer formulated his request in a query language and a DBMS evaluated the query and retrieved the relevant data from a database in which the timetable and the price list were stored—the result of which being unacceptable service quality for most customers. For someone who uses a train twice a year, it is unreasonable to have to learn a formal query language (even if the query language is very simple like pushing a combination of four buttons out of a menu of 50) for getting information on railway connections. Even if the customer would spend the time to learn the query language, the lack of expressive power of current database query languages compared with natural language, e.g. the absence of *indirect speech acts* and *anaphoric devices* as exemplified in 1, makes such a dialogue with an information system rather frustrating.

In our example scenario, a knowledge-based consultation system could provide an increased consultative capacity by combining a database system with a knowledge base, containing a formal representation of the linguistic, conceptual, and inferential knowledge of the clerk, as well as stereotypes for user modelling.

Although presently for each problem mentioned in 1–4 at least one experimental knowledge-based access system which can adequately handle this type of question exists, it is, of course, a long way from implementing the broad-based universal communication capabilities of a clerk into an integrated and robust real-time system.

A particular problem, far from being solved in any system, is the permanent *knowledge acquisition* of humans. In our example, one usually assumes that a clerk reads newspapers or watches TV news programmes. Therefore, he may know that this year the Davis Cup final takes place in Munich. Thus, if a customer asks for a return ticket to the Davis Cup final, the clerk will probably be able to offer him a return ticket to Munich. For a knowledge-based system today, it would be unrealistic to assume that the system updates its knowledge base daily with information potentially relevant for consultation purposes.

3. RESEARCH OPPORTUNITIES

Certainly, natural language (NL) processing has a broad range of possible application areas. But today, many existing NL systems break down when we begin to scale up to larger discourse domains where inherent limitations of the domain are no longer adequate to resolve ambiguities or to control inference. This means that more *breadth* for a NL system cannot be gained without more *depth* of representation and processing. For many possible applications the systems must have a very large vocabulary, deal with a wide range of linguistic constructions, and have a great variety of meaning representation constructions.

Further improvements of the semantic coverage, the richness of the discourse domains and the broadening of the conversational context in the next generation of NL systems will lead to an explosion in the number of semantic interpretations that the systems will have to process. Many ambiguities which are ignored in current systems will be dealt with. To cut down on the processing of spurious readings, future systems have to check a great variety of constraints imposed by user models and discourse models at an early stage of processing. This means that the improved functionality of future NL systems will lead to a considerable increase in the amount of processing resources required.

One possible solution for avoiding a decrease in response time, is to run the NL systems on suitable parallel machines. Today, machines like BBN's Butterfly or Thinking Machines' Connection Machine, both running parallel Common Lisp, seem to be most appropriate. A prerequisite for the success of such an approach is that *parallelisability* becomes a major design criterion.

There will have to be major breakthroughs in cognitive science in order to obtain general and principled solutions for the following research topics.

3.1 Integrated NL Interfaces

Today, a decision maker often has to access many different software systems in order to solve his problem. The next generation of NL systems should *interface intelligently to multiple underlying systems*. Such an integrated interface would allow the user to concentrate on decision making instead of spending his time on the details of which software system offers the information needed, how a problem should be devided to make use of the various systems, how to translate his query into the input language of the selected system, or how to combine the results from several systems into the desired answer.

For such interfaces meta-knowledge and a reasoning component are needed for determining which underlying system or which combination of systems can best fulfil a user's request. In order to choose the correct subset of systems, the interface has to exploit a model of the capabilities of the underlying systems together with a model of the user goals and intentions in the current conversational context.

An example of current research on this topic is JANUS, being developed by BBN in the Strategic Computing Program. JANUS will be an integrated NL interface to three systems:

1. A database which contains information about ships (IDB).
2. A graphics system which can display ships on maps (OSGP).
3. An expert system for force requirements (FRESH).

User-friendly natural language access systems must be able to deal *with extragrammatical language* and *metalanguage*. Users invariably commit errors of orthography, switch word order, violate agreement, omit function words, insert spurious words, or use incorrect punctuation (cf. Carbonell & Hayes, 1983). They often do not notice their errors, so that the system has to recover from sloppy user input, e.g. by exploiting its task and domain knowledge. Metalanguage, i.e. utterances about other utterances, also occur with some regularity in NL interactions, e.g. "when I say 'copy' I mean 'output on the laser printer'."

Thus, basic research on a theory of understanding metalanguage and extragrammatical language should be encouraged.

3.2 Multimodal Communication

In face-to-face conversation humans frequently use *deictic gestures* (e.g. the index finger points at something) in parallel to verbal descriptions for referent identification. Such a *multimodal* mode of communication can improve human interaction with machines, as it simplifies and speeds up reference to objects in a visual world.

The basic technical prerequisites for the *integration of pointing and natural language* are fulfilled (high-resolution, bit-mapped displays and window systems for the presentation of visual information, various pointing devices such as a light-pen, mouse, or touch-sensitive screen for deictic input). But the remaining problem for cognitive science is that explicit meanings must be given to natural pointing behaviour in terms of a formal semantics of the visual world.

Unlike the usual semantics of mouse clicks in direct manipulation environments, in human conversation the region at which the user points (the *demonstratum*) is not necessarily identical with the region which he intends to refer to (the *referent*). In conventional systems there exists a simple one-to-one mapping of a demonstratum onto a referent, and the reference resolution process does not depend on the situational context. Moreover, the user is not able to control the granularity of a pointing gesture, as the size of the predefined mouse-sensitive region specifies the granularity.

Compared to that, natural pointing behaviour is much more flexible, but also possibly ambiguous or vague. Without a careful analysis of the *discourse context* of a gesture there would be a high risk of reference failure, as a deictic operation does not cause visual feedback from the referent (e.g. inverse video or blinking as in direct manipulation systems).

Although the "common visual world" of the user and the system could be any graphics or image, current projects combining pointing and natural language focus on forms or geographic maps.

For example, the TACTILUS subcomponent of our XTRA (cf. Kobsa et al., 1986) system handles a variety of *tactile gestures*, including different granularities, inexact pointing gestures, and *pars-pro-toto deixis*. In the latter case, the user points at an embedded region when actually intending to refer to a superordinated region. XTRA provides NL access to an expert system, which assists the user in filling out a tax form. During the dialogue, the relevant page of the tax form is displayed on one window of the screen, so that the user can refer to regions of the form by tactile gestures. The syntax and semantics of the tax form is represented as a directed acyclic graph (including relations such as "geometrically embedded" or "conceptual part of"), which contains links to concepts in a KL-ONE knowledge base.

The deixis analyser of XTRA is realised as a *constraint propagation* process over these networks. In addition, TACTILUS uses various other knowledge sources of XTRA (e.g. the semantics of the accompanying verbal description, case frame information, the dialogue memory) for the interpretation of the pointing gesture.

While the simultaneous exploitation of both verbal and non-verbal channels provides maximal efficiency, most of the current prototypes do not use truly parallel input techniques, as they combine *typed* NL and pointing. In these systems the user's hands move frequently back-and-forth from the keyboard to the pointing device. Note, however, that multi-modal input makes even NL interfaces without speech input more acceptable (less keystrokes) and that the research on typed NL forms the basis for the ultimate speech understanding system.

Another restriction of current prototypes is that the presented visual material is fixed and finite, so that the system builder can encode its semantics into the knowledge base. While some of the recent NL interfaces respond to queries by generating graphics, they are not able to analyse and answer follow-up questions about the form and content of this graphics, as they do not have an appropriate representation of its syntax and semantics. Here one of the challenging problems is the *automatic formalisation of synthetic visual information* as a basis for the interpretation of gestural input.

Some of the open questions which have to be solved by future research in cognitive science are:

1. How can *non-verbally communicated information* be included in a formal semantic representation of discourse?
2. What is an *adequate architecture* of parsers and generators for multimodal communication?
3. How could a generator decide whether to use a pointing gesture, a verbal description or a combination of both for referent identification (*knowledge-based media choice*)?
4. What are the temporal interdependences of verbal and non-verbal output in deictic expressions (synchronisation of speech and gesture)?
5. How can we cope with complex pointing actions, e.g. a continuous movement of the index finger (drawing a circle around a group of objects, underlining something, specifying a direction or a path) or a quick repetition of discrete pointing acts (emphatic pointing, multiple reference)?

3.3 Spatial Descriptions

When seeing a series of TV pictures showing a part of a highway where several hundred vehicles are lined up one behind the other, each one moving forward only at a snail's pace, we can sum up the scene with the expression "traffic-jam". This is a typical example of a large class of situations that can be described with the statement "one word says more than a thousand pictures"—a reversal of the classical saying.

One of the major goals of cognitive science for the years to come is to gain a better understanding of how perception interacts with language production. A connection to the real world via perception is an optimal starting point for the investigation of *referential semantics* in natural language systems. Traditionally, referential semantics is the study of how phrases in a sentence connect to objects and events in the real world. One of the goals of language-oriented AI research is to attain a completely operational, extreme form of referential semantics that reaches down to the sensoric level.

However, because so far most NL systems have no access to sensory data, in NL research referential semantics often considers only the relationship of phrases to terms in the knowledge representation language. This means that the result of the referential analysis of a nounphrase like "the red car" is simply an identifier like "CAR123", which may be interpreted as an individual constant in a logic-based representation, a node in a semantic network, or a frame instance, depending on the particular knowledge representation language underlying the system. Moreover, a sentence like "The red car stopped now" is mapped onto some simple event representation, e.g. named "EVENT07" which links the referents for the nounphrase and the temporal adverb together. In the model-theoretic sense, for these systems, the knowledge base itself plays the role of the model, so that each syntactic constituent corresponds to an object in the knowledge base.

Such an approach obviously is inadequate for explaining the detailed semantics of spatial prepositions, locomotion verbs or temporal adverbs. Taking referential semantics seriously means that *tactile, acoustic* and *visual perception processes* must be coupled with language analysis and generation processes, so that their mutual dependencies can be studied. If an AI system is ever to use verbs like "hit", "push" and "touch" correctly, taking the subtle semantic differences between them into account, it has to rely on lexical entries for these verbs which establish explicit links to sensory information.

Some authors claim that for symbols to have meaning to an AI system, there must be *sensory symbols* to which the *nonsensory symbols* are related by some computational formalism (e.g. Woods, 1983). Even if one does not adopt this extreme position, it is clear that the semantic objects onto which spatial descriptions are mapped must be elements of a domain with a rich geometric structure. Unlike most other semantic theories, the model theory of *situation semantics* (cf. Barwise & Perry, 1983) explicitly refers to a sort of locations L, which consists of connected regions of space-time and various structural relations between them, so that is has much promise for application in natural language scene description (cf. Fenstad, 1988).

Whereas for many years there was little interaction between computer vision and language researchers, in the last few years this situation is changing.

A great practical advantage of natural language scene description is the possibility of the application-specific selection of *varying degrees of condensation* of visual information. The vast amount of visual data accumulated in medical technology, remote sensing and traffic control, for example, can only be handled by a machine. As opposed to a representation of the results of processing digitised image sequences in the form of graphical output, a natural language description of an image sequence can provide the user with more information in less time. If a system is capable of describing the results of interpreting an image sequence in a medical context as "stricture of the left kidney artery", the doctor can first classify this description according to the diagnostic context and later go back to specific segments of single relevant images.

Numerous open questions concerning the formal reconstruction of the interplay between "seeing" and "speaking" must be further explored and resolved.

A problem which is generally left unsolved is one where not only the course of a trajectory in time and space is of decisive importance for the selection of an adequate description. For example, even if all temporal and spatial requirements for the description of the observed trajectory of a moving vehicle are met, a description such as (1) might still be felt to be inadequate:

1. The car is parking in front of the traffic lights.

Only by taking the *intention behind an action* into consideration (cf. Retz-Schmidt, 1986) can an adequate description of the same trajectory be given as in (2):

2. The car is waiting in front of the traffic lights.

One criterion for the choice of soccer as a domain of discourse in the VITRA project (cf. Wahlster, 1988b) was the fact that the influence of the agents' assumed intentions on the description is particularly obvious here. Thus (3) and (4) describe the same process in time-space but imply different team membership for player Meyer:

3. Meyer kicked the ball out of play next to the goal.
4. Meyer barely missed the goal.

In (3), the player has no intention of getting the ball into the goal, but deliberately kicks it out of play. In (4), by comparison, the player's kick was clearly aimed at the goal as expressed in the verb "miss".

One advantage of this domain of discourse is that, given the position of players, their team membership and the distribution of roles in standard situations (e.g. penalties and corners), stereotypical intentions can be assumed for each situation. Given the current state of *plan recognition* research, then, the chances of successfully reaching the described research goal are better than in other less schematised situations.

A second problem arises from the fact that a system, in order to generate communicatively adequate descriptions, must construct a model of the visual conceptualisations which the system's utterance elicits in the hearer's mind. Such a user model (cf. Wahlster & Kobsa, 1986) can become relevant for the decision during sentence generation as to whether, instead of a definite description, a pronoun might also be understandable for the hearer.

Let us suppose that the system has just generated the following text as a description of an observed situation:

5. In the left half, Jones is running toward the goal with the ball. Meyer is chasing him and trying to attack him. But Meyer is too slow.

Because it is not possible for the hearer to visually follow the action on the field, s/he can only form a rough idea of the spatial setting. It is imperative that the system be able to put itself into the hearer's place and take the hearer's possibly imagined conceptualisation into account before continuing to generate sentences.

If the system is planning to generate sentence (6), it must decide, in order to conform with the conversational maxim of cooperativity, whether the referent of the pronoun "him" can be unambiguously determined by the hearer:

6. Now only the goal keeper is between him and the goal.

Only "Jones" and "Meyer" in the preceding text are possible referents for the pronoun. Because Meyer was mentioned last, this referent is the first to suggest itself to the reader in purely textual terms. In the sense of an *anticipation feedback loop* (cf. Jameson & Wahlster, 1982), however, the system could recognise that this resolution of the anaphora is inconsistent with the assumed spatial conceptualisation in the hearer's mind by accessing the *imagination component* of the user model. Therefore, "Jones" is the only unambiguous referent for the pronoun that is compatible with the user model. Only after such a successful understanding process has been anticipated should the planned sentence be generated. Otherwise, the system would not be able to employ pronominalisation to shorten its sentences but would have to resort to the use of proper nouns, for example.

3.4 Non-monotonicity in Understanding

Due to the serial nature of utterances and dialogues, non-monotonicity is pervasive in natural language processing. When reading text left-to-right, *default assumptions* made early in the sentence must often be withdrawn as reading proceeds (cf. Zernik & Brown, 1988). A similar problem occurs when following a dialogue, as assumptions about the dialogue partner, derived from his dialogue behaviour at an early stage of the conversation, often have to be retracted in a later phase of the dialogue (cf. Wahlster, 1988a).

During the last years, non-monotonic inference was identified as a central part of *common sense reasoning*. A number of formalisms for non-monotonic logic have been proposed, none of them completely successful (cf. Ginsberg, 1987). On the practical side there has been better success at integrating so-called *reason-maintenance systems* into AI systems for belief revision. However, the role of default reasoning in natural language processing is an important research question, which has barely been addressed.

Zernik and Brown (1988) show that even during the various processing stages for an apparently simple sentence [see (7a) and (7b) below] interpretations are asserted and retracted dynamically. Sentence (7a) yields the intitial hypothesis that "John got the battery".

7a. John needed a new battery. He took it

This interpretation is based on two assumptions: Unless otherwise observed, a generic word like "take" indexes the generic meaning of a physical transfer and the pronoun "it" refers to the last physical object mentioned in the discourse. However, as reading proceeds,

7b. John needed a battery. He took it up with dad

the initial interpretation must be revised, because a more specific lexical entry is found. The idiomatic sense of "He took it up with his dad" leads to to an interpretation in which "it" refers to John's goal of getting a battery and "take up" is understood as "raising an issue". However, the initial reading must be recovered when reading the end of the sentence.

7c. John needed a battery. He took it up with dad from the basement.

The *Non-Monotonic Grammar* (NMG) described by Zernik and Brown is a first attempt to use a reason maintenance package for enhancing a parser's capabilities. NMG uses dependency directed backtracking, so that unlike other current parsers it does not have to recompute the initial interpretation after retracting the idiomatic reading. Processing garden path sentences and parsing in the presence of lexical gaps are other tasks highlighting the role of default reasoning in text comprehension.

User modelling is another important research area in natural language processing where non-monotonic reasoning plays a crucial role. Consider the following dialogue (U = User, S = System) with a tutoring system (cf. Wahlster, 1988a):

8. S: Tell me about California.
9. U: San Francisco is the capital of California.
10. S: No, that's wrong.
11. U: I see. So, that's not the capital.
12. U: Then, what is the capital?
13. S: Sacramento.
14. S: Now, tell me why you mentioned San Francisco first, when you began to talk about California.

A simple consequence of the user's response (9) is an entry in the system's user model, which represents the fact, that the system believes that the user believes (B1). After (10), and certainly after (11), the model should contain (B1'):

B1.   capital (California, San-Francisco).
B1'. not (capital (California, San-Francisco).
B2.   capital (California, Sacramento).

This means that the user-modelling component has to remove (B1) from the user model [in a reason maintenance system this causes (B1) to be added to the set of beliefs, which are currently "out"]. After (13) the user's belief (B2) should be added to the system's user model. If the *a priori* user model contains "For each state there exists one and only one capital" as a mutual believed fact, then the user-modelling component can also remove (B1') after adding (B2). The GUMS system is a first attempt to integrate a belief revision component into a dialogue-based user-modelling component (cf. Finin & Drager, 1986).

3.5 Transmutable Systems

A general-purpose natural language dialogue system should be adaptable to applications that differ not only with respect to the domain of discourse, but also to dialogue type, user type, and intended system behaviour. In Wahlster and Kobsa (1986), we call such systems, which are transportable and adaptable to diverse conversational settings, *transmutable systems*. A first attempt to build a transmutable system was our design of the experimental dialogue system HAM-ANS (see Hoeppner et al., 1983), whose dialogue behaviour can be switched from a "cooperative" mode (e.g. the system answers questions about a traffic scene) to a "interest-based" mode (e.g. the system tries to persuade the user to book a room in a particular hotel).

When people communicate, they do so for a purpose specific to the conversational situation. On the other hand, most of the systems developed so far have no interest beyond providing the information-seeking user with relevant data. In the long run, natural language systems as components of advanced knowledge-based systems must perform a greater variety of illocutionary and perlocutionary acts: they may teach, consult, or persuade the user, inspire him to action or argue with him (see Bates & Bobrow, 1984; Wahlster, 1984; Webber, 1986; Woods, 1984). The major problem builders of transmutable systems are confronted with, is the lack of representational vocabulary for the declarative description of the relationship between the system and the user, the *system's intended dialogue behaviour* and the associated *conversational tactics*.

3.6 Text Generation

The task of text generation involves translating knowledge represented in a formal language in a computer's memory into natural language. For example, information encoded in a knowledge representation language like KL-TWO regarding the use or repair of a technical system could be used as the basis for the automatic generation of instruction manuals in a *variety of natural languages*. Moreover, from the same representation, different manuals could be generated for different audiences, such as beginners, expert users, or maintenance personnel. Ultimately, techniques of user modelling (cf. Wahlster & Kobsa, 1986) can tailor the documents to the background of each particular individual, making the text more understandable and generating the correct level of detail. Especially in a tutorial framework, it is important to make the generated text interesting. Heuristics for increasing the tension and fluency of a text must be integrated. In order to speed up the comprehension process the system has to generate *meta-utterances* like "as I have stated before" or "generally speaking" (cf. Zuckermann & Pearl, 1984).

There are two main aspects of generation: (1) deciding what to say, and (2) deciding how to say it. For the first task it is important to treat text generation as a special case of a goal-oriented action, which requires planning and reasoning. Combined with speech act theory the planning approach to text generation promises significant advances, but it presupposes efficient inference systems for reasoning about the beliefs, goals and actions of rational agents.

Another goal which requires considerable basic research is that of matching the NL production capabilities of systems with their comprehension capabilities. This is a prerequisite for building advanced *writer's workbenches*.

Such document preparation aids could detect errors in spelling and grammar, suggest paraphrases of passages of the text to make them more understandable, suggest ways to shorten the text or to restructure the document. This involves integrating work on text processing, document formatting and natural language processing.

3.7 Tools for NL Research

An investment in good tools for NL research and the development of NL systems will pay excellent dividends. Such tools make it possible to test new theories or methods and to build new systems more rapidly, by using *off-the-shelf components* for programs.

In order to speed up the development of large lexicons and grammars, and to ensure their well-formedness and consistency, specialised software tools must be developed, much like the structured editors and programming environments that improve programmer productivity. Utilities to trace the application of the lexicon and the grammar to a set of examples and to display the processing graphically can improve the debugging and the quality assurance processes.

We do need to have these tools well-documented, portable, reliable and widely distributed as public domain software. The sharing of tools should be encouraged by funding the development and maintenance of research tools, for example morphological analysers, parser generators, knowledge representation systems, planning and inference components, and language generators.

REFERENCES

Allen, J. (1987). *Natural language understanding*. Menlo Park: Benjamin/Cummings.

Barwise, J. & Perry, J. (1983). *Situations and attitudes*. Cambridge, Mass.: MIT Press.

Bates, M. & Bobrow, R.J. (1984). Natural language interfaces: What's here, what's coming, and who needs it. In W. Reitman, (Ed.); *Artificial intelligence applications for business*, pp.179-194. Norwood: Ablex.

Carbonell, J.G. & Hayes, P.J. (1983). Recovery strategies for parsing extragrammatical language. *Journal of Computational Linguistics, 9*, (3–4), 123-146.

Fenstad, J.E. (1988). Natural language systems. In R. Nossum, (Ed.), *Advanced course on AI*. Heidelberg: Springer.

Finin, T. W. & Drager, D. (1986). GUMS: A general user modeling system. In *Proc. of the 6th Canadian Conf. on AI*, pp.24-29. Montreal.

Ginsberg, M.L. (Ed.) (1987). *Readings in nonmonotonic reasoning*. Los Altos, Calif.: Kaufmann.

Hoeppner, W., Christaller, Th., Marburger, H., Morik, K., Nebel, B., O'Leary, M. & Wahlster, W. (1983). Beyond domain-independence: Experience with the development of a German language access system to highly diverse background systems. In *Proc. of IJCAI-83*, pp.588-594. Karlsruhe.

Jameson, A. & Wahlster, W. (1982). User modelling in anaphora generation: Ellipsis and definite descriptions. In *Proc. of 1st ECAI*, pp.222-227. Orsay.

Kobsa, A., Allgayer, J., Reddig, C., Reithinger, N., Schmauks, D., Harbusch, K., & Wahlster, W. (1986). Combining deictic gestures and natural language for referent identification. In *Proc. of COLING-86*, pp.356-361.

Retz-Schmidt, G. (1986). Script-based generation and evaluation of expectations in traffic scenes. In H. Stoyan, (Ed.), *GWAI-85. 9th German Workshop on Artificial Intelligence*. Heidelberg: Springer.

Wahlster, W. (1984). Cooperative access systems. *Future Generation Computer Systems*, *1*, (2), 103-111.

Wahlster, W. (1988a). Distinguishing user models from discourse models. In A. Kobsa, & W. Wahlster, (Eds), *Special issue on user modeling. Journal of Computational Linguistics*.

Wahlster, W. (1988b). One word says more than a thousand pictures. *Computers and Artificial Intelligence*,7.

Wahlster, W. & Kobsa, A. (1986). Dialog-based user models. In G. Ferrari (Ed.), *Special issue on natural language processing. IEEE Proceedings*, *74* (7), 948-960.

Waltz, D. (1983). Artificial intelligence: An assessment of the state-of-the-art and recommendation of future directions. *AI Magazine*, Fall, 55-67.

Webber, B.L. (1986). Questions, answers and responses: Interacting with knowledge base systems. In: M. Brodie, & J. Mylopoulos, (Eds), *On knowledge base management systems*. New York: Springer.

Woods, W. A. (1983). Under what conditions can a machine use symbols with meaning? In *Proc. of IJCAI-83*, pp. 47-48. Karlsruhe.

Woods, W. A. (1984). Natural language communication with machines: An ongoing goal. In W. Reitman, (Ed.), *Artificial intelligence applications for business*, pp.195-209. Norwood: Ablex.

Zernik, U. & Brown, A. (1988). Default reasoning in natural language processing: A preliminary report. To appear in *Proc. of COLING'88*, Budapest.

Zuckermann, I. & Pearl, J. (1984). *Listener model for the generation of meta-technical utterances in math tutoring*. Technical Report, UCLA, Cognitive Science Lab.

CHAPTER 8

Reasoning and Cognition: Towards a Wider Perspective on Logic

Johan van Benthem

Institute for Language, Logic and Information,
Faculty of Mathematics and Computer Science,
University of Amsterdam, The Netherlands

1. LOGIC AS THE SCIENCE OF REASONING

There are two main sources of knowledge, one being perception in its various forms, the other reasoning as a process of transforming knowledge structures and creating new ones. That the latter process has enough regularity to lend itself to systematic study was discovered in Antiquity, and the discipline of Logic has been concerned with the various aspects of reasoning ever since. Thus, logic is the study of *knowledge in action*.

Another way of describing the field to be studied is as the process of manipulating *information*: extracting it, modifying it, transferring it. This is reflected in the various *functions* of reasoning: to prove a statement, to refute it, to correct it, etc. A deeper account of these functions turns out to involve a study of the possible *forms* of information, and a common assumption, also in logic, is that these forms can be found, or at least be represented in some kind of language, whether natural or artificial. Thus, logic has a common cause with linguistics, and other disciplines where language plays a central role, such as computer science or artificial intelligence. Eventually, language may be taken in a very broad semiotic sense here to include any form of information carrier, be it written or spoken text, graphics, or even other means.

The general plan of a logical theory for some specific aspect of the above task is as follows. First, one chooses an appropriate *language* for representing the kind of information being considered. Then, one has to give an account of the *meaning* of this language, as it applies to reality, or to some *representation* of the latter. Such an account of meaning already determines a notion of *validity* for inferences from one statement to another. Finally, there is the computational aspect of describing explicit systems of *proof*, or other computational algorithms for establishing validity, whose individual steps may be viewed as atomic mental operations transferring information. Of course, within this broad scheme, there is a plethora of additional questions to be asked and studied: logical theories usually have a broad scientific fall-out.

This scheme again highlights what are the closest neighbours of logic, at least from a cognitive perspective: the language part leads to linguistics, meaning and representation also bring in psychology, and proof with computation creates additional links with computer science. More detailed illustrations of these interfaces will be given in due course.

2. A MINIATURE HISTORY

Logic found its origin, like most sciences, in Greek philosophy, where it was systematised by Aristotle as a tool for rational argument and deliberation. In a broad sense, including the theory of knowledge and general methodology, logic has been a major part of the philosophical curriculum ever since. This explains why departments of philosophy are still one of the major sites for this discipline. The other locations are departments of mathematics and, more recently, linguistics and computer science, something which will be explained presently.

In the nineteenth century, there was a growing rapprochement between logic and mathematics. By then, research into the foundations of mathematics had reached a degree of formal precision where it became imperative to be fully explicit about the actual patterns of inference admissible in mathematical reasoning. And this was precisely what logic supplied, in the hands of famous practitioners such as Gottlob Frege and David Hilbert. As is usual in good applications, however, the discipline being applied did not remain unaffected by the process. And indeed, logic itself became more and more mathematical in its outlook, both as regards its notions and techniques, and as regards its guiding perspective. Foundational questions, concerning the consistency or completeness of mathematical theories, became of paramount importance. Unfortunately, this also resulted, in some quarters, in a noticeable narrowing of concerns: wider questions of a more linguistic or psychological nature were ignored, and sometimes even publicly repudiated.

Two examples of the latter tendency have become famous. Frege, as well as many later followers, believed in a refutation of "Psychologism", a supposedly ill-founded doctrine ascribing mental reality to logical and cognitive concepts generally. As a purely methodological separation of concerns, this attitude may have some virtues, but the real danger has rather been a growing blindness to the common ground with cognitive psychology. (This is not a phenomenon peculiar to logic. A similar separatist tendency has made much classical Theory of Knowledge relatively sterile, whereas it took research in artificial intelligence, disregarding established academic watersheds, to revitalise many traditional epistemological discussions.)

Another separatist stance is enshrined in the so-called "Misleading Form Thesis", advocated vigorously by Bertrand Russell and the early Ludwig Wittgenstein (who repented eventually). For the purposes of smooth logical inference, it is often necessary—or at least convenient—to diverge from the surface forms of natural language, using autonomous "logical forms" instead. Indeed, natural language grammar can be systematically misleading, witness such similar grammatical structures as the following pair:

"Andreotti resigned."
"Nobody resigned."

Their two meanings do not have the same structure at all: in particular, there is no individual "nobody" who resigned in the second case. Lack of awareness of such pitfalls accounts for many errors in classical and contemporary philosophy, according to Russell and Wittgenstein. Hence they advocated an exclusive concentration on logical form, leaving the linguists to cope with the muddy waters of actual language.

Even if the mathematical turn brought this narrowing of concerns, it also compensated for it by a scala of tangible benefits. For instance, logic acquired a set of sophisticated mathematical tools for carrying out the above tasks, as well as a set of foundational results about their strength and limitations (famous examples are the Theorems of Gödel on Completeness and Incompleteness, the Turing analysis of Computability and Decidability, and the Hilbert-Gentzen development of Proof Theory). These tools have been applied quite succesfully to many questions in the foundations of mathematics, a lively enterprise which continues to this day.

Recently, the horizons of logic have started expanding again, with many wider questions returning into focus. These questions had often been kept alive in neighbouring disciplines. Linguists continued the study of meaning structures within natural language, and occasionally reaffirmed the ideal of a "natural logic", consonant with, rather than opposed to grammatical form. Philosophers of science worked on theories of explanation, confirmation, causality or truth-approximation, which can all be viewed as aspects of the various functions of reasoning set out in Section 1. And of course, in the last two decades, new disciplines such as computer science and artificial intelligence have started raising questions of computation and reasoning in more practically oriented forms.

Now, the interesting and promising fact is that many of the logical techniques developed in the foundational phase turn out to be applicable in this wider setting—or at least, they seem to provide the best scientific points of departure that we know of. This application cannot be a matter of mere translation of existing results into cognitive jargon, of course. New questions will emerge, and new situations subtly different from earlier ones. But their systematic exploration is virtually unthinkable without the level of logical sophistication given to us by Frege and his successors.

3. THE PRESENT STATE OF LOGIC

Current developments in "mathematical logic" and the foundations of mathematics are well-documented in the authoritative *Handbook of Mathematical Logic* (Barwise,

1977). Here, one will find the main technical subdisciplines which have evolved in this century, such as:

1. Model Theory (studying the relation between   formal languages and models).
2. Proof Theory (studying the formal structure of systems of proof).
3. Recursion Theory (studying the general aspects of computability).
4. Set Theory (being the mother theory for modern mathematics and logic).

As a counterpoint, there has also been a development of so-called "philosophical logic", which has tended to concentrate on those kinds of reasoning which have a special philosophical interest. A prominent example here is the logic of modalities, whether ontological (necessity, possibility, causality) or epistemological (knowing, believing). Around these themes, a technical field has sprung up of so-called intensional logic, trying to model the semantics of these notions using extensions of the Fregean paradigm in mathematical logic. This area is well- documented too, in the *Handbook of Philosophical Logic* (Gabbay & Guenthner, 1983-1987).

Finally, as for more recent developments in applied logic, two handbooks on "Logic in Computer Science" and "Logic in Artificial Intelligence" are in the making as well (Gabbay et al., in press a, b).

4. COGNITIVE TRENDS IN CONTEMPORARY LOGIC

To illustrate a certain cognitive trend in modern logic, we give an impression of how an "epistemic logic" would proceed. To study the behaviour of the notion of knowledge, expressed in the verb "know that", one takes a sentence forming operator K:

$K_x p$ (person x knows that p).

Then, various possible principles of cognitive inference can be formulated, such as the following:

- $K_x p$, $K_x(p \rightarrow q)$ implies $K_x q$
  (if x knows that p, and she knows that p implies q, then she knows that q),
- $K_x p \rightarrow p$
  (what is known is true),
- $K_x p \rightarrow K_x K_x p$
  (positive introspection: if one knows something, then one knows that one knows it),
- $\neg K_x p \rightarrow K_x \neg K_x p$
  (negative introspection: if x does not know p, then she knows that she does not know p).

There has been a good deal of philosophical debate about the validity or invalidity of these principles: in particular, about the introspection axioms. By itself, the introduction of a perspicuous logical *notation*, as in the above, was already an intellectual advance here.

A semantic analysis which illuminated this debate was found in the 1950s, starting from the following simple idea. A person can imagine a certain range of possibilities of how the world could turn out to be: her "epistemic horizon". If this range is very large, many alternative options are still open, which means that the person does not know very much yet. When more information comes in, certain options will drop out (being excluded by the new data): the smaller the range, the greater the knowledge. (In the limiting case, there is only one world left in the range, and the person knows the world completely.) Now, this picture suggests making knowledge statements themselves relative to worlds, viewed as epistemic perspectives, in the following manner:

$K_x p$ is true in world w

if and only if

p is true in all worlds which are epistemic alternatives to world w for person x.

Then, looking at the above principles, only the first is immediately validated by this scheme. (If p holds in all alternatives, and p implies q there, then q holds in all alternatives.) The other principles, however, presuppose certain requirements on the alternative relation describing epistemic ranges. For instance, the second one demands that every world always be an epistemic alternative to itself, and the third that alternatives to epistemic alternatives be still epistemic alternatives themselves. Thus, the semantics enables us to translate questions of epistemic reasoning into various associated pictures of what the pattern of knowledge states looks like. This correspondence has sparked off much research in intensional logic.

But also, the semantics sketched here has proven useful, in quite unexpected ways, in different areas, notably in computer science. For instance, informal reasoning about the behaviour of systems of distributed processors following some fixed protocol, has an epistemic slant. One tends to argue in patterns like "As long as processor x does not know if processor y has already completed its task, it will wait and ... ". To make this kind of reasoning precise, so as to allow for exact correctness proofs for protocols with respect to stated goals, the above epistemic calculus turned out to be just what is needed. Moreover, the above semantics has a very concrete explication here. The worlds are the global states of the system of processors. And, in any one of these global states S, a processor x has for its "epistemic" alternatives those global states of the system which it cannot distinguish from S. (Seen from S, these are all possible global states where x has the same local state.) Note that this relation does satisfy the requirements validating the second and third principles of epistemic reasoning, and in fact also the fourth: distributed protocols, on this view, have negative introspection.

Also, conversely, the computer science connection has invigorated epistemic logic itself. Notably, in the application just outlined, a crucial aspect is the interplay of *several* knowing agents at the same time: processor x has to reckon with what y knows about him and others, etc. But, this is precisely what is also going on in discourse between human knowers. In particular, successful communication presupposes a certain measure of *common knowledge*, shared by all participants, being such that everyone also knows that this is shared knowledge. There is a fast-growing literature on the possibility of (efficient) attainment of common knowledge, which is of equal interest to logicians, computer scientists and general philosophers.

Epistemic logic is by no means the only way in which cognitive concerns have entered modern logic (in the long run it may not even be the most significant way). A deeper connection is found, interestingly, in the foundations of mathematics. Within mathematics, there has alway been an interplay between two major viewpoints. On the one hand, mathematical objects can be thought of as existing in some abstract realm of numbers, sets, functions and the like—and the mathematician is an explorer describing what is true in this realm. On the other hand, mathematical objects can be viewed as human mental constructions, produced in the course of mathematical proofs and definitions. The latter perspective is stressed in so-called "constructive mathematics", of which a particularly important and well-developed species is called *Intuitionism*. When the creation of objects and the proof of their properties become part of the same process, it becomes natural to replace abstract truth by a fundamental notion of provability, or "assertability". Accordingly, in intuitionistic mathematics, the basic notion is "I know/have a proof that object x has property P".

This view has repercussions for general logic too. With the intuitionistic set-up for mathematics comes a so-called "intuitionistic logic", with a stronger constructive, knowledge-oriented character than the Fregean standard logic. It differs from the latter in several respects. For instance, a disjunctive statement p-or-q can only be asserted if one knows (or, can find out effectively) which disjunct is true. (Therefore, an intuitionist cannot accept the usual logical law of Excluded Middle p-or-not-p; because for many statements p, we do not know whether p holds or not-p, and may not even have the slightest idea how to settle the matter.) Likewise, an existential statement "There exists an object x with property P" will only be true, intuitionistically, if we can *construct* an example of such an x satisfying P. Thus, truth and knowledge become closely intertwined, and the semantics for intuitionistic logic (of which there exist quite a few) all have a definite epistemic flavour.

Constructivist ideas have not remained confined to the foundations of mathematics. Various logicians have argued that a similar perspective can be taken, and perhaps should be taken with respect to meaning in general. Michael Dummett has argued forcefully, since the early 1970s, that the above general approach is almost forced upon us, once we assume a Wittgensteinian account of meaning, as being determined by *language use*. The crucial notion, then, is when one can *state* (or *reject*) a sentence, rather than when it is true *in abstracto*. This general cognitive trend is quite conspicuous in contemporary semantics, where more concrete cognitive "information-based" proposals abound.

Again, these discussions also have a practical side, which shows in a connection with computer science. The usual division of labour in the latter area has been to first write a program, embodying a certain algorithm for performing some specified task, and only then to enquire into its correctness, trying to prove that the algorithm does the specified job. The practical problem with this approach is its complexity: correctness proofs can be of forbidding length (if at all possible). A better approach, as was found by workers in the field, is to proceed in tandem: developing algorithms hand in hand with the skeleton of a correctness proof for it (that is, a particular form of "structured programming"). Now, here is where intuitionistic logic is particularly suitable, thanks to its integrated philosophy. Proving that an object exists already amounts to giving an algorithm for computing it; so, the two processes are really one! This observation is the basis for various current attempts to apply intuitionistic, or more generally constructive systems of logic to program development and verification.

5. CONTACTS WITH LINGUISTICS

Gradually, in the twentieth century, the isolationist tendencies described in Section 2 have lessened. For instance, the Misleading Form Thesis, once an article of faith for analytic philosophers, has receded into the background. As modern linguistics progressed, natural language grammar turned out to be much more systematic than had been assumed, and hence capable of being linked up with logical forms as developed within the Frege-Russell tradition. Especially when Noam Chomsky introduced his Transformational Generative Grammar, incorporating a basic distinction between linguistic "surface structure" and its underlying more stable "deep structure", the road seemed open to an identification of deep structure with logical form. This was in fact proposed in the so-called "Generative Semantics" movement around 1970. Eventually more fruitful, however, was a different approach, put forward by the logician Richard Montague around the same time. In what has come to be called *Montague Grammar*, grammatical structures are translated into logical formulas, whose already available semantic interpretation can then be enlisted to serve natural language as well. Afterwards, the ladder may be thrown away, and we can interpret natural languages directly, just as systematically as formal languages.

Through this channel, an intensive mutual traffic has started flowing. Linguists have discovered that their grammatical theories can be linked with a rigorous semantics (despite earlier leanings to an "autonomy of syntax"), even if this imposes certain constraints on how their grammars should be arranged. But also, logicians have become inspired to search for logical formalisms and accompanying semantics optimally suited to match various phenomena in natural language. Several mutual concerns of cognitive import have arisen in this way. For instance, there are several levels now where knowledge representation can take place: close to grammatical form (sentence or discourse representation), but also further away, in logical semantic structures (recall the above semantics for epistemic operators in terms of knowledge states). And the systematic connections between these various loci invite us to study the links between more language-internal knowledge, and more external manifestations of the same, all the way to the eventual bridge with physical reality.

Another shared interest is the locus of inference. We have the option now of describing this human competence entirely within the logical side of the spectrum—but also, if only by borrowing, inference can be described at the level of grammatical forms (using a montagovian translation). The latter approach would already realise some form of the earlier-mentioned "natural logic". Using currently available insights, however, the picture becomes much more delicate and sensitive. Certain mechanisms of inference seem to operate very close to surface syntax, with relatively low algorithmic complexity. An example is so-called Monotonicity reasoning, which allows replacement of one expression by another with a "larger extension". For instance, sentence patterns headed by a determiner expression "all", "some" or "most" are monotone in their right-most position:

Det X Y.

Thus, since "having an entrance" is a property with a larger extension than "having a door",

> "Most houses *have a door*" implies
> "Most houses *have an entrance*".

It turns out that such monotone positions, allowing this type of replacement, can be marked systematically during the parsing process constructing grammatical forms, and thus, this type of inference can take a free ride on the syntax. Other types of inference, however, are not as easy to describe, requiring pre-processing of grammatical forms to either some kind of linguistic representation, or even a rather different logical form. In this way, the earlier Misleading Form Thesis dissolves into a spectrum of research as to what fits where.

There is another noteworthy aspect to the above monotonicity reasoning. The inferential step consists really in a very simple operation on syntactic structures: *replacing* one item by another. Thus, the question arises whether a calculus of logic can be set up using only such simple concrete transformations, so that conclusions are literally reached by transforming premises in just these admissible ways. One other basic transformation of this kind is *deletion* of components, a pattern which is reflected, indeed, in another basic logical rule:

> "A (and) B" implies A.

Perhaps more interesting is the operation of *copying*. There is in fact a large class of natural language inferences which consist in copying parts of expressions elsewhere. A well-known case is the rule of "Conservativity" for determiner expressions, as illustrated in the following pair of sentences:

> "Most roofs leak"

implies (and is itself implied by)

> "Most roofs are leaking *roofs*".

In a more general form, such copying rules are found in the Peircean calculus of natural logic (see Guenthner, Chapter 5). The intriguing possibility here is that such calculi may correspond much more closely to the actual physical operations of hard-wired inferential processes in the human brain.

The preceding type of research can be classified as the use of logical *tools* in setting up systems of inference, or natural language processing generally. This is certainly one immediate, practical way of applying logic. But, there is a more fundamental use of logic, in this area too. Logical theory provides insights into why, and to which extent, such calculi will work—and what are their general semantic and computational properties. Thus, in various areas of semantics, a body of logical results has sprung up bringing out the deeper mathematical content of the enterprise. As is usual with formal mathematical approaches, another spin-off is the stimulation of creative phantasy: seeing one mathematical structure at once suggests another. Thus, foundational studies serve as a "laboratory of ideas" for further practical developments.

Many additional contacts between logic and linguistics are surveyed in van Benthem (Chapter 4).

6. CONTACTS WITH PSYCHOLOGY

The influence of anti-psychologistic ideas in logic has been longer in the waning than that of the anti-linguistic ones. To be sure, there were promising contacts in the nineteenth century, when thinkers like Helmholtz saw profound analogies between the basis of perception and the foundations of geometry, and Heymans proposed a foundation for logical reasoning in developmental psychology. But, these lines were not followed up in this century—with the exception of an interesting collaboration between two well-known representatives of their respective areas, viz. Jean Piaget and Evert Beth, who wrote a book underpinning Piaget's developmental psychology in various stages of logical foundational research. Another positive contemporary example worth mentioning is Gibson's "ecological realism", whose emphasis on transformations and invariants in perception is quite reminiscent of the Helmholtz program.

Generally speaking, contacts between logic and psychology in this century have been confined to more mathematical, methodological areas. This is not to say that these are without intrinsic interest. For instance, there is an extensive body of work on *Measurement Theory* which links questions in the foundations of mathematics and psychology. And, more recently, there has been a noticeable flourishing of a mathematical *Learning Theory* modelling psychological views of knowledge acquisition using tools from the logical theory of computation. Viewing human learners as fallible producers of hypotheses, in the face of ever growing amounts of data, subject to severe limitations of memory space and access, leads to interesting conclusions as to what are humanly learnable collections of theories.

Another obvious area of contact between logic and psychology would seem to be the psychology of reasoning itself. But in fact, recent work in this area has tended to look at linguistic, rather than logical inspiration—sometimes even with polemical undertones concerning the latter. Nevertheless, with the present confluence of approaches in logic and linguistics, conditions are changing nowadays. In particular, recent work on semantics and discourse carries the promise of producing a framework of *knowledge representation* which might serve both logicians and psychologists (compare Guenthner, Chapter 5 in this volume, and Noordman, Volume 1, Chapter 6).

A special case where such overlaps have already been recognised is in the study of time and temporal representation. Psychologists have long been interested in problems of temporal measurement, an interest resulting in various connections between the psychology of time and more logical theories of measurement. This raises issues of a most plausible representation of time and duration which are very similar to those investigated in current logic and linguistics. We shall return to this example in the section on Artificial Intelligence, an area which has proved quite fruitful as a meeting ground for logical and psychological concerns about cognition.

7. CONTACTS WITH COMPUTER SCIENCE

Unlike the previous cases, computer science has been an area without any prohibitions on border-crossing, at least for logicians. From its inception, this whole field has been tied up with logic in many ways. The general theory of computation and complexity was developed by recursion theorists, such as Turing and Kleene—and even von Neumann himself had been a field worker in the logical foundations of mathematics, at an earlier stage of his career. Likewise, the development of programming formalisms shows an unmistakeable influence from logic, evident in such "logic programming" languages as LISP or PROLOG, but also in various imperative languages. And, finally, as has been explained in van Benthem (Chapter 4), there is a great overlap between logical semantics in the more traditional sense, and the semantics of programming languages, as applied to questions of correctness and design. The various areas of complexity and semantics in computer science are thriving these days, so much so that various handbooks are coming out, to chronicle the first round of achievements.

One conspicuous focal point nowadays is the enterprise of *logic programming*, as exemplified in the European language PROLOG. Here, the predicate-logical formalism itself serves to describe the relevant knowledge about the data upon which computation is to be performed, as well as the requests for information triggering such computations. Moreover, the mechanism by which answers are obtained is a logical proof-generator: answers are to be deduced from the knowledge base. As the basic ideas of logic programming are widely known, it will be sufficient to make a few general observations. First, logic programming shows that logical formalisms with their accompanying proof algorithms, whatever their original theoretical motivation, can be put to use in the actual practice of computing. But also, as the PROLOG formalism is so close to those being used in formal semantics anyway, it may come to serve as a suggestive medium for computational thinking about current semantic theories, as well as a possible testing ground for such theories as to their computational feasibility. This computational view is already being implemented in so-called "conditional logics", a species of intensional logic describing inferences between conditional statements of the form:

"A ⇒ B" ("if A, then B").

These become dynamic systems of rules, when viewed as PROLOG instructions. Put somewhat vividly, a static "theory" of abstract implications between statements becomes a dynamic expert system, once a PROLOG engine is built in.

There is a caveat here. Often, the point of logic programming is presented as its being a completely *declarative* language, with the step-by-step *control* of the computing process (as exerted in imperative programming) being delegated to the system, i.e. the underlying theorem prover. Unfortunately, so the story continues, one has to make some concessions to reality (viz. efficiency): a certain amount of control remains necessary, in various ways, in order to protect the system from entering fruitless searches. So, logic programming would not yet have reached its ideal form. This presentation may actually be very misleading from a general cognitive perspective, for our cognitive capacities certainly seem to consist in *processing*, not just contemplating, declarative knowledge, an activity where control is as important as content. So, instead of downplaying imperative control aspects, one should rather integrate these into the study of knowledge. For instance, as with the constructive logic discussed in Section 4, logic programming makes algorithmic thinking and proving closely related activities ("Computation as Deduction"). But this should surely mean also that the control structure of proofs deserves more logical attention than it has hitherto received. Actual deduction is a game of manoeuvering information into the right position at the right time—witness such control instructions in discourse as "suppose", "let", "take", etc. Our rational competence consists not just in creating logically valid proofs, but also intelligible and convincing ones.

Thus, logic programming is one important, but by no means the only traffic link between logic and computer science. Other examples which may be mentioned are the theory of *databases* and knowledge bases, or the theory of *complexity* of computations (itself largely inspired by logical recursion theory). Especially nowadays, the latter area poses the great challenge of finding an analysis of *parallel computation* of equal elegance and power as Turing's analysis of sequential computation.

8. LOGIC AND ARTIFICIAL INTELLIGENCE

As was remarked earlier on, the study of inference has been expanded in various beneficial ways by researchers in AI, working in the more practical setting of describing "active intelligence", when designing, for example, expert systems for planning purposes. Such an enterprise forces one to tackle a broad spectrum of theoretical problems, disregarding traditional academic boundaries. In the process, many connections with logic have emerged.

Before giving some examples illustrating this phenomenon, a warning should be stated. As befits a frontier discipline, AI is an area where disputes not only flourish, but are also often pursued at gunpoint. In particular, the use of "logic" in AI itself has generated some controversy, including attempts at shoot-outs during scientific conferences. Here, we shall side-step this issue, letting the examples speak for themselves as to what is being pretended and what is not.

One conspicuous outcome of the above work in AI is the renewed interest in various forms of *plausible*, as opposed to absolutely *demonstrative* reasoning. This has generated various forms of quantitative probabilistic or inductive logic, but also several discoveries closer to deduction in its usual qualitative sense. One notable phenomenon in the latter vein arising here, which has attracted a lot of attention lately, is so-called *non-monotonicity* (the connection with the earlier "monotonicity inference" is only oblique): "What has been plausibly inferred in a certain state of knowledge (and ignorance!), may have to be abandoned when that state of knowledge grows". Under this heading, various previously scattered types of research suddenly become related. Non-monotonicity calls for an account, not just of inference, but also of *revision* of inferences, and of knowledge generally. Here is a topic where logically oriented philosophers of science have been active for quite a while—and it is interesting to observe how current research in artificial intelligence is trying to integrate ideas from logic and the philosophy of science, to arrive at workable models of knowledge revision. For instance, one major issue to be settled here, and one which had already been encountered by the philosophers, is if such processes of revision adapting inferences (and one might say, of *learning* in general) can be handled purely deductively, or whether some form of probabilistic analysis is needed in the end. This is reminiscent of the discussion between Popper's deductivism in the general theory of knowledge versus Carnap's inductivism (the latter finding a formal vehicle in so-called inductive logic). Of course, in line with earlier remarks, there might be room, or even a need for both approaches to the dynamics of knowledge.

A distinction commonly made in AI is that between *representation* of knowledge and *computation* with it (including inference). The former aspect has generated numerous contacts with logic too. Indeed, there are often striking analogies between discussions of advantageous formal modellings as found in AI and within logical semantics.

One telling illustration of this phenomenon is the study of *time*, and in particular the choice of basic temporal representations. It is now often agreed in psychology and artificial intelligence that what is needed are not so much physical, scientific models of time (or other basic concepts, for that matter), because these tend to get computationally intractable. What is needed are rather simple *common sense models* of time, such as those (presumably) governing our ordinary speech and domestic actions. This is one instance of a general program, toward recapturing a so-called "naive physics", consisting in the common sense theories of important clusters of spatio-temporal or causal concepts. Proposals in artificial intelligence for concrete samples of naive physics show striking parallels with earlier philosophical and logical studies on the interplay between the worlds of common sense and of science, with various systematic connections linking one to the other.

Here is a concrete example, where many research lines converge. In the 1970s, following Montague's original proposals for treating the semantics of temporal expressions, an old discussion about the structure of time was reopened. There has always been a certain duality between more continuous views of time, as consisting of extended chunks ("intervals"), and more discrete ones, where time is a succession of mathematical points. The latter view had gradually become dominant, not just in science, but also in logic and linguistics. But, empirical studies of linguistic temporal expressions suggested that our temporal representation rather consists in an ordered structure of events, with underlying intervals, which can be further subdivided or extended, as more pieces of information come in about what happened. Events do not occur at durationless points, they always "take time". Consequently, interval models were developed for linguistic purposes, with appropriate temporal logics to perform inferences with respect to them. Independently, a similar observation was made in the context of intelligent planning systems, where efficient storage and manipulation of temporal information requires interval-based, rather than point-based models. By now, the two research lines have started merging. In this process, many other themes turned out to be common concerns. A notable example is that of temporal monotonicity, or loss of it: "When, and for how long, can time-dependent information obtained about a certain interval be expected to hold good into the future?" Eventually, one would expect these issues to become challenges for the general psychology of time as well.

This concludes our list of examples illustrating the interaction between logic and artificial intelligence. It is far from being an exhaustive survey. One might elaborate with equal ease on such topics as *reasoning about knowledge* (as exemplified in epistemic logic) or *self-reflection* (a topic with deep roots in the logical foundations of mathematics.) Right now, however, we will move on.

9. CROSS-CONNECTIONS

As has been noted repeatedly in the story so far, there are many unifying themes in current logic, linguistics and computer science (including artificial intelligence). The phenomenon is so striking that many people already see one new discipline emerging here, centred around common cognitive problems. To increase the weight of evidence, we present a few examples of interdisciplinary convergence in a little more detail than has been done so far. The selection made is relatively arbitrary: often, one can start from any given significant problem in this area, and find that the intellectual thread will run from one established science into another.

Remark: This Section can be skipped without loss of continuity.

9.1 Categories and Types

Our first illustration concerns the mechanism of semantic interpretation. Frege has remarked that a fundamental mathematical pattern is to be observed in the construction of meanings for natural language expressions, viz. *function/argument* structure. This shows when a predicate is applied to an individual object ["(Mira) hates (Dorothy)", "(2)<(3)"], but also when a predicate itself is modified [as in "intensely (hate)", "(f)^2"], or when a determiner is being used ["every (midwife)(worries)", "$\forall x(Px)$"]. Frege's idea was carried further in the foundations of mathematics by Russell, who designed his "Theory of Types" as a formal language where all expressions are subdivided into their mathematical levels: individual objects, functions, functionals (i.e. operators on functions), etc. These levels reflect precisely the structure of the mathematical universe, according to Russell. In the subsequent history of mathematical logic, many results have been obtained about such type theories in the so-called *Lambda Calculus*.

Another historical line, however, takes us from Frege to the Polish logician Kazimierz Ajdukiewicz, who pursued the above analogy between functional types and grammatical categories. For instance, when the proper names "Mira" and "Dorothy" denote individuals, then the verb "hate" becomes a function from individuals to truth values, and the adverb "intensely" already a functional from verb phrases (predicates) to more complex verb phrases (predicates). Out of these observations arose so-called *Categorial Grammar*, which tries to describe natural languages by means of suitable assignments of types to all their syntactic categories. Correct expressions will then be exactly those for which the types assigned to their component words can be combined, by repeated function application, to one single final type.

Example
Let e be the type of individuals, t that of the truth values. Let (a,b) stand for the functional type "from type a to type b". Here are two categorial grammar parses for one single string of words:

On Monday Mira sings regularly
(t,t)   e   (e,t) (t,t)

Note how the expressions "on Monday" and "regularly" are taken as functions taking sentences to sentences here, the latter being the expressions denoting a truth value t. Now, the combination process can go two ways, deriving two possible readings for the above string:

First reading: ["on Monday (regularly...)"].

(t,t)   e   (e,t)   (t,t)
             ....
                   t
              ....
                          t
    ....
              t

REASONING AND COGNITION 199

Second reading: ["regularly (on Monday...)"].

```
   (t,t)    e          (e,t)   (t,t)
            ....................
                   t
   ...................
         t
           ...............................
                  t
```

The attractive feature of this procedure is that one kills two birds with one stone: we describe syntactic modes of combination, in parallel with a mathematical semantics.

In recent years, the two mentioned traditions are coming together, and this movement has brought to light some surprising connections between mathematical logic and linguistic questions. Here is one example, which also shows how unorthodox one has to be in one's expectations about what will turn out applicable where. The first practical problem confronting a linguist, once she has written a grammar, is that of *parsing* a given string of words. In categorial grammar, this question has the following form. Given some string of grammatical types, how can we determine effectively if it can be combined to a certain desired final type? The central step here is, as said before, repeated function application:

function type (a,b) together with argument type a yields value type b.

Already in the 1950s, mathematical logicians had observed the following analogy: in many respects, a *function type* (a,b) resembles a logical *implication* "if A, then B". Thus, function application becomes a basic rule from conditional logic, viz. Modus Ponens:

from A and *if* A, *then* B, infer B.

And this again means that the parsing problem can be regarded as a problem of logical *proof*: to infer, from a set of types viewed as implications, some final type with the rules of conditional logic. To give due credit, this analogy was first exploited by computer scientists, who, characteristically, summed it up in a vivid slogan: "Parsing as Deduction". Along this road, many methods developed in logical Proof Theory have turned out to be applicable in the theory of grammars—an unlikely employment for a subject conceived in the more esoteric regions of mathematical foundations.

With this connection, the applications of the Theory of Types are by no means exhausted. For instance, the Lambda Calculus is being used extensively in the syntax and semantics of programming languages, and various theories of types are presently being discussed in the semantics of natural languages too.

9.2 Inference and Minimalisation

For a second illustration, we take up an earlier-mentioned theme in artificial intelligence. As we said before, this area has produced a remarkable revival in studies of actual human reasoning, in its many facets. One central feature of this actual

200 8 VAN BENTHEM

reasoning is that it has to take place within tight constraints of complexity. We have only partial information about the world, and possess only limited powers of computation, and yet we have to make inferences, if only temporary ones.

One important strategy coming to our rescue here is what might be described as *minimalisation*. We assume that the situation at issue only validates our positive information, whereas "what we do not know, is not true". For instance, if a rule has exceptions, and we have a case at hand which might be one where it is applicable, then we will assume until further notice that it does in fact fall under the rule. (Only proven exceptions are allowed.) Technically, this idea is implemented, for a given set of data, by considering not all its possible models, but only the "minimal" ones among these, in some suitable mathematical sense. The number of inferences which can be made increases then:

> B follows from A, if B is true, not in all models of A (the usual criterion
> for logical validity), but if B is true in the smaller set of all minimal
> models of A.

For instance, as long as we know only swans that are white, all swans will be white in the minimal models for our knowledge.

The coin does have a reverse, obviously. Further incoming information may bring extended data, with a different set of minimal models, where not all earlier conclusions need be true. The first black swan encountered on our Australian vacation undermines the earlier generalisation. This is again the earlier-mentioned non-monotonicity, which calls for a second counter-balancing mechanism, viz. strategies of optimal revision of earlier assumptions.

Some clues as to a general treatment of non-monotonicity and knowledge revision may already be obtained from existing conditional logic. A conditional sentence such as: "If I catch the late-night train, I will be home in time", refers to *ordinary* circumstances: no explosions, sudden bankruptcy of the National Rail, or reversal of the laws of Nature. Technically, this feature has been modelled by introducing an ordering on the relevant worlds or situations, some of which are "closer" to each other than others. The conditional sentence then expresses that the consequent is true in those situations verifying the antecedent condition which lie closest to the actual world from which the speaker takes his perspective. With this semantics, conditional implication loses some of its classical features, such as:

> *Transitivity*:
> "*if* A, *then* B", "*if* B, *then* C" imply "*if* A, *then* C".

Nevertheless, there still remains a set of principles for inference, often replacing the now invalid classical cases by more subtle substitutes. For instance, we do have that:

> "*if* A, *then* B", "*if* A-*and*-B, *then* C" imply "*if* A, *then* C".

Thus, existing logical theory provides a common ground for many diverse kinds of non-monotonic reasoning considered in current artificial intelligence.

Upon reflection, minimalisation has a much wider scope than has appeared so far.

Thus, it figures at various places in the semantics of natural language. For instance, it has been argued that answers to questions often have a surplus meaning over and above their narrow informative content:

"Who is joining us?" "Mira and Dorothy",

suggests that *only* Mira and Dorothy will be joining. Thus, again, the predicate in question is being minimalised with respect to the information received. Something similar holds for the following piece of dialogue:

"Doctor, how shall I get better?"
"If you do as I say".

There is a promise here ("if you do, then you will..."), but also a threat ("if you don't, then you won't..."). The latter example also has its analog in computer science. Conditional clauses in PROLOG programs,

"*if* condition C, *then* goal D",

are also interpreted in a stronger converse sense, to the effect that the antecedents indicated are the only means of achieving the goal. (Technically, this is described by taking the "completion" of the program.) And this *modus operandi* is justified, of course, by the use of so-called "minimal (Herbrand) models".

Finally, we can even return to mathematics itself. Minimalisation has two aspects:

1. Do not postulate more objects than are explicitly mentioned in your language.
2. Do not postulate more facts concerning these objects than are enforced by the information at your disposal.

Now, the first type of minimalisation is encountered whenever we use an "inductive definition", as in the paradigmatic case:

"0 is a natural number.
If n is a natural number, then so is n+1."

There is a hidden clause here, viz. "no other thing is a natural number", which is justified by an appeal to the minimal model of the standard natural number line. (By contrast, "non-standard models" of arithmetic are non-minimal, carrying a tail of supernatural numbers.) Minimalisation of predicates is less frequently observed in mathematics—but, once observed, we might in fact look for further opportunities for putting it to use as well.

9.3 Stabilisation and Monotonicity

For a third, and last unifying theme, we return once more to the PROLOG example. Programming in PROLOG may be viewed as asking questions about a certain data structure. A popular example is that of family relationships, stored in some genealogical tree—and we are interested here in the relation of being an ancestor. The program might have the following rules relevant to this question:

Parent(x,y) → Ancestor(x,y)
(parents are ancestors),
Parent(x,y) & Ancestor (y,z) → Ancestor (x,z)
(parents of ancestors are ancestors themselves).

(Thus, speaking mathematically, we are asking for the transitive closure of the Parent relation.) Querying the extension of the Ancestor relation now amounts to asking for which pairs (x,y) the above rules prove the formula Ancestor (x,y).

A remarkable feature of the above two rules, when viewed as a definition for the Ancestor relation, is their self-reflective, or recursive character: the definition contains the definiens. In a formula:

Ancestor(x,y) ↔ Parent(x,y) *or, for some* z,
Parent(x,z) *and* Ancestor(z,y).

What guarantees that such definitions, being essentially circular, will lead to meaningful answers? The solution lies in the following observation. The search procedure may be viewed as an iteration, proceeding in stages. First, nothing is known about the Ancestor relation, it is empty. Next, this preliminary approximation can be plugged into the above definition, yielding a second approximation (being the Parent relation). Then, the latter may be plugged in again, yielding a third approximation, and so on. This process stabilises in a certain number of rounds, depending on the data structure considered.

What is the reason for this stabilisation? There is a connection here with "monotonicity" as mentioned in Section 5. The "next approximation" operation used in the above is *monotone* in the usual mathematical sense: if a couple (x,y) belongs to its argument set, then it will not be thrown away in the next round—the values can only increase, up to the stabilisation point. But, not all forms of circular definition guarantee such stabilisation. For instance, if we had used a scheme such as:

Ancestor(x,y) ↔ Parent(x,y) *or not* Ancestor(x,y),

the approximation sequence would have entered an endless alternation: empty relation, universal relation, Parent relation, universal relation, Parent relation, etc.

The difference is due to a typical point of mathematical logic, concerning the interplay between linguistic forms of definition and their semantic properties. In the first definition above, the predicate term "Ancestor" occurs only *positively*, in the same syntactic sense mentioned in Section 5 when discussing monotonicity inference in natural language. In the second definition, the "Ancestor" predicate does not occur positively (being in the scope of a single negation). Now, we know from general Model Theory that only the first type of definition will produce semantically monotone iteration functions, and hence eventual stability for the notion being defined.

Again, we recall that this notion of monotonicity is not confined to logic or computer science. We observed it also with determiner expressions in natural language. In fact, there is a proposed semantic universal to the effect that the basic determiners, across all human languages, are monotone. It is surely not far-fetched to speculate that this regularity has its basis in the "stability" behaviour of such monotone expressions, being the ones relatively insensitive to changes in information. A good deal of logical theory has been developed concerning precisely such properties of determiners and related categories of expression, characterising, for example, precisely which are the mathematically possible monotone ones among them, and to which extent the latter are definable using the resources of natural language. But also, the above PROLOG example may point at a special use for such expressions in the functioning of ordinary questions in natural discourse.

The point in presenting this list of cross-connections has been to emphasise that many of the general threads in the previous sections are not mere promises, or good intentions: "there is money in the bank". Another moral to be derived from these examples is the necessity of free-flowing theorising across existing academic boundaries. This advances not only the concerns of cognitive science, but may also produce new perspectives for the parent disciplines themselves.

To illustrate such a course of events, we conclude by returning to an earlier topic, mentioned in Section 4, viz. reasoning about the knowledge of others. That this is of practical importance, may be seen as follows. There is a great difference between a group of pirates individually knowing that the treasure is under the second palm-tree to the left of Captain Sharkey's coffin, and the same individuals also knowing that the others know this. And higher iterations are possible. In fact, it has been claimed that even ordinary linguistic communication, for instance in planning common action, presupposes an arbitrarily deeply embedded "common knowledge" among the partners. An urgent question, then, is to develop a good representation for such epistemic situations, as well as a perspicuous way for arguing about/inside them. What has been found by practically oriented researchers in this area is the necessity of drawing upon ideas stemming from such diverse sources as philosophical logic, general philosophy of knowledge and action, and the foundations of set theory. Conversely, applications to such mundane subjects as protocols for distributed systems of processors (to which knowledge is only being ascribed by courtesy) have stimulated philosophical thinking about the emergence and maintenance of norms in human communities. Incidentally, ascription of knowledge to our environment (including machines) is not just an anthropomorphic idiosyncracy of humans. It also has quite practical value as a form of representation: protocols for distributed processes which would normally be of forbidding complexity, have been verified easily in epistemic terms. Thus, it literally pays to be flexible in one's cognitive interests.

10. THE NEW TURN

Our panorama of research in logic directed toward cognitive representation and processing, as it is being pursued on the border or philosophy, mathematics, linguistics, psychology and computer science, suggests various directions for the next decade of logical research.

One direction to be stimulated is the ongoing cognitive or epistemic trend in semantic modelling, looking for suitable knowledge or *information structures*. On the technical side, this involves both more cognitively oriented notions of semantic "models" and the recognition of a variety of *modes of inference* appropriate to these. In particular, this calls for a better understanding of the model theory of *finite*, and *partial* structures, and logical systems of inference exploiting these. This will require a development of new logical systems; but also, various existing theories in constructive mathematics might turn out to be adaptable for this wider purpose. Only thus, by attacking over a broad front, can one hope to overcome such practical obstacles as the Frame Problem (concerning the explosion of facts to be stored in one's knowledge representation), and other monsters barring the road to truly intelligent systems. And likewise, here lies the obvious path toward establishing meaningful contacts with current studies of mental modelling in psychology. In this perspective, the relations between the various possible *levels* of knowledge representation will have to be investigated in more depth, as to their logical properties.

A second trend to be encouraged is the incorporation of *dynamic* aspects of cognition into current logical theories. We need an account of the actual procedures used in interpreting language, which build up local information structures—but also, of the various more global mechanisms of addition, retraction or modification of information which characterise intelligent activity. This is an issue with many sides, which range from the interplay of proof structure and algorithm development (which calls for constructive logics) to the interplay of knowledge and action (as modelled, to some extent, in current "dynamic logics", especially when coupled to epistemic logic). What is needed here is a level of theorising closer to computational realities than is usual in earlier "static" approaches (though not so close as to become tied up with ephemeral details of implementation). There are some ground-breaking publications here, proposing dynamic systems of semantic interpretation and general handling of knowledge, but as yet no full-fledged theory.

The time may be ripe to take a great leap ahead, trying to integrate larger clusters of research. We need theories at the level of *text and discourse*, doing justice to the various functions of language, such as statements, questions and commands. In operational semantics for even the simplest programming language, it is taken for granted that one will have to say something about all these aspects; so, can logicians and semanticists of natural language be content with anything less? (After all, even the simplest logical *proof* is already a piece of text, with its own architecture beyond the sentence level.)

More generally, in this field, we will have to study *rules* governing language use, over and above mere linguistic *forms* of information. Some first cues may be taken here from existing dialogical or game-theoretical approaches developed in philosophical logic. The difficult point will be to increase descriptive coverage of earlier theories with a more modest scope, without sacrificing former standards of precision.

Finally, the computational turn also suggests a further, bolder step. As Schnelle (Chapter 6) argues, cognitive competence may be divided into two varieties. One consists of conscious achievements, using modifiable sequential algorithms, whereas the other is unconscious, at the neurophysiological level, using rigid but fast parallel computation. The former processes have been the traditional domain of logic. But, in a unified cognitive science, there is certainly a "naturalistic challenge", to logic as much as to linguistics: Can logical theory also cover the unconscious level, and say something enlightening about the interface between consciously controlled and "hardwired" reasoning? This is an attractive, though still highly speculative project. To be sure, there have been early attempts at bridging the gap, using concepts such as "neural nets" which can easily be related to the usual logical notions of Automata and Recursion Theory. But as to deeper contacts, even quite new ideas will have to be developed. One encouraging sign may be discerned, however. If it is true that *parallellism* is of the essence at the level of neurophysiology, it is at least worth pointing out that many logical systems of proof are in fact parallel, or can be made to work that way. (For instance, various current projects trying to build a fast so-called Reduction Machine are trying to capitalise on the parallelism inherent in the logical Lambda Calculus mentioned in Section 8). Even so, whether we can use already existing theory or not, there is certainly an intriguing challenge to logic in the project of penetrating below the conscious surface of rationality.

11. POSTSCRIPT

The thesis of this paper has been that *logic* can play a useful role in the ongoing convergence of concerns in the various disciplines feeding into cognitive science. This is not to say that *only* logic has such an integrating contribution to make. Notably, also its two traditional sister disciplines (see Section 2) should be able to find general employment. For instance, *mathematics* still supplies notions and techniques across the spectrum of cognitive science; not just discrete mathematics, but also more classical continuous mathematics, as in the most recent development of "connectionism" in neurophysiology. And likewise, several branches of philosophy have turned out relevant in various ways: many insights from the philosophy of language, the philosophy of science, and general epistemology have inspired developments set out in the preceding story.

BIBLIOGRAPHY

This is not a comprehensive bibliography, but merely a list of useful publications illustrating some of the main themes in the text.

Sections 1 and 2.
Barwise, J. & Perry, J. (1983). *Situations and attitudes*. Cambridge, Mass.: Bradford Books / MIT Press.
Bolzano, B. (1837). *Wissenschaftslehre*. Sulzbach: Seidelsche Buchhandlung.
Doyle, J. (1983). *An essay on non-monotonic reasoning*. Pittsburgh: Carnegie Mellon University. Department of Computer Science.
Dummett, M. (1973). *Frege. The philosophy of language*. London: Duckworth.
GAMUT (1989). *Logic, language and meaning*. Chicago: Chicago University Press.
Glymour, C. (1980). *Theory and evidence*. Princeton: Princeton University Press.

van Heyenoort, J. (Ed.) (1967). *From Frege to Gödel*. Harvard: Harvard University Press.
Hintikka, J. (Ed.) (1969). *The philosophy of mathematics*. Oxford: Oxford University Press.
Kneale, W. & Kneale, M. (1962). *The development of logic*. Oxford: Clarendon Press.
Troelstra, A. & van Dalen, D. (1988). *Constructivism in mathematics*. Amsterdam: North-Holland.

Section 3.

Barwise, J. (Ed.) (1977). *Handbook of mathematical logic*. Amsterdam: North-Holland.
van Benthem, J. (1985). *A manual of intensional logic*. CSLI Lecture Notes, Vol.1. Stanford: Center for the Study of Language and Information. (Also published by Chicago University Press, 1988.)
Gabbay , D. & Guenthner, F. (Eds) (1983). *Handbook of philosophical logic, Vol.I: Elements of classical logic*. Dordrecht: Reidel.
Gabbay, D. & Guenthner, F. (Eds) (1984). *Handbook of philosophical logic, Vol. II: Extensions of classical logic*. Dordrecht: Reidel.
Gabbay, D. & Guenthner, F. (Eds) (1986). *Handbook of philosophical logic, Vol. III: Alternatives to classical logic*. Dordrecht: Reidel.
Gabbay, D. & Guenthner, F. (Eds) (1987). *Handbook of philosophical logic, Vol. IV: Topics in the philosophy of language*. Dordrecht: Reidel.
Gabbay, D., Hogger, C., & Robinson, J. A. (Eds) (in press a). *Handbook of logic in artificial intelligence and logic programming*. Oxford: Oxford University Press.
Gabbay et al. (Eds) (in press b). *Handbook of logic in computer science*. Oxford: Oxford University Press.

Section 4.

Dummett, M. (1977). *Elements of intuitionism*. Oxford: Clarendon Press.
Halpern, J. (Ed.)(1986). *Theoretical aspects of reasoning about knowledge*. Los Altos: Morgan Kaufmann.
Hintikka, J. (1962). *Knowledge and belief*. Ithaca, N.Y.: Cornell University Press.
Lenzen, W. (1980). *Glauben, Wissen und Wahrscheinlichkeit*. Wien: Springer.
Martin-Löf, P. (1982). Constructive mathematics and computer programming. In L. Cohen, J. Los, H. Pfeiffer, & K. Podewski (Eds), *Logic, methodology and philosophy of science VI*, pp.153-179. Amsterdam: North-Holland.
Sundholm, G. (1986). Proof theory and meaning. In D. Gabbay & F. Guenther (Eds), *Handbook of philosophical logic, Vol. III: Alternatives to classic logic*, pp 471-506. Dordrecht: Reidel.
Veltman, F. (1984). Data semantics. In J. Groenendijk, T. Janssen, & M. Stokhof (Eds), *Truth, interpretation and information*, pp.43-63. Dordrecht: Foris.

Section 5.

van Benthem, J. (1986). *Essays in logical semantics*. Dordrecht: Reidel.
Creswell, M. J. (1973). *Logics and languages*. London: Methuen.
Davidson, D. & Harman, G. (Eds) (1972). *The semantics of natural language*. Dordrecht: Reidel.
Fenstad, J.E., Halvorsen, P.K., Langholm, T., & van Benthem, J. (1987). *Situations, language and logic*. Dordrecht: Reidel.
Kamp, H. (1984). A theory of truth and semantic representation. In J. Groenendijk, T. Janssen, & M. Stokhof (Eds), *Truth, interpretation and information*, pp.1-41. Dordrecht: Foris.
Montague, R. (1974). *Formal philosophy* (edited by R. Thomason). New Haven: Yale University Press.
Peirce, C. S. (1960). *The collected papers of C. S. Peirce. Vol. IV* (Edited by Ch. Hartshorne & P. Weiss). Cambridge, Mass.: Harvard University Press.
Reichenbach, H. (1966). *Elements of symbolic logic*. New York: The Free Press. (Reprint of 1947.)
von Stechow, A. & Wunderlich, D. (Eds) (forthcoming). *Handbook of semantics*. Berlin: De Gruyter.

Section 6.

Beth, E. & Piaget, J. (1966). *Mathematical epistemology and psychology*. Dordrecht: Reidel.

Gibson, J. (1979). *The ecological approach to visual perception*. Boston: Houghton Mifflin.

Heymans, G. (1923). *Die Gesetze und Elemente des Wissenschaftlichen Denkens*. Leipzig: Teubner Verlag.

Johnson-Laird, P. (1983). *Mental models*. Cambridge: Cambridge University Press.

Krantz, D., Luce, R., Suppes, P., & Tversky, A. (1971). *Foundations of measurement*. London and San Diego: Academic Press.

Kugel, P. (1986). Thinking may be more than computing. *Cognition, 22*, 137-198.

Michon, J. & Jackson, J. (1985). *Time, mind and behaviour*. Berlin: Springer.

Osherson, D., Stob, M., & Weinstein, S. (1986). *Systems that learn*. Cambridge, Mass.: Bradford Books/MIT Press.

Wason, P. & Johnson-Laird, P. (1972). *Psychology of reasoning*. London: Batsford.

Section 7.

Apt, K. (1987). *Introduction to logic programming*. Report CS-R8741. Amsterdam: Centre for Mathematics and Computer Science.

Barendregt, H. (1984). *The Lambda Calculus: Its syntax and semantics*. Amsterdam: North-Holland.

Bergstra, J. & Klop, J.W (1984). Process algebra for synchronous communication. *Information and Control, 60*, 109-137.

Bratko, I. (1986). *Prolog programming for artificial intelligence*. Wokingham: Addison-Wesley.

Ginsberg M. L. (Ed.) (1987). *Readings in nonmonotonic reasoning*. Los Altos: Morgan Kaufmann.

Goldblatt, R. I. (1982). *Axiomatizing the logic of computer programming*. (Lecture Notes in Computer Science 130). Berlin: Springer.

Goldblatt, R. I. (1987). *Logics of time and computation*. CSLI Lecture Notes 7. Stanford: Center for the Study of Language and Information.

Harel, D. (1984). Dynamic logic. In D. Gabbay & F. Guenthner (Eds), *Handbook of philosophical logic, Vol. II: Extensions of classical logic*, pp. 497- 604. Dordrecht: Reidel.

Hodges, A. (1983). *Turing. The enigma of intelligence*. London: Allen and Unwin.

Hopcroft, J. & Ullman, J. (1979). *Introduction to automata theory, languages and computation*. Reading, Mass.: Addison-Wesley.

Janssen, T. (1986). *Foundations and applications of Montague Grammar*. Amsterdam: Mathematical Centre.

Kowalski, R. (1979). *Logic for problem solving*. New York: North-Holland.

van Leeuwen, J. (Ed.) (forthcoming). *Handbook of theoretical computer science*. Amsterdam: North-Holland.

Section 8.

Allen, J. (1983). Maintaining knowledge about temporal intervals. *Communications of the Association for Computing Machinery, 26*, 832-843.

van Benthem, J. (1983). *The logic of time*. Dordrecht: Reidel.

Charniak, E. & McDermott, D. (1985). *Introduction to artificial intelligence*. Reading, Mass.: Addison-Wesley.

Gardenfors, P. (1988). *Knowledge in flux: Modelling the dynamics of epistemic states*. Cambridge, Mass.: MIT Press /Bradford Books.

Hayes, P. (1977). In Defense of logic. *Proceedings IJCAI 5*, 559-565.

Hofstadter, D. (1979). *Gödel, Escher, Bach*. New York: Basic Books.

Kowalski, R. & Sergot, M. (1985). *A calculus of events*. Department of Computer Science. University of London: Imperial College.

McDermott, D. & Shoham, Y. (1985). Temporal reasoning. In S. Shapiro (Ed.), *Encyclopedia of artificial intelligence*. New York: Wiley-Interscience.

Nute, D. (1986). *LDR: A logic for defeasible reasoning.* Advanced Computational Methods Center. Athens, GA.: University of Georgia.

Russell, B. (1926). *Our knowledge of the external world.* London: Allen and Unwin.

Shoham, Y. (1988). *Reasoning about change: Time and causation from the standpoint of artificial intelligence.* Cambridge, Mass.: MIT Press.

Sosa, E. (Ed.) (1975). *Causation and conditionals.* Oxford: Oxford University Press.

Stegmuller, W. (1957). *Induktive Logik und Wahrscheinlichkeit.* Wien: Springer.

Section 9.

Aczel, P. (1977). An introduction to inductive definitions. In J. Barwise (Ed.), *Handbook of mathematical logic*, pp. 739-782. Amsterdam: North-Holland.

Barwise, J. (1988). *On the model theory of common knowledge.* Report CSLI-88-122. Stanford: Center for the Study of Language and Information.

Buszkowski, W., Marciszewski, W., & van Benthem, J. (Eds) (1988). *Categorial grammar.* Amsterdam: John Benjamin.

Chierchia, G., Partee, B., & Turner, R. (Eds) (1988). *Categories, types and semantics.* Dordrecht: Reidel.

Davis, M. (1980). The mathematics of non-monotonic reasoning. *Artificial Intelligence, 13,* 73-80.

Fitting, M. (1985). A Kripke-Kleene semantics for logic programs. *Journal of Logic Programming, 4,* 295-312.

Harper, W., Stalnaker, R., & Pearce, G. (Eds) (1981). *Ifs.* Dordrecht: Reidel.

Lewis, D. (1969). *Convention. A philosophical study.* New Haven: Harvard University Press.

McCarthy, J. (1980). Circumscription—a form of non-monotonic reasoning. *Artificial Intelligence, 13,* 295-323.

Oehrle, R., Bach, E., & Wheeler, D. (Eds) (1988). *Categorial grammars and natural language structures.* Dordrecht: Reidel.

Veltman, F. (1986). *Logics for conditionals.* Dissertation. University of Amsterdam: Department of Philosophy. (To appear with Cambridge University Press.)

Section 10.

Arbib, M. (1964). *Brains, machines and mathematics.* New York: McGraw-Hill.

Barwise, J. (1987). Noun phrases, generalized quantifiers and anaphora. In P. Gardenfors (Ed.), *Generalized quantifiers. Linguistic and logical approaches*, pp.1-29. Dordrecht: Reidel.

van Benthem, J. (1987). Semantic automata. In J. Groenendijk, D. de Jongh, & M. Stokhof (Eds), *Studies in discourse representation theory and the theory of generalized quantifiers*, pp.1-25. Dordrecht: Foris.

van Benthem, J. (forthcoming). Semantic parallels in natural language and computation. In M. Garrido (Ed.), *Logic Colloquium. Granada 1987.* Amsterdam: North-Holland.

Groenendijk, J. & Stokhof, M (1985). *On the semantics of questions and the pragmatics of answers.* Dissertation. University of Amsterdam: Department of Philosophy. (To appear with Oxford University Press.)

Groenendijk, J. & Stokhof, M. (forthcoming). Dynamic predicate logic. *Journal of Semantics.*

Gurevich, Y. (1985). *Logic and the challenge of computer science.* Ann Arbor: Computer Research Laboratory, The University of Michigan.

Kamp, H. (forthcoming). *Discourse representation.* Dordrecht: Reidel.

Moore, R. (1984). *A formal theory of knowledge and action.* Menlo Park: Artificial Intelligence Center, SRI International.

Stalnaker, R. (1972). Pragmatics. In D. Davidson & G. Harman (Eds), *Semantics of natural language*, pp.380-397. Dordrecht: Reidel.

Author Index

An index of authors cited in the text. For further reading see the Reference Sections and Bibliographies which follow individual chapters.

Subject Index